VENDORS' CAPITALISM

VENDORS' CAPITALISM
A Political Economy of Public Markets in Mexico City

Ingrid Bleynat

Stanford University Press
Stanford, California

Stanford University Press
Stanford, California

© 2021 by the Board of Trustees of the Leland Stanford Junior University. All rights reserved.

No part of this book may be reproduced or transmitted in any form or by any means, electronic or mechanical, including photocopying and recording, or in any information storage or retrieval system without the prior written permission of Stanford University Press.

Printed in the United States of America on acid-free, archival-quality paper

Library of Congress Cataloging-in-Publication Data

Names: Bleynat, Ingrid, author.
Title: Vendors' capitalism : a political economy of public markets in Mexico City / Ingrid Bleynat.
Description: Stanford, California : Stanford University Press, 2021. | Includes bibliographical references and index.
Identifiers: LCCN 2020050941 (print) | LCCN 2020050942 (ebook) | ISBN 9781503614604 (cloth) | ISBN 9781503628298 (paperback) | ISBN 9781503628304 (ebook)
Subjects: LCSH: Markets—Mexico—Mexico City—History. | Vending stands—Mexico—Mexico City—History. | Markets—Government policy—Mexico—Mexico City—History. | Vending stands—Government policy—Mexico—Mexico City—History. | Capitalism—Mexico—Mexico City—History. | Mexico City (Mexico)—Economic conditions—19th century. | Mexico City (Mexico)—Economic conditions—20th century.
Classification: LCC HF5473.M62 B54 2021 (print) | LCC HF5473.M62 (ebook) | DDC 381/.1097253—dc23
LC record available at https://lccn.loc.gov/2020050941
LC ebook record available at https://lccn.loc.gov/2020050942

Cover photo: Inside the Abelardo Rodríguez Market, Mexico City. Archivo General de la Nación, Fondo Hermanos Mayo. Undated (ca. 1950–1970).
Cover design: Rob Ehle
Typeset by Motto Publishing Services in 10/14 Minion Pro

To Paul

To Lucas and Camilo

Contents

Acknowledgments ... ix

Introduction: Market Vendors and the History of Capitalism in Mexico, 1867–1966 ... 1

1 Taxes and Compassion, 1867–1880 ... 12

2 A Cloak of Magnificence over Beggars' Rags, 1880–1903 ... 38

3 Vendors, Workers, or *Pueblo*? 1903–1928 ... 63

4 Political Experimentation in a Time of Crises, 1929–1945 ... 94

5 Vendors' Developmentalism, 1945–1966 ... 124

Epilogue ... 156

Notes ... 161

Bibliography ... 207

Index ... 233

Acknowledgments

This book has been made possible by the support of several institutions and many individuals both inside and outside of academia. The initial research and writing were funded by the History Department, the Graduate School of Arts and Sciences, and the Rockefeller Center for Latin American Studies at Harvard University, and the Mellon Foundation. The Department of International Development at King's College London has provided the encouragement and research support necessary for the completion of this project.

My first thanks must be to John Womack Jr. I could have not hoped for a more inspiring, generous, and knowledgeable mentor, who also had the wisest and most compassionate words when life turned both dark and bright. I cherish all he has taught me, and continues to teach me, about so much more than Mexican or Latin American history. John Coatsworth's brilliance and intellectual energy never fails to convey excitement for our field, and I always left our conversations inspired and ready to take on new challenges. Aurora Gómez-Galvarriato has been a generous friend and guide since my first trips to Mexico more than a decade and a half ago, where she welcomed me into her home, provided me with connections and archival tips, and helped me to find my way around an entirely new country. Pablo Piccato's engagement at the earlier stages of this project helped it come to fruition, and his insightful comments clarified and sharpened key arguments.

In Mexico City, the staff at the Archivo General de la Nación, the Archivo Histórico de la Ciudad de México, and the Biblioteca Lerdo de Tejada were often obliging beyond the call of duty. In particular, I want to thank the late Victoria San Vicente for helping me locate the "lost" Actas y Versiones del Consejo Consultivo. During 2005 and 2006 I spent many days at La Merced market, asking questions of anybody kind enough to humor me. Víctor Manuel Martínez Cruz, of the Locatarios Unidos de La Merced, made sure I had plenty to drink and eat while there and saved me from some uncomfortable situations. Ernesto González Aldana and Yttzé Quijada provided excellent research assistance.

At the Department of International Development at King's College London I have found a wonderful academic home among a group of caring and brilliant scholars. Among them, I am particularly grateful to Peter Kingstone, who hired me right after graduate school and always insisted that I continue to work on this research, even when it made more practical sense to put my energies to other purposes. Jelke Boesten has been a fantastic mentor, and I feel privileged to be able to learn from her. Juan Grigera commented on the introduction of this book and has offered support in the latest stages of the process of publication. Anna Grimaldi, teaching and research assistant extraordinaire, has not only helped me to bring this project to a close but has also become a dear friend along the way.

I have very special to debts to Raphael Folsom, Guy Geltner, Olga Gonzalez-Silen, Sandra Mendiola, and Louise Walker. Raphie, Guy, and Sandra generously read the first iteration of this manuscript and shared their knowledge and insight as it developed. This book is much improved for their suggestions, and my life richer for their friendship. I was lucky to meet Louise Walker at a cantina in Mexico City as I started my doctoral research in 2005, and I do not exaggerate when I say I learned what I know about the practice of history from her. Her work, as well as her warmth, intellectual creativity, and professionalism have been major sources of inspiration. I hope we will share many more adventures in years to come. I owe my deepest gratitude to Olga, both as a friend and as a scholar. Her passion for history and her generosity know no bounds, and I have been blessed to have her by my side at every step of the way since the early days of graduate school. Her careful reading of multiple drafts, incisive comments, and stylistic suggestions shaped every page of this book. We have shared this project and so much of our lives over the past fifteen years, and I look forward to more.

Other friends and colleagues have been integral to this long journey. Nicolás Kwiatkowski encouraged my adventure into history and has never stopped amazing me with his kindness and breadth of knowledge. At Harvard and since, Alison Adams, Amílcar Challú, Hal Jones, Rob Karl, Dan Gutierrez, Mónica Ricketts, Miles Rodriguez, Julia Sarreal, Sergio Silva Castañeda, Bill Suarez-Potts, and Rainer Schultz read earlier versions of these chapters and gave invaluable advice. I treasure the fun, intellectual exchanges, and camaraderie we have shared over the years. In Mexico City, Louise, Raphie, Bomee Jung, Susanne Eineigel, and Thom Rath made the vagaries of research much more enjoyable and productive. All throughout and even before, Paula Porroni and Gwen MacKeith have showed me the beauty of writing and the importance of being true to our own voices. More recently, Marcela López Levy kindly offered writing advice and helped me finish this book during a pandemic without (fully) losing my mind. Pilar Piqué and Facundo Alvaredo also provided intellectual and moral support as I was completing this work. I hope I can now pay back in dedication to our project together.

I am grateful to Margo Irvin at Stanford University Press for believing in this project and for guiding me through the protracted process of publication. Also at SUP, Cindy Lim and Susan Karani patiently answered my questions and oversaw the edits that refined the format and content of text. Thanks to Dawn Hall for the careful copyediting and to June Sawyers for the indexing. Two anonymous reviewers offered thoughtful feedback and excellent suggestions, which helped improve the book significantly. Megan Pugh provided brilliant developmental editing on the final manuscript. Marlene Pérez García from the AGN helped me obtain permission for the cover. Tomas Jaehn from the Center for Southwest Research and Special Collections at the University of New Mexico somehow managed to scan and share images in the middle of the current pandemic. Roberta Vassallo generously sent me her photographs of Porfirian market plans. Enrique de la Rosa provided the newspaper covers of the 1924 vendor demonstration. Parts of chapter 5 appeared as "The Business of Governing: Corruption and Informal Politics in Mexico City's Markets, 1946–1958" in the *Journal of Latin American Studies* 50, no. 2 (2018): 355–81. I thank the editors of the journal and the anonymous referees for their comments.

My parents deserve a big thanks for encouraging me to pursue my PhD even if it did not really fit in their worldview and it meant I had to move abroad. My mother has always had a way of making me feel free and able to achieve anything I set my heart to. I wish my father had lived to see this book published, but I know he would be proud. Along the way, I gained the most terrific mother-in-law, who not only has provided much-needed support over the years but has also been a wonderful grandmother to my children. Paul Segal, my wonderful husband, shrewdest critic, and best friend deserves the most credit for this book, which should be as much his as it is mine. I am grateful for his laughter and delicious meals as well as for his unwavering belief that, no matter what I said or did, this day would come. Finally, our sons Camilo and Lucas, still so little, have already taught me much about the meaning of love and work. I dedicate this book to them. I owe them the world over.

VENDORS' CAPITALISM

Introduction

*Market Vendors and the History of
Capitalism in Mexico, 1867–1966*

"MEXICO IS TO BE FOUND IN ITS MARKETS," wrote the Chilean poet Pablo Neruda of his experiences traveling the country in the 1940s.[1] Struck by their eruptions of humanity, the piles of vegetables and chiles, the colors of the textiles, the sliced fruit asking to be tasted, Neruda followed a long line of visitors enthralled by the vitality of Mexico's marketplaces and their vibrant social interactions. Yet there is more truth in his words than he knew: Mexico City's public markets were integral to the development of the country's economy, bolstering the expansion of capitalism in the century spanning from the definitive restoration of the Republic in 1867 to the heyday of the so-called Mexican miracle in the 1960s. These markets were embedded in a wide network of social and economic relations, which gave the vendors who sold in them an influence far beyond the running of their stalls. As they fed the population of the capital, they interacted daily with customers, suppliers, and government officials. Fighting to protect their livelihoods, vendors shaped the city's public sphere and extended the scope of popular politics. Furthermore, they left their mark on official programs of urban renewal as well as on the institutions of state. In short, market vendors played a central part in the intertwined processes of economic development and state formation.[2]

Mexico City's markets remained publicly owned and regulated throughout the century this book covers. They supplied households with everyday necessities and generated much-needed revenue for the local authorities. The importance of public markets grew as the city industrialized, because the provision of affordable wage goods became key to maintaining a measure of peace between workers and capitalists. Public markets were also the focal point of repeated attempts by the national government to turn the capital city into the elegant—or at least presentable—face of the nation. For these reasons, their management was a matter of public interest. Governments invested financial capital in the building and upkeep of markets and political capital in brokering the relationships within them. However, running these markets was difficult. The competing interests of multiple stakeholders—vendors, workers, suppliers, government officials, and politicians—repeatedly tested the institutional capacity of the state.

The vendors who earned their living in Mexico City's public markets occupied a particular position within the broader political economy. They were not wage workers, in the sense that they did not sell their labor power in order to make a living. They were not capitalists either, because they did not hire people to work for them, and in most cases they never managed to accumulate any capital. For better or for worse, market vendors remained locked in what I call the proprietary mode of production: people who work for themselves, more often than not with the help of their families, running small-scale operations with at best a modest working capital, usually on credit. The term that best fits them is probably the Spanish *trabajadores por cuenta propia*, which in English would translate as self-employed or own-account workers. In a typical workday market vendors visited wholesale depots, bought goods, transported them to their stalls, sorted them, displayed them, promoted them, and sold them to the city's residents. This is how they created value. The conflicts that pervaded their economic lives revolved around the distribution and appropriation of this value through buying, borrowing, and selling. That is, they experienced exploitation through exchange.

In making this case I build on John Womack Jr.'s insight that the single most notable and consequential feature of social life in twentieth-century Latin America was that different modes of production continued to function simultaneously alongside capitalist businesses.[3] Slavery was no longer legal (Cuba and Brazil had been last to abolish it, in 1886 and 1888 respectively), but feudalism, in a host of varieties, remained the organizing principle of agricultural life in large parts of many countries well into the 1930s, with some of its elements informing domestic service relations ever since. In addition, myriads of peasants, artisans, and other small-scale producers, along with small-scale traders, engaged in the proprietary mode of production in every village, town, city, and province of every country in the region. But while slavery and feudalism faded away, proprietary production and trade expanded together with capitalism throughout the century, as they continue to do to date. The fact that slavery and feudalism gave way not just to capitalism but also to an extensive proprietary mode, meant that for a large proportion of the population of Latin America progress did not lead to increasing productivity, the accumulation of capital, stable employment, or the protection of a welfare state. Instead, it took the form of individualistic self-exploitation, precariousness, and bitter competition for meager incomes.

The capitalist and proprietary modes of production not only coexisted throughout the twentieth century but also interacted with one another through supply chains, credit arrangements, and other economic relations such as subcontracting and subleasing.[4] Such interactions resulted in complex class antagonisms—conflicts *within* modes of production continually ran into conflicts *across* modes. Conflicts within modes of production included the familiar class struggle between workers and capitalists over pay, hours, and conditions. Within the proprietary mode were conflicts between artisans or peasants and the proprietary traders that commercialized their products, both sides trying to increase their respective share of the value realized in final sales to consumers. Conflicts across modes of production, on the other hand, pitted proprietary producers and traders against capitalist middlemen, creditors, and merchants in struggles over the appropriation of value through commercial transactions, rents, and loans. At the same time, these compounding class antagonisms were often diffused and further obscured by the many other vital social relations that people in Latin America established through bonds of kinship, friendship, religion, and politics, in their search for some security, or at least stability, for themselves and their families.

Although Mexico City's market vendors experienced multiple and shifting forms of struggle as well as solidarity across the century, the internal logic, technology, and productivity of their commercial activities stayed relatively constant. They acquired goods through interactions with their suppliers and creditors, often the same people, who tried to charge them as much as they could for their merchandise and loans. In the 1860s and 1870s some of these were small-scale producers within the proprietary mode of production, local artisans or peasants from the city's hinterland, but from the 1880s onward vendors dealt mostly, if not exclusively, with capitalist operations involved in broader commercial networks. Market vendors then sold these goods to their customers, who wanted to pay as little as possible for their products. Archival evidence suggests that on both sides these relationships were fraught. As soon as vendors formed coherent organizations, they demanded a state-funded bank that would help them finance collective purchases and would empower them vis-à-vis their suppliers and creditors. Equally, as the public-facing end of the supply chain for everyday necessities, vendors suffered the anger of consumers in periods of high inflation. During the Mexican Revolution desperate women and children stormed the city's markets. In the late 1930s and late 1940s, when workers mobilized to protect the purchasing power of their wages, vendors faced fines and government censure. As the twentieth century progressed, vendors also had to learn to compete with supermarkets and chain stores while bearing the brunt of government attempts to control the prices of basic goods.

Along with these conflicts with other social classes, the most recurrent and bitter antagonisms vendors experienced were among themselves, as a result of competition over customers and market space. Sometimes they took the form of a group within a market hall denouncing the street vendors that blocked the entrance to their places of work, accusing them of illegal or inappropriate behavior. Other times, of outright street battles over the best vending spots. Archival sources show that vendors were aware of how disruptive this intraclass competition could be to their livelihoods. They responded with forms of collective action such as group petitions for state intervention in specific disputes and, eventually, the creation of organizations aimed at curbing tensions within their markets.

Mexico City's market vendors stood apart from other proprietary classes because they performed a key public service. The official denomination *mercados públicos* underscores this uneasy overlap between the pursuit of individual gain and the common good. Public markets were physical and social spaces successive governments committed to build, manage, and regulate so vendors could effectively supply essential goods to urban residents. Their indispensability for the daily provision of the population of the capital city gave these vendors a degree of political leverage that was beyond the reach of most other small-scale producers and traders. Whether vendors sold from a shop in a purpose-built hall or from a stall on the city's streets—the lines that divided public markets from street thoroughfare shifted back and forth in the period covered by this book—their right to occupy their workplace resulted from constant negotiations with government officials. The levels of rents, fees, and taxes market vendors paid were often contested. The archives are full of successful petitions for rent and fee reductions during the late nineteenth and early twentieth century. In the 1920s, vendors organized demonstrations to protest tax hikes, and in at least one instance they went on strike, though threats to abandon markets to take to the streets, where evasion of fiscal charges was easier, seemed to have been more effective. Likewise, government attempts to ensure public health and public order, or to improve the appearance of the capital city, which in practice always involved vendor relocations, frequently led to cycles of disputes and concessions, both when particular groups of market vendors found that regulations threatened their interests, and when they made use of those same regulations to attack their competitors. The ability of vendors to disrupt the daily business of the capital gave them veto power over any urban development project that excluded them.

Since public markets were indispensable to the economic life of the capital, the government agents stepped in not just to regulate access to stalls and taxation levels but also to broker the conflicts that market vendors had with their suppliers, creditors, and consumers as well as with street vendors. This had consequences far beyond the markets themselves. The specific interventions public officials and politicians made to resolve these conflicts involved institutional innovations that extended the reach and the capacity of the state. In 1943, for example, the government opened the state-funded Bank of Small Commerce in response to vendor demands for support against their creditors, which officials then used to intervene in vendor organizations. The creation of the Partido Revolucionario Institucional (PRI) in 1946 broadened and institutionalized vendor politics through the Confederación Nacional de Organizaciones Populares (CNOP). This signified a loss of independence for vendor organizations, but it gained them a seat at the political table. Tens of thousands of vendors obtained improved market facilities, subsidized credit, and protection from competition. The government's effectiveness in managing vendors' social relations, and more broadly its success in incorporating a significant portion of the city's proprietary classes into its probusiness compact, underlay the economic growth and political stability of these years. It is no coincidence that the heyday of Mexico City's markets was also the heyday of both Mexican state capitalism and the PRI's rule.

· · ·

The location of Mexico's markets at the intersection of private enterprise and public service makes them an ideal focus for a political economy of what

Jeremy Adelman and Jonathan Levy call "the fuzzy and shifting boundaries between the economic and noneconomic."[5] It also means that vendors appear in an array of primary sources, whose provenance reflects the changes in the governance of the city. This book is therefore based on extensive research across a range of archives. At the Archivo Histórico de la Ciudad de México I studied ayuntamiento minutes and publications, petitions by vendors, complaints by merchants, responses by city councilors, and reports from market administrators for the years between 1867 and 1903. During the Porfiriato, the growing power of the federal government can be seen in the higher incidence of interventions by the governor of the District, the District's director of Public Works, and the president of the council of Public Health. After the Mexican Revolution, vendor voices began to feature more prominently in federal government archives such as the presidential collections, the files of the Labor Department, and those of the Secretariat of the Interior, all housed at the Archivo General de la Nación. The minutes of the meetings of the Consejo Consultivo allowed me to track vendors' disputes with other organized urban interest groups after 1928.[6] In the late 1940s, Mexico revamped its intelligence services, and the reports produced by the Directorate of Federal Security and the General Directorate of Political and Social Investigations provided an unexpected window into vendor politics. Their files suggest that intelligence agents spent as much time policing the groups that constituted the PRI as persecuting those who opposed it.[7] These sources partly compensate for the two main missing pieces of the mid-twentieth-century archival puzzle, the files of the office of the head of the Federal District, and those of the Confederación Nacional de Organizaciones Populares (National Confederation of Popular Organizations, CNOP), the branch of the party to which vendors belonged.[8] In addition, my work draws on published travel accounts and on newspaper collections from the Biblioteca Lerdo de Tejada and the Hemeroteca Nacional. I also benefited from informal conversations with vendors and leaders of several organizations from La Merced Market, still the largest of its kind in the city.

The story unfolds chronologically. Chapter 1 shows that the relationship between market vendors and the ayuntamiento was at the heart of the moral economy of the capital of the Restored Republic (1867–76).[9] At the time, the city was home to less than a quarter million people and retained important traditional elements. The economy was well-integrated but sluggish, and capitalist businesses coexisted with artisanal production and proprietary trading in public markets. Market vendors reliably generated a significant portion of the council's yearly fiscal income, driving the ayuntamiento to try to find ways to expand the number of fee-paying stalls and raise the rates they paid.[10] Yet local officials also responded to a second, less tangible set of principles. An imperative to show compassion toward vendors, a combination of councilors' private Catholicism and political good sense, pushed the ayuntamiento in the opposite direction.[11] Councilors' concern with the plight of the poor, thus, often overturned their fiscal prudence, with the result that vendors' petitions for reductions in market fees were frequently answered favorably.

This delicate balance between taxes and compassion informed the everyday interactions between the city authorities and market vendors. But chapter 1 further argues that the same moral economy that ensured the viability of vendors' small businesses precluded their participation in the public sphere, where politicians, councilmen, and journalists discussed market policies and, more generally, constructed their version of the common good.[12] In other words, market vendors were barred from policy debates. Instead, compassionate politicians and journalists mediated their views, representing vendors' interests and acting as their protectors. In this low-growth and low-stakes environment, an exclusionary benevolence based on custom and a respect for social hierarchy kept the city relatively at peace.

After 1880, a capitalist boom took hold of Mexico.[13] The combination of economic growth and political stability allowed politicians, businessmen, and journalists to entertain the fantasy of transforming Mexico City into a modern metropolis, worthy of their imagined Republic.[14] Chapter 2 analyses how their attempts to turn this fantasy into reality played out in the city's markets.[15] The ayuntamiento took the lead. Full of optimism, it contracted out the building of elegant iron and glass halls. It also passed bylaws stipulating acceptable and unacceptable forms of vending. Yet old market practices persisted. Many vendors continued to set their stalls on the city's streets, now joined by a growing number of peddlers who disregarded government regulations altogether. As capitalist merchants moved their stores to private premises, the new halls remained undersubscribed and partially vacant.

The Porfirian elite soon became frustrated with what they saw as the ayuntamiento's inability to exercise authority over public spaces. A repressive consensus emerged in the 1890s, leading to the criminalization and police harassment of all vendors outside the officially sanctioned halls.[16] Chapter 2 contends that this process entailed a differentiation among the city's proprietary vendors, with those who chose to become *locatarios* within the new markets supporting the changes, including the repression of those unable or unwilling to secure a stall. By joining the new halls these vendors embraced a modernity that promised to reduce competition and legitimize their self-interest. Their determination to benefit from the expansion of capitalism was as implacable as the elite's.

The year 1903 marked a turning point in the history of Mexico City, as the capital was politically and administratively reorganized and the ayuntamiento stripped of its powers.[17] Whereas markets had been a social and infrastructural priority for the city council, the responsibility for their management was now dispersed across multiple ministries. As chapter 3 lays out, the resulting jurisdictional overlaps created power vacuums that brought uncertainty to stallholders and government officials alike. As a result, the police took a bigger role in the day-to-day running of markets, assisting in fee collection, dispersing unlicensed peddlers, overseeing porters, ensuring vendors kept their stalls clean, and even reprimanding customers who disposed of their garbage on the nearby streets. Vendors learned they could no longer rely on pleas for protection from a receptive local government, so they began to enunciate their collective grievances. The onset of the Mexican Revolution in 1910 catalyzed the emergence of new attitudes and expectations among the city's laboring classes.[18] Vendors soon adopted the political lexicon of the revolution and joined the period's proletarian struggles.[19] After the Constitution of 1917 enshrined labor rights, vendors formed their own unions, through which they joined the newly created workers' confederations. Together workers and vendors reconfigured the city's politics and public sphere.

Vendors repeatedly challenged the postrevolutionary authorities, whose approach to markets lagged behind the changing social landscape. At times, these challenges turned into open confrontations. During a demonstration against a hike in market fees on August 2, 1924, two vendors died and eleven were wounded at the hands of local government forces. How does "a petition become a protest march, which gradually takes the shape of a riot?" asked *El Demócrata*, one of the country's leading newspapers.[20] The press blamed local politicians for the violence and described the vendors as the nondescript "pueblo," which had been "machine-gunned by political interests."[21] While journalists exonerated vendors of any responsibility for the deaths and injuries, by the same token they reduced them to passive victims, denying them any political agency. But a close reading of the printed media's coverage of the events reveals that by 1924, market vendors were not only active but also organized.²² In tune with the militancy of the labor movement, vendors had discovered novel ways to claim their rights and defend their material interests, forming unions the authorities would sooner or later have to reckon with.

Chapter 4 examines how vendors' multiple class conflicts constrained attempts at state building. During the Great Depression, the capital witnessed intense political and economic experimentation, starting in 1929 when the federal government created the Consejo Consultivo, a corporatist body designed to supplant the labor movement as the intermediary between the state and the city's popular classes.²³ Managing the local political economy proved harder than the government anticipated. With the then forty-year-old Porfirian market halls overwhelmed by population growth, the proliferation of street stalls became, once again, a major source of tension. Wealthy capitalist merchants clashed with proprietary vendors over price controls, commercial regulations, and the use of public space.²⁴ Large industrialists, property owners, and urban planners joined merchants in opposing all types of street vending, while street vendors, knowing that market vendors would not take their side, looked to workers and to the head of the Markets Office for support. Mired in these overlapping, entangled disputes, the consejo faltered.

Postrevolutionary governments struggled to handle a mobilized but increasingly divided vendor movement. From 1932, economic recovery allowed the Department of the Federal District, now fully in charge of the city, to pour resources into public markets. Driven by demands from market vendors, construction companies, and other interested parties, it kick-started a redevelopment program in another attempt to move vendors off the city's streets and into purpose-built facilities.²⁵ But building halls was not enough. Chapter 4 finds that even the flagship Abelardo Rodríguez Market foundered because the department failed to solve conflicts among market and street vendors.²⁶ Without effective institutional mechanisms to manage competition between vendors, their commitments to relocate to the new hall remained tentative, all deals prone to falling apart. The situation deteriorated further in 1936 as a result of mounting inflation. In order to appease industrial workers, President Lázaro Cárdenas intervened to protect the purchasing power of wages by imposing price controls on everyday necessities.²⁷ The prospect of a reduction of vendors' profit margins only worsened their relations with the state. The highly contested presidential election of 1940 alerted Cárdenas's successors to the risks of alienating the city's vendors, spurring the authorities' determination to gain greater control over their organizations.

Mexico City's market vendors continued to feel squeezed during the major economic transformations that took place in the country in the years after World War II. The economy grew and industrialized, driven by a state that provided support to capitalists and invested heavily in infrastructure.[28] To ensure workers' compliance the government tried to guarantee the availability of affordable wage goods.[29] Official efforts focused on fixing prices and promoting direct sales to urban consumers by subsidized large- and small-scale agricultural producers. Vendors resented these policies, which increased competition and short-circuited their own place in the city's supply chains. At the same time, migration and population growth led to increasing numbers of peddlers, who also clashed with established vendors over sales and trading spots. It took significant compromise and creativity on the parts of both government officials and the vendor movement to resolve the tensions that played out in the streets and markets of the capital.

In 1946, organized vendors joined the new Partido Revolucionario Institucional (PRI) where, as members of the Confederación Nacional de Organizaciones Populares (CNOP), they hoped to have a greater say in developmentalist policies. The incorporation to the party of the self-employed popular classes represented by the CNOP was the key political innovation of the period. But scholars have paid little attention to corresponding changes in the city's political economy. To the extent that they have, it has been interpreted as a maneuver to reduce the influence of the national confederations of industrial workers and peasants—thereby removing any constraints they might have placed on economic growth.[30] Implicitly, the urban self-employed were deemed marginal, or at best secondary. But the experiences of vendors demonstrate this was not the case. From the vantage point of Mexico City's markets, the formation of the CNOP, which soon became the largest branch of the party, was the corollary of two decades of government efforts to learn how to mediate their social relations and respond to vendors' quests for proprietary progress.

While state actors used the new political connections to reconfigure the vendor movement, eliminating certain organizations and promoting others according to political (and personal) imperatives, vendors in turn used the PRI to channel their own demands. They mobilized effectively to elect sympathetic congressmen and made their voices heard during national election campaigns. Chapter 5 argues that, like industrialists and urban developers, vendors requested more, not less, state intervention—but on their terms. They wanted the government to upgrade markets and provide them with social services. They also expected officials to crush their competitors, especially street vendors. Their hopes were not misplaced. A combination of economic growth, public investment, and repression allowed politicians and vendor organizations to negotiate a successful program of urban renewal.[31] Between 1952 and 1966, the Department of the Federal District built 160 markets with a capacity for over fifty thousand stalls.[32] In these markets proprietary traders earned their piece of the Mexican miracle, constructing a way of life that promised they too could become middle class.[33] Nevertheless, further tens of thousands remained on the streets, where they suffered the repressive side of Mexico's state-led development—a reminder of the limits of the midcentury's achievements.[34]

Today, vendors remain in the same public markets the city government built in the 1950s and '60s, defending them against all odds from the combined threats of gentrification, Walmart, convenience stores, and an ever-growing number of street stalls.[35] These markets were the product of the interactions of multiple groups that systematically used whatever advantages they had to further their social aspirations and material interests. Their history does not fit a teleological framework; their future is as uncertain now as it was then. The mid-twentieth century offered capitalists and the state an array of possible institutional arrangements to supply the city's residents with everyday necessities, including supermarkets, small private shops, and government stores. They could have allowed itinerant peddlers to dominate retail trade in at least certain areas of the city. Instead, if in the 1960s market vendors provided upwards of 90 percent of the capital's food supply, and their halls epitomized the height of Mexico's high modernism, it was because of their unrelenting collective efforts, whose success was by no means guaranteed.[36] Over the course of the century this book covers, vendors adapted to and reshaped the urban political economy, sometimes deliberately, sometimes unintentionally, their actions always embedded in dynamic power structures that generated and reproduced inequality. Looking closely at vendors' dealings with their suppliers, customers, competitors, market administrators, urban planners, redevelopers, and politicians, we can see both proprietary traders' role in the story of capitalism and statecraft in Mexico, and the messy, constrained contingency of historical change.

1 Taxes and Compassion, 1867–1880

IN THE SUMMER OF 1867, Mexico once again became a republic. Though nobody could have known it at the time, this year marked the end of Mexico's postindependence civil wars and foreign military interventions, which had threatened the very existence of the country and cost its inhabitants so dearly in blood and territory. A year after Napoleon III withdrew French troops from Mexico, on June 19, Liberal forces executed Emperor Maximilian of Hapsburg alongside two of his Conservative military commanders.[1] Three weeks later, and six days before President Benito Juaréz's triumphant return to the capital, José María Cadena and ten other vendors of secondhand ironware, maize, matches, and balls of yarn at El Volador Market wrote to the Ayuntamiento de la Ciudad de México, or city council, with an urgent petition for a rent reduction.

Sales were poor on the dead-end street opposite the university where they had their stalls, and they were suffering from the higher rates imposed during Maximilian's rule. "The government of the traitors and their worthy Ayuntamiento," they maintained, "had no other aim than to squeeze the people to the last drop of blood. They left us in the most deplorable condition, as our little capital has disappeared and now we subsist on credit. In this state we appeal to you, our natural protectors, so that, aware of our situation, you might use your powers to render it less onerous."[2] The city council, which was the official body in charge of markets and the traditional arbiter of urban social relations, found the claims fair. Two months later it reduced their rents back to the level they had paid in 1863, before the French intervention.

In the years of the consolidation of the Republic, Mexico City's market vendors played a central role in the construction of political legitimacy at the different levels of government. The visibility of vendors in the city's streets and plazas shaped elite and popular conceptions of public space and made markets a focal point of discussions of what amounted to good urban governance. What is more, the vast majority of the urban population depended on public markets for reliable access to essential goods such as charcoal, oil, hats, chiles, and beans. A disruption of market supply could cause unrest in the national capital, home to most of the country's rich and powerful. Public markets were not just a social necessity, but a strategic service.

The responsibility for administering markets and managing the social relations within and around them fell to the ayuntamiento, which in return received fees and rents. Fiscal needs drove much of its market policy in this period as vendors and merchants provided on average 10 percent of the city council's yearly income. Their contributions to the city's coffers gave vendors a certain leverage. Yet, as the signatories of the July 1867 petition to their "natural protectors" were well aware, a second, less tangible factor also informed the ayuntamiento's attitude toward markets. An imperative to show compassion toward vendors, a combination of councilors' private Catholicism and political good sense, featured prominently in the ayuntamiento's decisions and in wider public debates about market policies. Concern for the plight of the poor could trump the need for fiscal revenues, with the result that vendors' pleas for lower market fees were frequently answered favorably.

In this quiet capital city not yet ruffled by economic growth, the local authorities carefully weighed the competing imperatives of taxes and compassion on the basis of their knowledge of vendors' personal circumstances. If the ayuntamiento could claim such knowledge it was because its officials regularly engaged with vendors in discussions about the terms under which their businesses operated. But these discussions did not imply that vendors were able to participate in the restricted local public sphere, where Liberal politicians, councilmen, and journalists decided market policies and, more generally, what amounted to the public good. When vendors' views and interests appeared in policy debates, they did so indirectly, mediated by the politicians and journalists who, responding to their pleas, spoke and wrote on their behalf and acted as their protectors. This chapter argues that in a city of low stakes, elites and proprietary vendors remained embedded in a set of customary relations rooted in Catholic ethics and the preservation of social hierarchy. These bonds of exclusionary benevolence enabled the local government and vendors themselves to manage the city's social inequalities, with minimal conflict and minimal change.

Mexico, a City of Commerce

After four years of French occupation, and having witnessed the loss of almost half of the country's territory to the United States of America earlier in the century, Mexico's political elites were acutely aware of the risks of continued civil strife.[3] As President Juárez sought political conciliation, Conservatives either withdrew from public life or were assimilated into Liberalism, a project that perceived the stability of republican forms as a necessary condition for the country's survival as a sovereign state. Thus it was essential to the construction of a viable polity to curtail the power of the Catholic Church, which under Pope Pius IX had supported the French intervention in Mexico and universally condemned the separation of church and state, freedom of speech and religion, and other Liberal principles as modern errors.[4] Liberals banned Catholicism from official politics even though it remained the professed faith of virtually all the citizenry and was fundamental to how Mexicans of all political persuasions made sense of the world around them.

Still, the ascendancy of secular constitutionalism did not mean the end of conflict. Violence, including banditry and agrarian social unrest, remained widespread outside Mexico City. More significantly, bitter Liberal factionalism and struggles for power resulted in continued political turbulence. Reforms to the federalist constitution of 1857 provided for a stronger central government, leading to fervent opposition to the national executive and revolts in several states. The last successful Liberal uprising would bring General Porfirio Díaz to the presidency in 1876.[5]

Like the quest for peace, economic prosperity turned out to be elusive in this period. The scant data available suggest that gross national product grew slowly, while indicators such as federal revenues and railroad construction improved only slightly before 1880. An empty treasury made repayment of foreign debts difficult and infrastructure works impossible. Lack of investment and employment opportunities meant that political appointments and military actions provided the only sure path to upward social mobility. Mining, mostly silver, and the production of sisal revitalized foreign trade, but expensive internal communications, deficient capital markets, and other institutional constraints prevented domestic economic integration and economic growth.[6]

Mexico City had over 200,000 residents in a territory stretching 8.5 square kilometers.[7] As the seat of the federal government and the bureaucratic center of the country, it formed a hub for officials on public payrolls and anybody seeking connections and concessions. It was also the heart of the country's conspicuous consumption, where the rich spent their fortunes on mansions and townhouses, organized balls and banquets, and kept stables and servants. Yet a quarter of the local population were described as *léperos*, a term that encompassed petty thieves, vagrants, and beggars, making the capital a city of stark contrasts.[8]

Trade of all types dominated the urban economic landscape. The city council registered 1,200 businesses, three-quarters of which were devoted to purely commercial activities, wholesale and retail, while the remaining quarter combined production with commercialization, as in the case of bakeries, carpenters' shops, cobblers, and blacksmiths.[9] The most elegant stores lined Plateros Street, where Mexico's elite could purchase the latest French fashion and other imported luxuries. Those seeking out domestic luxuries packed what one guidebook described as "some of the very best shops in Mexico," the "tailors, hatters, milliners, jewelers" of the Portal de Mercaderes.[10] More ordinary garments could be bought in specialized stores on Monterilla Street, and in less central areas artisans opened their workshops to the street, improvising spaces to sell their goods.[11] Licensed butcher shops were scattered throughout the city, including many in lower-class areas.[12] Businessmen of French, German, and Spanish origins were prominent figures in high-end, highly profitable retail activities catering exclusively to the upper and middle classes, while Mexicans ran most retail ventures marketed to the masses.[13]

As varied as these businesses were, they formed just one end of the commercial spectrum. At the other end were countless peddlers selling all manner of items, from toys and rebozos, the traditional Mexican shawl, to flowers, foodstuffs, and herbs. No contemporary observer, whether foreign or national, failed to comment on them.[14] As John Lewis Geiger, a British traveler in the 1870s, reminisced:

> Flower-girls exhibit their magnificent bouquets, which they offer for a few *reales*, spread out temptingly on a wide part of the pavement; *aguadores* cased in their leather garments with huge water-jars on their backs, suspended by straps from their foreheads . . . ; *carboneros*, men and women, bending under their dingy huacalitos, wander from house to house; whilst countless hawkers of confectionary, dulces, agua fresca, tamales (a species of savoury roll, made

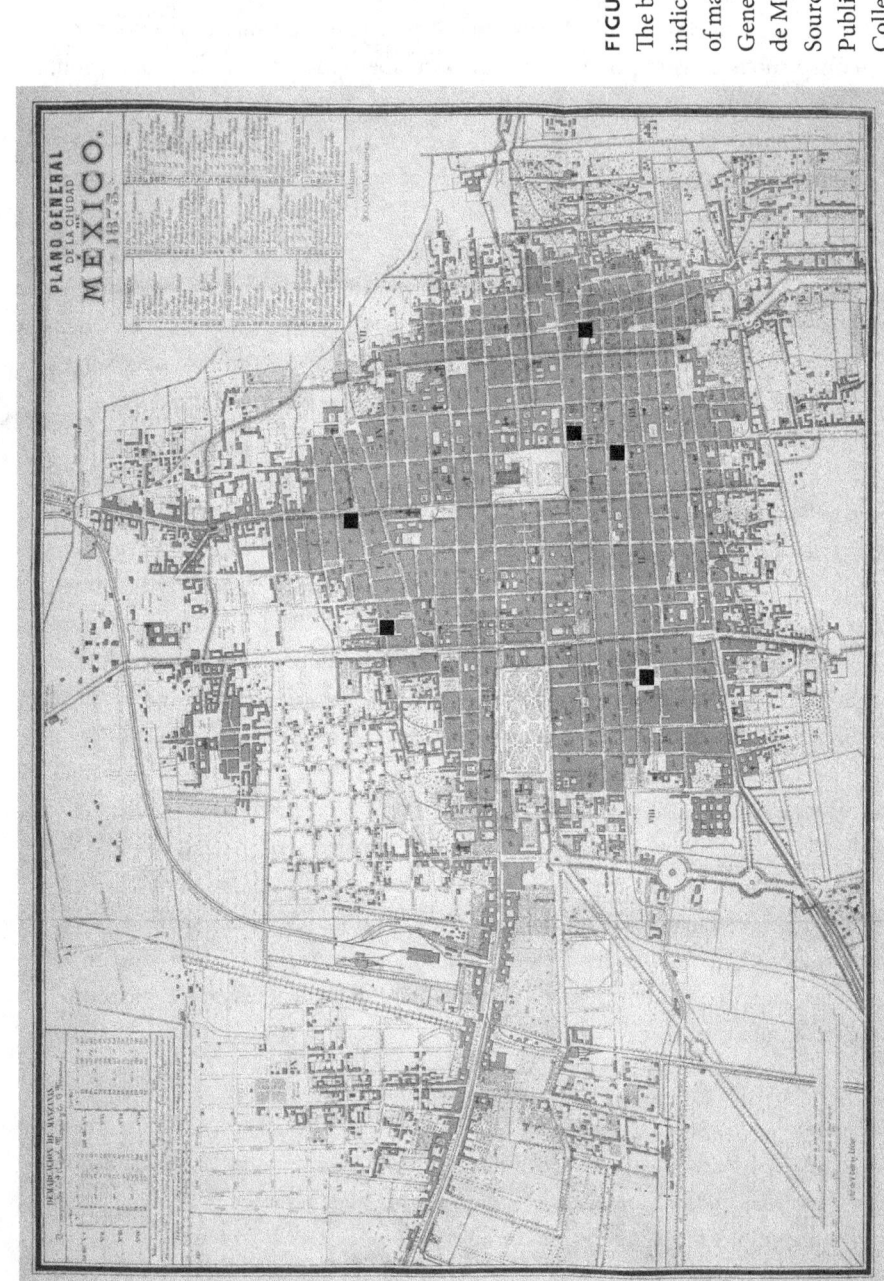

FIGURE 1.
The black squares indicate the location of markets. Plano General de La Ciudad de México, 1875.
Source: The New York Public Library, Digital Collections.

of maize-dough and meat), and a hundred other dainties, carry their wares on their heads, and make the air ring with their motley cries.[15]

Many single mothers and widows struggling to provide for their families took to peddling, alongside wives and children of factory workers and artisans trying to supplement their household incomes. Some of them offered prepared foods to the city's laboring classes who, pressed for time and lacking cooking facilities at home, took their meals on the city's streets.[16] Other peddlers were artisans who, unable or unwilling to find an outlet for their products in established retail stores, sold their wares on the city streets. Small-scale producers of flowers, vegetables, and fruits from the city's hinterland also participated in this trade.

In between the worlds of the established, registered stores and the unregulated peddlers were the city's public markets—public in the sense that they were a service to be provided by the ayuntamiento for local residents, with their accessibility, adequate supply, order, and cleanliness treated as paramount matters of good urban governance.[17] While the more affluent city dwellers purchased many goods in the retail shops just described, the vast majority of the urban population depended on these markets for reliable access to everyday necessities. The city council thus sought to ensure their smooth functioning.[18]

In 1868, Mexico City's six existing public markets were in bad shape. Some markets were housed in old or poorly constructed buildings, while others were mere gatherings of vendors in open spaces.[19] La Merced was an undeveloped lot overlooking the colonial cloisters of the convent that gave the market, and eventually the neighborhood, its name. Vendors had been carrying out their transactions in precarious stalls of their own construction, or directly from mats placed on the ground, since they had been moved there from other locations around the city three years earlier.[20] The markets of Santa Catarina, Iturbide (also called San Juan after the plaza on which it was built), and El Jardín had been remodeled in the late 1840s and early 1850s but were already in disrepair, while the unfinished but active Jesús Market had been under construction since 1857.[21] The largest market in the city, El Volador, needed constant work, not least because its wooden-framed stalls frequently caught fire.[22]

Public markets were highly heterogeneous places, and within a single market the infrastructure varied considerably. In El Volador, for example, the main hall contained one hundred internal fixed stalls (*cajones interiores*), and

FIGURE 2. *Iturbide Market on Plaza San Juan.* Lithograph by Casimiro Castro, 1856. Note how the market is depicted as encompassing the hall and the sombras outside. Source: México y sus Alrededores. Colección de monumentos, trajes y paisajes. Mexico City: Imprenta Litográfica de Decaen, 1875.

another hundred overlooking the streets (*cajones exteriores*). An upper floor was used as a warehouse. At the center were four open pavilions and eighteen open sheds housing a variety of stalls, including movable booths or *puestos eventuales*. Outside the hall, other vendors, many of them women, carried out their business under *sombras*, tripod parasols, while clusters of stalls dotted the surrounding streets.[23] El Volador's physical boundaries, like those of all the city's markets, were ill-defined, encompassing a variety of vending practices within and in the vicinity of the building that gave it its name.

According to regulations, the city council was supposed to privilege requests from merchants and vendors of foodstuffs when allocating stalls in public markets, because concentration would facilitate the monitoring of prices, qualities, weights, and measures.[24] But rules and reality did not necessarily match. Market stalls sold everything necessary for running a household, from fruits, vegetables, and flowers to cloth and construction materials. In El Volador Market, the two hundred fixed and most expensive cajones sold mainly nonperishables, as only these generated enough profit to pay for their rents. Fresh foodstuffs were relegated to the market's four less costly open pavilions or the nearby streets, where they were sold in puestos eventuales and sombras—that is, in movable booths and under parasols.[25]

To simplify municipal control, a detailed bylaw partitioned Iturbide Market into distinct sections selling different types of goods. Internal stalls numbered one through six were reserved for butchers, while stalls numbered eight through ten were reserved for dealers of earthenware and glass objects. The rest of the cajones interiors were meant for those selling pork, poultry, fish, game, and salted meats. The sale of cotton cloth, shawls, serapes, washtubs, trays, and large earthen jars was allowed as long as the practice did not displace any trade in foodstuffs. Stalls in the exterior facing part of the market were primarily intended for vendors of fresh produce, but these stalls could also house trade in charcoal, tar, bricks, sand, and lime. Some of these products, due to their combustible nature, were to be traded there in order to avoid fires inside.[26]

Different ways of doing business coexisted in public markets. Hidden behind the homogenizing rubric of *comerciantes*, or traders, were two distinct types. On the one hand there were capitalist merchants, some of whom operated multiple stalls. Rules governing markets did not restrict the size of the space an individual could rent,[27] so at El Volador, for example, butcher Donasiano Serna rented three stalls, while his competitor Antonio Ocaranza rented four.[28] Inside this market, there were ten to twelve stores run by the richest merchants in dry goods, hardware, and nonperishable foodstuffs, each occupying up to forty square meters.[29] They sold the products of factories and artisans' workshops, and staples such as beans and meat, which they bought from the wholesalers in charge of bringing such goods into the city.[30] These merchants hired employees to take care of customers and signed leases securing their stalls for up to ten years.[31]

On the other hand, larger numbers of less affluent proprietary vendors, who dealt mostly in perishable foodstuffs and flowers or other essential items like straw hats and petates, traded independently with no help beyond that from their families, paying daily fees to occupy much smaller booths and sombras.[32] During 1869, according to a report by markets administrator Juan García Brito, an average of 2,322 vendors paid daily fees to the city's collectors for the use of puestos eventuales alone.³³ Many of these vendors, however, had to adapt to the seasonal availability of goods, and therefore some of their stalls remained vacant during part of the year, especially the winter months.³⁴ Their position in the city's commercial networks depended on the line of business they were in. Sellers of hats and mats might have produced the wares themselves or bought them from artisans. Vendors of offal sourced their produce from the slaughterhouse workers in charge of the killing floor.³⁵ Retailers of maize usually bought from wholesalers. Produce vendors often resold flowers, fruit, and vegetables they purchased from small-scale producers of the *chinampas*, the floating gardens to the south of the city.³⁶ These man-made islands, constructed atop lakes and canals and irrigated by the surrounding waters, had been supplying Mexico City since before colonial times.³⁷ Every morning at daybreak, an English visitor wrote, peasants from the chinampas piloted "hundreds of Indian canoes, of different forms and sizes" through the busy Chalco canal, loaded with "the finest cultivated vegetables which are produced in European gardens" and "the numberless fruits of the torrid zone," all "piled up in pyramids, and decorated with the most gaudy flowers."³⁸ In the early 1860s, these canoes were estimated to carry about 80,000 loads per year, providing the city with most of its daily needs.³⁹

Proprietary vendors' working capital was small, and they often depended on credit, which might explain why vegetable producers protested that La Merced vendors did not pay them for their wares on the spot but instead delayed payments for several days.⁴⁰ When such disagreements arose, the ayuntamiento stepped in to mediate. The local authorities had to ensure the city's ubiquitous and highly heterogeneous networks of commerce functioned smoothly. At stake were not just vendors' livelihoods and residents' access to everyday necessities. Public markets also helped to generate tax revenue, and to legitimize the city council as a governing body.

Markets and the Fiscal Needs of the Ayuntamiento

By 1867, the ayuntamiento had secured the exclusive prerogative to build, open, tax, and administer public markets, along with the concomitant responsibility of maintaining and managing them. This was no small task, and to fulfil it the ayuntamiento appointed an *administrador de mercados*, a markets administrator who supervised the collection of market rents and fees, enforced markets' rules and regulations, ensured the cleanliness of markets and their fountains, and solved minor conflicts between comerciantes and their customers as well as among vendors and merchants themselves, all with the assistance of municipal employees.[41] In addition, a market commission formed of three councilors received and processed all correspondence related to markets, made proposals for their improvement, and acted as the liaison between the ayuntamiento and the administrador de mercados.

The consolidation of the ayuntamiento's power over markets had been part of a broader and protracted process establishing the city council's competence and administrative jurisdiction relative to other authorities. Under the Spanish Empire, the governing of cities, towns, and pueblos had been in the hands of municipal councils, which among their many duties oversaw the cleanliness of streets and markets, the appropriate supply of basic goods, and the conservation of public fountains. After independence in 1821, ayuntamientos throughout Mexico continued to fulfill most of the same functions as before but within a new set of republican institutions: they were now regulated by state constitutions and overseen by state governments with veto powers over their decisions. Mexico City's case was more complicated. Once it became the capital of the Republic in 1824, it was not subject to the authority of any state. The ayuntamiento's executive responsibilities and the relationship with the "higher authorities" of the national government remained legally unsettled until the issue of the Ordenanzas Municipales of 1840.[42]

The Ordenanzas of 1840 defined and regulated the city council's functions and its obligations to provide public services. At the same time, they also determined that any decision made by the ayuntamiento had to be approved by the governor of the Department of the Federal District, which in practice meant the consent of the secretary of the interior and the president of the Republic. As Ariel Rodríguez Kuri has documented, the Ordenanzas formalized the national government's political control over the Ayuntamiento de la Ciudad de México while simultaneously confirming a certain degree of autonomy for the ayuntamiento to exercise a series of functions with immediate implications for the local population.[43] Tensions between the different levels of government persisted, but the Ordenanzas created a stable framework for the working of the ayuntamiento.

Fiscal laws passed in 1848 ratified the Ordenanzas' assertion of the city council's authority over markets, which could not be challenged either by private interests or by other authorities.[44] This encouraged the ayuntamiento to purchase the plazas of San Juan and Jesús and, to the extent afforded by municipal resources, to improve markets' material conditions. Between 1850 and 1851, the council rebuilt seventy wooden stalls in Villamil Market. In Santa Catarina it refurbished stalls, put up masonry walls, and paved the surrounding sidewalks. It also inaugurated the refurbished Iturbide Market on the recently acquired Plaza of San Juan.[45]

For most of the nineteenth century, funding for these improvements, and for the city council's budget more generally, came from two sources: *arbitrios* and *propios*.[46] The arbitrios represented the share of certain taxes collected by the national authorities that were allocated to the ayuntamiento. The city council could lobby for an enlargement of its arbitrios, but had no decision-making power over these transfers. The most significant arbitrios were the *derechos municipales*, or the portion of internal customs passed on to the city council. Between 1869 and 1880, the derechos municipales supplied on average 46 percent of the ayuntamiento's total revenue, making them the largest item in the budget (table 1). The city also counted on the propios, the inflow of fiscal income derived from municipal assets such as markets and abattoirs and from charges on local services including water provision and carriages for hire. The city council collected these revenues directly, but—despite the control suggested by their name—the national executive, under authorization from Congress, set the rates at which propios were charged.

During the first half of the nineteenth century this fiscal structure had allowed the city council to attend to the city's material needs adequately, if imperfectly.[47] After Liberal attacks on Church and other corporate holdings were enshrined into the so-called desamortization laws of the 1850s, however, the ayuntamiento was stripped of many of its income-generating properties. The Lerdo Law of 1856 and the 1857 Constitution forbade civil and religious institutions from owning or administering properties other than those "directly and immediately used for their purpose and object."[48] The Catholic Church, peasant communities, and government bodies were forced to divest themselves of valuable assets. In Mexico City, the ayuntamiento had to sell such a large portion of its real estate that the share of urban property owned by the public sector fell from over 6 percent in 1848 to less than 1 percent in 1864.[49] Public markets were among the few city properties that the ayuntamiento could still legally own, manage, and exploit, thanks to the codification of the Ordenazas.[50]

The city's coffers were subsequently somewhat replenished by the *leyes de dotación municipal* of 1863 and 1867, but scarcity remained the norm.[51]

Mexico City was better off than the rest of the country, but given the general sluggishness of the economy, and the constraints on generating its own revenue streams, members of the ayuntamiento complained repeatedly that the council lacked sufficient resources to deliver public services to the local population. In every published yearly report between 1867 and 1880 there are disclaimers about how little could be done in public works, or even maintenance, for lack of funds. For example, in 1870 the council declared: "Unfortunately, for quite a while the city has been in a deplorable state, not due to the negligence or lack of will of those responsible for its conservation, but because improving its situation would require large sums [of money] that the Ayuntamiento cannot afford."[52] This statement was a defense against the criticisms that circulated in the press about the state of the city's built environment. It was also a political intervention, an implicit denunciation if not of the political order then of the decisions made by the national executive on how to allocate available resources.[53]

Public markets seemed to offer the ayuntamiento the most viable option for obtaining more revenue. While federal fiscal laws dictated the rates to be charged for different types of stalls, they granted the city council the right to decide on the number and location of markets. If the ayuntamiento could increase the number of fee-paying stalls, it could expand its resource base. Markets already provided the ayuntamiento its second largest source of revenue (after the derechos municipales), producing on average 10 percent of the council's resources each year between 1869 and 1880 (table 1). They also represented the most stable flow of income month to month.[54] Market revenues were composed of two accounts, *arrendamientos* and *viento*. The few hundred fixed stalls in the existing market halls paid into the ayuntamiento's arrendamientos account, while thousands of vendors "out in the wind" paid into the viento account. This second account included fees from stalls and booths in designated streets and plazas throughout the city as well as from puestos eventuales and sombras within and around market halls. The spaces where viento vendors worked might have looked more ad hoc than indoor stalls, but they constituted well-established, clearly regulated commercial outlets. In the 1870s, for example, the viento category included most vendors of fresh produce in El Volador as well as everybody trading in La Merced Market, where no hall existed. Viento vendors were an essential part of public markets, producing three-quarters of the city council's market revenues, and over 7 percent of its total resources (table 1). In other words, in this period there was no

TABLE 1. Ayuntamiento revenues.

Year	Total revenue (current pesos)	From derechos municipales (%)	Total from markets (%)	Of which viento (%)	Of which arrendamientos (%)
1869	830,793	47	11.4	7.6	3.8
1870	839,509	48	9.8	7.5	2.3
1871	874,402	47	9.5	7.7	1.8
1872	848,703	47	8.2	6.2	2.0
1873	897,609	47	8.0	6.1	1.9
1874	921,969	46	9.0	7.1	1.9
1875	869,845	48	9.8	7.3	2.5
1876	839,043	43	9.8	7.0	2.8
1877	745,256	39	10.9	7.6	3.3
1878	869,578	48	9.7	7.0	2.8
1879	941,845	47	10.7	8.0	2.7
1880	1,006,547	44	11.0	8.5	2.5
Average		46%	9.8%	7.3%	2.5%

SOURCES: Total revenue and derechos municipales from Rodríguez Kuri, *La experiencia olvidada*, 120; market revenues for 1869–1879 from *Memoria 1879*, 220, and for 1880 from *Discurso 1880*, 12.

clear dividing line between markets and streets. In the eyes of the city council, the relevant distinction was between vendors who paid taxes, wherever they might be located, and those who did not.

The income-generating capacity of public markets, together with the fact that market revenues went directly into the city's coffers, convinced the ayuntamiento of the desirability of increasing the number of fee-paying stalls. The council thus contemplated building new halls, which would increase the size of the arrendamientos account. But in a context of chronic scarcity, major public works projects were financially unfeasible. In fact, in these years the city council struggled to afford anything beyond basic repairs. This explains why the articulate lobbying of markets administrator Juan García Brito fell on deaf ears. He argued repeatedly and eloquently that more and better markets would bring additional revenue while improving the provision of daily necessities for the city's population. On several occasions, for example, García Brito made the case for moving the always-crowded El Volador Market away from the city's main square. Its narrow aisles, he complained in 1868, were permanently covered in all manner of waste, and owing to the absence of a proper unloading platform, the adjacent streets of Portacoeli, Flamencos, Universidad, and Meleros bore witness to a "confusion of men and beasts" as the elegant carriages of the well-to-do collided with carts transporting merchandise.⁵⁵ Such a spectacle, he lamented, clashed with the order and elegance of the Palacio Nacional and its surrounding neighborhood, which deserved better.⁵⁶

García Brito proposed building a hall at La Merced to relocate the merchants and vendors of El Volador and to provide a roof for those already there. He believed that La Merced could replace El Volador as the city's main market thanks to its favorable location next to the Chalco Canal, still one of the most important entry points for produce. La Merced was close enough not to inconvenience those who were used to shopping at El Volador but far enough to avoid disturbing the owners of near-by stores selling luxury goods—not to mention their wealthy customers.⁵⁷ Despite García Brito's persistence, the ayuntamiento found it impossible to erect a new hall for the comerciantes of El Volador, even after a fire consumed the market in March 1870.⁵⁸ The city authorities took five years to rebuild it, despite the lost revenue that this delay entailed. La Merced would have to wait even longer, until 1880, for a masonry hall. Only in 1882 did the arrendamientos account return to its 1869 prefire value.⁵⁹

Increasing the number of viento stalls appeared to provide an alternative means to generate additional market revenues without costly investment in infrastructure.⁶⁰ In principle, the ayuntamiento could grant permission to vendors to set up fee-paying stalls wherever it saw fit. But expanding the *ramo del viento* effectively posed its own challenges. The ayuntamiento would need to be able to monitor extended parts of the city to prevent the embezzlement of fees by collectors and their evasion by vendors. After all, these vendors often sold their goods from mats placed on the ground, or from movable booths, making it easy for them to stay one step ahead of collectors. Scattered viento vendors could easily avoid the council's control altogether by joining the ranks of unregulated peddlers. For this reason, the ayuntamiento sought to concentrate viento sales in the streets adjacent or close to existing market halls where it was easier to enforce their fiscal obligations. A complementary strategy for increasing revenue, therefore, was to try to improve oversight of the ramo del viento. Several attempts were made, but it proved prohibitively expensive to hire the necessary personnel, and efforts were soon abandoned.⁶¹

Due to the ayuntamiento's lack of investment funds and its persistent need for revenue, the city authorities continued to encourage viento sales, despite having limited capacity to regulate them. But if the city turned to market vendors to help fund the government and feed its population, vendors turned to the city to request fee reductions and other forms of support. Their mutual dependency, however lopsided, shaped the local political economy.

Councilors' Compassion: Moral Economy or Catholic Duty?

The ayuntamiento's attempts to generate income from public market resources was tempered by a paternalistic notion of responsibility for the livelihoods of the vendors who worked there. As the council's 1877 records put it:

> Two considerations have weighed, alternately, on the minds of our legislators, or those in charge of public life, when dictating the rules pertaining to Mexico [City]'s markets; at times they have considered their primordial objective to enrich municipal coffers, on which rest the demands of the culture and refinement of a great capital; at others, they have yielded to compassion for those unfortunate people who, with their labors like those of ants, the bearing of wild fruits of the earth, or the traffic in products of primitive agriculture or industry, hardly obtain enough for the most miserable diets and for clothes.[62]

This imperative to "yield to compassion" weighed heavily on social relations and political communications throughout the period.[63] That so many of the city's poor lived off proprietary retail activities, or undertook them to supplement their meager household incomes, made streets and markets an obvious outlet for the authorities' moral duties. In exchange for deference and obedience, vendors could expect the ayuntamiento to tolerate a certain amount of untaxed peddling and to grant fee reductions for struggling viento vendors and market stallholders.

Historians and anthropologists working across a host of eras and geographies tend to place such bonds and obligations within the framework of E. P. Thompson's "moral economy."[64] Given the country's deep Catholic past, any moral economy in place in Mexico City in the 1860s and 1870s must have necessarily been constructed on Catholic ethics and doctrine. The Laws of the Reforma and the Liberal Constitution of 1857 had officially separated church and state, but Catholicism remained the professed faith of the citizenry, and the new laws would have done little to transform people's long-held views and beliefs. In other words, religion might have been banned from official politics, but it was still fundamental to how Mexicans made sense of the world around them, whatever their social standing or political inclinations.

Compassion, intimately related to charity (*caritas*) and mercy (*misericordia*), remained a fundamental Catholic duty, shaping the attitudes of rich and poor alike. Paul the Apostle called charity, or Christian love, a virtue greater than faith and hope. Thomas Aquinas affirmed this view in the thirteenth century, holding that "the merit of eternal life rests chiefly with charity."[65] According to Aquinas, charity leads us to perform compassionate acts of mercy, which, building on Augustine, he declared to be a "heartfelt sympathy for another's distress, impelling us to succor him if we can. For mercy takes its name 'misericordia' from denoting a man's compassionate heart for another's unhappiness."[66] Aquinas's teachings were undergoing a revival in the second half of the nineteenth century, and Thomism became central to the development of Catholic social teachings in this period.[67]

These were not distant references in Mexico. The Catholic press frequently discussed the importance of charity, with its emphasis on good works, in social and political matters. An 1871 editorial from *La Voz de Mexico*, for example, argued that without charity, "which blends all Catholic virtues into one," there could be no family, friendship, city, or nation.[68] Moreover, in 1875, to counteract the limitations the Liberal government had imposed on the Church, the archbishops of Mexico City, Michoacán, and Guadalajara admonished the faithful to prove that they were good Christians through "the sweet perfume of their true piety, and the pure gold of their multiplied compassionate acts of mercy toward the sick, the poor, and the helpless orphan."[69] A concern with moral duties was ubiquitous enough that the theme for the 1883 biennial painting competition of the Escuela Nacional de Bellas Artes was "A Sublime Act of Mercy." The winner was José María Ibarrarán y Ponce's *La caridad en los primeros tiempos de la Iglesia*. The work, which depicts two men bringing a basket of food and a woolen robe to a prisoner in shackles, can be read as a commentary on the Church's attempts to return to its origins in order to reinvigorate itself and to find solutions to pauperism and other contemporary "social problems."[70]

Liberal politicians had compelling reasons to show Christian compassion for the less privileged. Many of them remained fervent Catholics in their private lives. As historians Robert Buffington and Rafael Barajas Durán point out, Liberal ideology, even anticlericalism, did not necessarily undermine their religious faith.[71] Beyond satisfying personal religious imperatives, performing acts of mercy also made good political sense as a demonstration of a virtue-centered morality to a Catholic public. The importance of Catholicism

FIGURE 3. José María Ibarrarán y Ponce, *La caridad en los primeros tiempos de la Iglesia*, 1883. Source: Museo Nacional de Arte, Mexico City.

to the construction of the social identities of Mexico City's popular classes could be seen in the frequent use of religious language and imagery by the writers, illustrators, and readers of the local penny press.[72] What is more, politicians were quite aware of the risks of ignoring popular religiosity. In 1873, for example, when federal authorities expelled seventeen Jesuits from the country on the grounds that they were "pernicious foreigners," a group of Liberals led by a former president of the ayuntamiento argued vocally though newspaper articles and in the national Congress that the expulsion not only betrayed Liberal principles but also unwisely antagonized the majority of Mexicans, threatening to "renew old and bitter religious disputes."[73] Finally, Liberals might have accepted their Christian duties in the hope that upholding a traditional moral order would preserve the subordination of the laboring classes and thus help bring about economic prosperity.[74]

Where city councilors were concerned, the legal framework of the 1870s allowed them to act compassionately toward individual vendors by reducing their rents or, if a vendor's pecuniary situation was bad enough to justify it, by waiving his or her market fees altogether.[75] But broader-reaching measures were beyond their remit, and at times the council found that these bounds on their compassion were too tight. By appealing to what he referred to as their "enlightened and generous feelings," ayuntamiento president Eduardo F. Arteaga persuaded his fellow councilors that female viento vendors of tortillas, vegetables, and flowers in markets and their adjacent streets should be exempt of all taxes. He insisted that it was high time they repaired the "iniquity" being committed against this "most unhappy and helpless people who almost without exception belonged to the Indian race," for they were paying up to four times their small working capital in fees every month, while constantly being ill-treated by the fee collectors. Arteaga lamented that these poor women's pleas almost never reached the authorities, and that in the few instances they did, they were often ignored. Their predicament, he confessed, broke his heart. Arteaga acknowledged that municipal revenue would suffer with the exemption—fees from the tortilla vendors alone totaled 4,000 pesos per year. But "between this ill and the injustice being committed" he said, he "did not hesitate to accept the former."[76] The council was powerless to modify fiscal laws on its own, so in late January 1872 it petitioned President Benito Juárez, through the governor of the Federal District, to change the Ley de Dotación del Fondo Municipal along these lines.[77]

President Juárez's response must have been an unnerving surprise. On February 14, 1872, a presidential decree granted full tax exemptions to "the most destitute" vendors, regardless of their gender, race, or place of trade. This included not just female viento vendors of tortillas, vegetables, and flowers in the vicinity of markets but also many other small-scale independent producers and sellers of basic consumption goods. The list of exempted items included prepared meats, palm leaf hats, baskets, feather dusters, brooms, mats, multiple types of herbs, eggs, butter, cheese, white fish, and poultry. To aggravate the matter, the decree stated that vendors should not be restricted to carrying out their trade in designated areas but should be free to move around the city as their trade required.[78] The ayuntamiento's attempt at a controlled, selective exemption had backfired.

The markets commission called the decree a "disastrous innovation."[79] Had it been fully enforced, its effects would have been dramatic, for it promised to reduce not only the ayuntamiento's revenues but also its jurisdiction. Deregulating viento sales would have severely curtailed the city council's control over the large swaths of commercial activities that took place in the city's streets. Public markets would have shrunk to coincide with market halls, the category of regulated street vending lost. However, the ayuntamiento was able to interpret the decree in such a way as to protect its jurisdiction over viento sales, claiming it was only fair that vendors were charged for their use of the city's thoroughfare. Stalls in streets and plazas, the ayuntamiento maintained, would continue to pay for their use of the public space, no matter what sorts of items they sold.[80] Market revenues accruing from viento still fell significantly in 1872, and the year 1873 also yielded relatively low viento revenues. However, the ayuntamiento managed to avoid its worst-case scenario, and by 1877, revenues had already recovered to a level consistent with the council's projected loss from their original, more restrained, petition.

The same year the decree was repealed, a new rule took hold. The ayuntamiento decided that only vendors who declared they could not possibly afford to pay would have their charges waived, and consequently were forbidden by fee collectors from staying in the same place for any period of time. In return, these vendors had to commit to carrying out only itinerant sales.[81] These compromises allowed the ayuntamiento to retain the distinction between viento sales and untaxed peddling, together with the control over what it meant to be a market vendor and what constituted a market. It also permitted councilors to continue to profess compassion. Whether or not they felt the Catholic imperative on an intimate level, in Mexico City in the 1870s it was both prudent and good political sense to make frequent displays of it.

Vendor Politics: Negotiating at the Fringe of the Public Sphere

Running the city's public markets required a cautious management of local socioeconomic conditions. On top of balancing the imperatives of tax collection and compassion, the ayuntamiento faced conflicting demands from vendors and other interested parties, which councilors were expected to arbitrate based on their intimate knowledge of the community. As a result, markets were sites of brokering and negotiation. This need to juggle fiscal needs, moral obligations, and competing material interests often translated into flexibility in the enforcement of market policies.

When El Volador burned down in 1870, for instance, the council offered the comerciantes who had lost their stalls to transfer to either La Merced or Jesús Market. As the markets commission explained, this would help to minimize the fall in the city's revenues.[82] Those already in La Merced, however, did not necessarily share the priorities of the council. Unhappy with the overcrowding and the new competition in their market, they protested the relocation in a letter:

> We beg you to have the kindness to tell us what the law is for those of us who have for so long suffered the inclemency of every season's weather, now that the main market called El Volador has suffered the unfortunate accident of a fire, and the people who were there are occupying our places, where we had established ourselves with so much work and effort.[83]

Complicating matters further, the rainy season then arrived to flood their market, prompting many vendors to move their businesses to other parts of the city.[84] As might be expected, the ayuntamiento did not approve, arguing that the behavior "produced a noticeable harm to the population due to the scattering of basic essential goods, and a further decline in fee collection." In an attempt to remedy the situation it offered vendors from La Merced priority in the allocation of stalls in the soon-to-be-inaugurated Guerrero Market. When they refused the offer, the ayuntamiento allowed those who had been there before to return to El Volador, albeit provisionally, to ply their wares among the ruins.[85]

Given the nature of the sources available, it is much harder to read the motivations of vendors and merchants than it is to unpack the ayuntamiento's markets policy. They did not leave diaries, and there are no records of their discussions. The most informative documents they generated during this period were petitions like those from the vendors in La Merced as well as complaints and other letters they wrote to the authorities.[86] While biased and written with a specific purpose in mind, these exchanges reflect how comerciantes in public markets positioned themselves with respect to the city council. In particular, they shed light on what they expected of the local government. A petition from the spring of 1868, for example, illustrates that vendors counted on the ayuntamiento's role as an arbiter in disputes among them, on its protection of their fee-paying businesses, and on its public health role in monitoring of the trade in foodstuffs. In this missive, three butchers from La Merced Market by the names of José Rosas, José Puerto, and Dolores Aguilera complained that a group of new vendors were stealing their business by luring their clientele with lower prices. They asked the ayuntamiento to remove their competition so they could continue to afford their stalls. In addition to their economic grievances, they stated that the recent arrivals hurt the city's most humble residents, the *clases menesterosas*, who bought from them, because they were obviously selling "meat of the lowest quality, which given its color and value was possibly not even cow meat," or if it was, they said, "it must surely be harmful."[87]

The available sources indicate that these comerciantes appropriated, interpreted, and recast the council's concerns with taxation, the livelihoods of the poor, and the adequate supply of the city in ways that helped them protect their own interests. Capitalist merchants renting the most expensive stalls, and thereby making the greatest fiscal contributions, could assume the ayuntamiento would respond favorably to requests for maintenance and repairs. Public works commissioners continually described works done as "demanded" and "required by market tenants," even in years when they claimed that little else was done due to lack of resources.[88] Poorer proprietary vendors could credibly expect to bargain down the level of fees the authorities charged them.[89] Sometimes they justified their petitions by discussing their personal economic circumstances, typically by comparing the modesty of their working capital with the fees they were expected to pay. When the city council tried to transfer the burden of infrastructure expenditures on La Merced vendors by forcing them to substitute masonry and metal stalls for their wooden ones, a group of "*comerciantes* of fruits and vegetables" appealed to the president of the Republic, claiming that building their precarious stalls had cost them "many days of fasting and sleepless nights," and that they could not possibly afford the replacement because their working capital was so small that it generated only modest profits, "barely allowing [them] to eat and pay taxes."[90]

On other occasions, market vendors disputed the logic behind the ayuntamiento's fees. One Adolfo Fernández appealed what he considered an excessive rent by drawing what he described as "a very judicious comparison" between La Merced Market, where he had recently established himself, and San Juan Market, which was "notoriously better" and where stalls were "built with all the desirable conditions of good construction and safety." He argued, in addition, that his wooden stall in La Merced was smaller than those in San Juan, providing measurements down to the centimeter to prove his point.[91] Out of such exchanges emerged the norms for a social contract to be respected by vendors and authorities alike. In other words, these very personal negotiations bestowed legitimacy on the ayuntamiento's policies toward public markets and on the social and economic relations within them.

Yet there were limits to what public market vendors and merchants could negotiate with the city council. Their relationship with the authorities rested on the premise that their appeals would remain in the private domain of individual self-interest. True, comerciantes would sometimes pool together to address the government collectively, but when this happened the groups they formed were fleeting, constructed ad hoc in response to specific challenges. Unlike artisans and workers, market vendors did not form civil associations during this period.[92] While they could successfully engage the authorities in defense of their individual businesses, they were excluded from the discussion of matters affecting them as a class, such as the regulations pertaining to markets.

When vendors nonetheless attempted class-based interventions, the authorities were quick to dismiss them. In 1878, after the ayuntamiento decided to charge merchants and vendors the full rents and fees allowed by existing fiscal laws, and to revise the rules that guided tax collection to incentivize its employees' compliance, a group of vendors from El Volador petitioned the city council and the president of the Republic to demand a repeal. The vendors argued that the higher fees would either negatively affect consumers if they passed them on or would force them to close their businesses and sink into misery or crime. They also rejected the claim that the upcoming modifications to the bylaws would improve the administration of markets. The city council responded that their arguments were flawed, and, what is more, that they had no right to make them.[93] The governor of the Federal District, speaking for the national executive, agreed, writing that "after examining the matter, I have determined that [the vendors] are wrong, and that they have erred in the channel they chose to avoid the harm they are complaining about." Instead, he admonished, each of them should have appealed to the ayuntamiento, which under article 116 of the Ley de Dotación del Fondo Municipal could reduce their fees if their individual circumstances so merited it. He continued:

> Beyond that, whether the disputed bylaw is inappropriate for the goals of the Ayuntamiento, which were that fee collection be as exact as possible, and whether the application of this same bylaw entails higher expenses, are matters that in good faith should not be of concern to the *comerciantes*, because they are of the exclusive incumbency of that corporation.[94]

In the minds of both the members of the ayuntamiento and the federal authorities, market vendors and merchants were not entitled to participate in policy debates. In their economic role as comerciantes, they were not members of the "public" that the city council recognized as responsible for "observing," "evaluating," and "deciding" whether the councilors were "guilty of negligence" or had "wandered from the rules mandated by justice and reason."[95] Instead, discussions of official market policies belonged in a restricted public sphere in which local notables and Liberal politicians—some of whom could well have had commercial interests—formed a "public" who, "informed of the facts," "warn[ed] and advise[d] the Ayuntamiento, through the press or private conversations, about matters pertaining to the city's good."[96]

Vendors' and merchants' exclusion from this public sphere did not mean that debate was muted. Newspaper owners, editors, and writers actively discussed and influenced the ayuntamiento's actions. In fact, according to the council minutes, the changes in the bylaws that were opposed by El Volador vendors were a response to the fact that,

> for quite a while, public opinion had been set in its desire for a sensible organization of all things related to markets; the press, preoccupied with this thought, had prompted the Ayuntamiento, denouncing abuses and calling for an end to them, always repeating its demands on the basis of the general welfare.[97]

These journalists were not detached observers but interested parties with important Liberal political connections, especially with presidential contenders and aspiring governors. They took sides in the political struggles that dominated the period, received subsidies from politicians, and, in many cases, became elected officials themselves or received government appointments.[98] The responsiveness of the ayuntamiento to the opinions of the press stemmed, in part, from this overlap between the media and politics.

In this manner, a selective group of men used the press as a forum in which to discuss policy and build consensus over local political and administrative issues. Between 1867 and 1880, in the context of Liberal factionalism and a relative freedom of the press, newspapers expressed a range of perspectives and competing interests.[99] Debate, sometimes rational and sometimes less so, produced a public opinion that legitimated the ayuntamiento's actions. But unlike the norms that emerged from the negotiations between vendors and the authorities, this source of legitimacy belonged in a narrow political space defined by the confines of Liberal power networks.

The two arenas, however, intersected every time vendors reached out to journalists to seek their support. Just as the ayuntamiento was obliged to dispense justice to poor vendors, journalists were expected to act according to the same duty of compassion in representing their interests. In the spring of 1878, for example, the ayuntamiento received two proposals to contract out the administration of markets, one by a former employee, Francisco de P. Castañares, and the other by Francisco Lizardi.[100] Three newspapers, *El Foro*, *El Federalista*, and *La Colonia Española*, supported the proposals, calling them "extremely advantageous" on the grounds that they "would save the city council the twelve thousand pesos per year that running markets now costs."[101] But the Liberal *La Patria* strongly disagreed:

> We expect and are positive that the Ayuntamiento would decline the offers after considering what is being said about it, especially that the subcontractors would ruthlessly tax the miserable small-scale vendors, with the sole goal of enriching themselves at the expense of the poor. Or does the Ayuntamiento suppose that the subcontractors only want to do a good deed, helping commerce while augmenting municipal income?[102]

El Monitor Republicano, another leading Liberal newspaper, shared this view, going as far as to refer to the project as "the ruin of poor vendors."[103] *La Patria* elaborated, "At present the Ayuntamiento, due to its sense of equity and justice, and taking into account the poverty of the people as well as their pressing needs, does not charge . . . the rates allowed [by fiscal laws] but only two thirds to some, one third to others."[104]

El Monitor's opposition went further, demanding debate and defending the role of the press in the construction of what passed for the city's common good. "It is necessary to take time to act correctly, and to make these proposals known to the public so that they can be discussed by the press, before they are accepted."[105] What is more, in their attempt to influence the ayuntamiento's decision, journalists claimed to represent the interests of market vendors, who had sought their protection:

> The poor market vendors have not eaten or slept with ease since the discussion about contracting out of markets began. . . . They have just sent us a document urging us to take on the matter, because, it is rumored that, they say, an onerous contract is about to be finalized. . . . We believe they are right, and for that reason we repeat what we have already said on previous occasions.[106]

Unable to participate openly and directly in policy debates, vendors could appeal to the "court of public opinion," which would judge whether they had a fair claim worth publicizing.[107] The liberal press could then act as an interlocutor for popular groups that otherwise were excluded from the public sphere.

In the end, journalists persuaded the ayuntamiento to abort the idea of contracting out the administration of markets—not only by building consensus but also by threatening the reputations of the councilors who had promoted it. Historian Pablo Piccato has demonstrated that the city's public sphere was defined by a juxtaposition between the public and private realms in which honor and opinion were intimately related.[108] The press convinced the ayuntamiento to discard the proposal because its members were sensitive to how the media portrayed them. The city council conceded that the view that it would harm the city and its vendors

> had become so generalized that, while the resolution by the markets commission was still pending, the recurrent attacks of the press forced Mr. Segura and Mr. Monteverde, both members of that commission, to withdraw their proposal and to resign, a notable occurrence, given that these two men are persons of great integrity and civic courage.[109]

Councilors Segura and Monteverde must have known all too well that only those perceived as honorable could claim to represent the common good. They also probably knew that if they did not show sympathy for the poor their honor would not hold.

The Low-Stakes City

In the 1870s, Mexico City was still a relatively small, low-stakes capital city. A deep-seated moral economy arbitrated by the ayuntamiento dictated that streets and markets formed a continuum in which proprietary vendors and capitalist merchants worked side by side. Vendors could count on the city council's backing for their small businesses in return for supporting the local government with the fees and taxes they paid. They could also expect politicians to act on the moral imperative to protect their modest livelihoods, whether in response to direct, personal appeals to the ayuntamiento or to sympathetic press coverage. The economy was sufficiently stagnant that fiscal needs and moral duties could remain in balance. Customary rights and responsibilities associated with Catholic compassion helped maintain respect for social hierarchy and keep the city relatively at peace.

Debates in the public sphere, as well as among those excluded from it, show that the city's residents for the most part understood both the ayuntamiento's capacities and its limits. In early 1875 a journalist called attention to the "sad and terrible" state of the Jesús Market, which he described as a "heterogeneous and repulsive *totum revolutum* [sic]" that completely obstructed all adjacent streets and generated "deleterious miasmas in the city center."[110] Yet he made only the simplest of requests: that the council limit trade to the center of the streets so that transit could flow around the stalls, and that it ensure its employees clean the area every night. In other words, despite criticisms, demands on the ayuntamiento during this period were modest. Journalists and politicians, as well as merchants and vendors, acknowledged that public monies were scarce, and that such a dearth of funds meant that the cityscape could not be substantially altered; for now, only minor improvements were within reach. But that would soon change. The 1880s would usher in a capitalist boom and with it an urban renewal drive that would place public markets at the center of attempts to build a modern capital city.

2   A Cloak of Magnificence over Beggars' Rags, 1880–1903

IN THE LAST TWO DECADES OF THE NINETEENTH CENTURY, capitalism took hold of Mexico City. The combination of economic growth and political stability allowed politicians, businessmen, and journalists to entertain the fantasy of transforming the national capital into a modern metropolis worthy of their imagined Republic. In the 1880s they embarked on an ambitious program of urban renewal and a cultural crusade against what they cast as the backwardness of the popular classes. The overhaul of municipal markets featured prominently in their plans due to vendors' indispensable and very visible role in the economic life of the city. The ayuntamiento contracted out the construction of elegant iron and glass halls and passed regulations to create clear boundaries between streets and markets, two spaces that up to this point had not been fully differentiated.

But the optimism did not last. The new market halls remained underoccupied, and vendors continued to set up their stalls on the city's streets, now joined by a growing number of peddlers who disregarded municipal regulations altogether. The Porfirian elite became frustrated with what they saw as the city council's inability to eradicate old market practices. Once the ayuntamiento accepted its failures, it gradually surrendered responsibility for managing markets to the national government. A coercive consensus emerged in the 1890s, leading to the criminalization and increased police harassment of all vendors outside the officially sanctioned halls. This chapter argues that this consensus did not simply reflect a clash between the elite and popular classes over how to provide everyday essentials or how to inhabit public spaces. Rather, many vendors actively supported the transformation of their markets, including the repression of those unable or unwilling to secure a stall. By joining the new market halls, these locatarios embraced a modernity that promised to legitimize their self-interest and help reduce competition. They shared in the work of reorganizing social relations in the capitalist boom, undermining the customary norms and institutions that had governed the city "since time immemorial."[1] Paramount among them was the ayuntamiento itself.

The Business of Modernity

The overhaul of Mexico City's markets, and of the social and political institutions of the city more broadly, was driven by the responses of national political actors, businessmen, and journalists to the expansion of the international economy. In the period covered in this chapter, and for some years after, Mexico managed to make US, British, French, and German imperialism look like a positive-sum game. Through apt diplomacy, shrewd domestic politicking, and the allocation of economic favors, presidents Manuel González (1880–84) and Porfirio Díaz (back in office from 1884) channeled the forces of global capitalism into what at the time seemed like a virtuous circle of peace and economic growth. As international trade and loans expanded and foreign direct investment flourished, mostly but not exclusively in railroads and mining, US, British, French, and German ambassadors and business representatives replaced military threats with diplomatic pressure and deal making. For Mexico, these commercial and financial relations became the cardinal matters of state. While US influence was growing faster than that of European powers, competition among them gave Mexican authorities confidence in the sustainability of their outward-looking strategy.[2]

Domestically, the end of Liberal infighting had brought a degree of political stability that allowed for resources to be diverted from the armed forces into repaying debts and building infrastructure. Concessions to railroad promoters now yielded physical investments, with kilometers of track increasing rapidly after 1880. Railroads, in turn, helped to integrate Mexico's different regions into more unified and profitable consumer markets for agriculturalists and industrialists. Targeted protectionism and tax incentives, especially after 1890, combined with worsening terms of trade to encourage domestic production of cotton textiles. Businessmen also invested in breweries and soap, paper, and cigarette factories. International demand for silver, sisal, coffee, cochineal, and sugar as well as industrial metals such as copper, zinc and lead, generated a decent flow of foreign currency, which helped finance imports of machinery and industrial inputs in addition to luxury goods. The federal government earned revenue from import duties and from selling vacant and publicly owned land, often to businesses for further development.[3] When revenue and profits from these sales did not suffice to cover expenditures, the government could turn to liquid international financial markets to procure the needed cash or to renegotiate existing foreign debts.[4]

The motto of the era was "order and progress." As was true across Latin America, Mexico's national government became the guarantor of suitable conditions for the expansion of capitalism. Congress passed laws clarifying and securing private property rights, and the executive branch made sure they were enforced. The civil code, mining code, and banking regulations were updated. When rival capitalists had conflicts that could not be solved, President Díaz himself would mediate. He also arbitrated between capitalists and their workers and between landowners and peasants. Steady economic growth helped maintain the hard-won and much-praised political stability of these years. It allowed the government to coax potential opposition into compliance by extending patronage in the form of public employment, public works contracts, or profitable intermediation for foreign capital.[5] Peace had become, as historian Mauricio Tenorio puts it, the first real political consensus since independence.[6] But there were limits to this consensus: the Pax Porfiriana was also sustained by the repression of rural uprisings and workers' protests as well as electoral manipulation and censoring of the press. Overall, these tactics were effective, and between 1880 and 1903, real gross domestic product (GDP) grew two and a half times.[7]

Mexico City was at the heart of the country's economic boom. Though it was neither a port nor a hub for industry, mining, or agriculture, it nonetheless controlled a large share of the country's growing wealth thanks to its status as the national commercial, financial, administrative, and political center. The president and his cabinet expected the capital of the Republic to showcase the prosperity they had engineered. By the time the Mexican Central Railway linked Mexico with the United States in 1884, the desire had become an obsession. Mexico City had to be overhauled to woo foreign and domestic investors and to keep interest rates in check by reassuring lenders of the safety of their assets. Moreover, as the national executive consolidated its authority and concentrated it in the capital, urban renewal projects would remind state governors, other powerful political operators, and the population in general where power resided.

Mexico City thus embarked on a process that, if we are to trust foreign visitors and the government's propaganda, amounted to an almost alchemical transmutation from a backward provincial capital into a bustling modern metropolis.[8] Without a coherent plan, but following well-established trends in European and US urbanism, local authorities opened new roads and avenues, designed sculpted parks and green spaces, and built iron and glass market halls with the goal of improving the city's aesthetics, public health, and traffic circulation.[9] By the turn of the century, the city also boasted luxurious department stores and hotels, modern factories, grand public buildings, busy railroad stations, and a new sewer system that solved, albeit temporarily, the centuries-old problem of chronic flooding.[10] Still, the pattern of economic development of the Porfiriato brought about a dramatic increase in inequality, which manifested itself in the cityscape.[11] Public and private resources were funneled to the busiest and most visible downtown areas and to new, affluent neighborhoods that sprang up as upper- and middle-class residents moved to the outskirts of the city. For generations, different classes had lived side-by-side in mixed-use residences. Now, the city was increasingly segregated, with the majority of the population left behind to make do in overcrowded tenements and precarious shacks.[12]

For the Porfirian elite, the transformation of the capital represented more than an economic or political imperative; it was also a cultural mandate. In their urban renewal plans, and their attempts to modify the behaviors of the popular classes, politicians and businessmen projected onto the city their identity as men of newly acquired or increased power and fortune. Seeing themselves as the bearers of progress, they were possessed by an intense drive to perform, as the governor of the Federal District put it, "the works demanded by the state of culture of the first city of the republic."[13] Although their actions often benefited their own small social group the most, they rhetorically presented the projects as a response to "our city's exigencies" in terms of "beauty, comfort, and elegance."[14] In the market halls, railroad stations, and factories they erected in the capital, the Porfirian high and mighty expressed their confidence in their own ability to lead the city, and the nation, into capitalist modernity.

The ayuntamiento was initially optimistic about its ability to carry forth these visions for the city. City councilors praised the "firm but prudent" government in the National Palace for preserving the domestic peace that permitted industrial and commercial activities to develop, with the resulting increase in fiscal income.[15] They also celebrated Mexico City's population growth, because it implied an enlarged tax base.[16] There were some grounds for their optimism: in the 1880s, real municipal revenues increased by a third.[17] But local politicians soon discovered that more resources and more residents carried growing expectations to deliver more and better public works and services as well as increased tensions. The city council came under pressure from the national executive, from journalists, and from businessmen. Acting both separately and in unison they would shape the council's actions and redirect its efforts. Ultimately, they would weaken it beyond recognition.

The *Discursos* of the ayuntamiento show that the governor of the Federal District, who represented the national executive in local affairs, interfered with council business with increasing force as the years went on. The annual publication of these documents provided the ayuntamiento's outgoing and incoming presidents the opportunity to leave on record a description of projects that were completed or under way as well as a commentary of the challenges ahead. Starting in 1882, the *Discursos* began to include the transcription of addresses given by the governor at the council's first annual meetings. Initially, his speeches "indicated" to councilmen what he thought were the needs of the city and what he expected them to accomplish in that year.[18] By the end of 1883, he had come to believe that this was his "duty."[19] The shift aligns with Rodríguez Kuri's finding that, from the early 1880s onward, the National Palace operated a political machine aimed at manipulating the election of council members, completing what this author calls the "domestication" of the ayuntamiento by 1890.[20]

The press amplified both the Porfirian narrative of progress and the corresponding pressure on the ayuntamiento to modernize Mexico City. Newspaper writers and editors had long engaged in debates over the management of the city, but now their diatribes became particularly piercing, with bitter complaints about the slow pace of urban improvements.[21] Given the national government's control over the press, such views were not surprising. By 1888 the national executive was subsidizing thirty publications in Mexico City alone and routinely jailing journalists who dared criticize the regime.[22]

Local and foreign capitalists also exerted substantial influence on the ayuntamiento. As they built new *colonias*, or neighborhoods, and established new factories and shops, they tried to persuade the government to provide infrastructure to support their investments. Meanwhile, more and more bankers, developers, and industrialists sought contracts for public works and for the private provision of public services. Once they gained the backing of the national executive (in part due to the material gains some government officials obtained from these deals as brokers or partners) the combined actions of politicians and capitalists forced the ayuntamiento to outsource many activities that, until then, it had performed through inner cadres of professionals, employees, and workers. In this way, capitalists pushed for an expansion of works beyond the institutional capacity of the city council to execute or control, encouraging the transfer of responsibility over urban renewal from the ayuntamiento to the national government.[23]

Under pressure from these three fronts, the ayuntamiento planned a flurry of public works. Yet it still faced serious fiscal limitations. How would the city council pay for large projects such as drainage, public lighting, or market halls? Ramón Fernández, governor of the Federal District, estimated that in comparison with "the great cities of the world," Mexico City had less than half their municipal budget per inhabitant.[24] This figure was in all probability an exaggeration—he put the population of the city in 1882 at 350,000 when it was probably closer to 300,000—but his worry does not seem to have been out of place.[25] Many times during this period the council expressed the hope that the national executive and congress, which had control over the fiscal structure of the city, would pass new laws increasing the council's revenues and fiscal powers. But these hopes remained unfulfilled, in part due to competing claims over available resources between the federal and municipal governments. Expanding the existing tax base was equally challenging. With almost 70 percent of residents earning less than the income required to support a small family of four, the poverty of the great majority of the population put a check on the amount of revenue that local authorities could collect from them.[26] At the same time, a higher tax burden on the upper and middle classes threatened to generate resistance and jeopardize the existing political consensus. While income from taxes on production and real estate transactions rose in the following decade, the city's revenues failed to keep up with projected expenditures.[27]

Acknowledging its financial constraints, the council turned to private initiative and capital. The ayuntamiento president for 1883, Pedro Rincón Gallardo, insisted that "unless residents start contributing at least small quantities from their own resources, it will take a long time for Mexico to reach the stature it merits given its importance and its large population." Thus, starting that year, the ayuntamiento encouraged the cooperation of residents' assemblies, which, organized and overseen by a group of former councilors, promised to translate their members' concerns about the "public health and beauty of Mexico City" into concrete actions.[28] Originally called the Junta de Mejoras Materiales, this association of residents and former councilors hoped to contribute actively to the transformation of the city. Its first accomplishment was to collect funds from well-off property owners on the central Cinco de Mayo Street to pay for a new pavement for their street.[29] Though the junta received some early publicity, its initiatives failed to meet the council's expectations, and within a few years, it disappeared from the records.[30]

When reliance on the civic responsibility and sense of community of the local elite proved inadequate, the ayuntamiento considered privatizations. However, proposals to allow capitalists to supply and manage key urban infrastructure were controversial. The heated debates that ensued were framed by the question of whether the adequate provision of municipal public services was compatible with private profit.[31] For example, after failing to entice wealthy residents to finance the purchase of pipes for water distribution in the early 1880s, in 1884 the ayuntamiento sought to privatize water supply services. President González and the governor of the Federal District backed the project, but it faced so much opposition from other members of the political establishment and from the press that the council had to annul the contract. The ayuntamiento, in partnership with the national executive, resorted instead to outsourcing the works, forming *contratas* with private investors under which the council remained in charge of, and thus responsible for, the supply of "life's most necessary element."[32] While contratas would come to dominate public works such as road openings and paving, the construction of public buildings, and the overhaul of the city's drainage system, other large-scale projects involving new technologies such as the introduction of electricity and tramways took the form of concessions, under which private companies provided public services in return for subsidies and direct payment from users.[33]

The multiple contratas the ayuntamiento entered into in these years entailed significant financial obligations, which it sought to meet by issuing debt. Councilors hoped that borrowed money would afford them a semblance of control over the process of urban renewal and more leverage in negotiations with the capitalists performing the works. After a succession of short-term loans by the Monte de Piedad and the Banco Nacional Mexicano to cover working deficits, councilors set their sights on a large long-term foreign loan.[34] Such a loan, they believed, ought to be invested in the "most necessary, and productive works such as water distribution, markets, and an abattoir."[35] They had the support of Governor Fernández, who urged the council to embrace the opportunities offered by international credit markets and private initiative. Were the councilors to succeed, he anticipated the dawn of the new era for the ayuntamiento, finally free from the "cruel and unending struggle to cover with a cloak of magnificence the city's beggar's rags."[36] The following year Fernández was no longer governor but on a diplomatic mission in Paris, where he acted as legal representative of the ayuntamiento in the negotiations. Despite his best efforts, it would take until 1889 for the city to earn the privilege of owing millions of pesos to foreign creditors.[37]

New Halls, New Troubles

Public markets were probably the most visible and widely discussed subject of the period's push to modernize the Mexican capital. In response to the demands of the national government and the pressures of businessmen and the press, between 1880 and 1903 the ayuntamiento discussed, approved, and executed projects to renovate and reorganize the city's markets and to modify its long-standing commercial practices. The council's approach was two-pronged: on the one hand, after giving up on having its own employees and officials build them, it contracted out the construction of state-of-the art glass and iron halls;[38] on the other, the council passed bylaws restricting street sales and, more generally, instructing vendors and their customers how to inhabit the new spaces. Brought into what Elías Palti calls the positivist project of a "pedagogic republic," markets and vendors became the target of a cultural crusade to reshape collective and individual public behaviors.[39] Along the way, the formal and informal institutions governing urban life suffered dramatic transformations.

The ayuntamiento began its overhaul of the city's commercial landscape with La Merced Market, which the president of the council for 1880 described as little more than a "group of people busy in transactions under the only shelter of imperfect and disgusting sunshades." The sale that year of the underutilized Guerrero Market to Benito Arena, an entrepreneur seeking a site to open a textile factory, provided the necessary funds to build a hall.

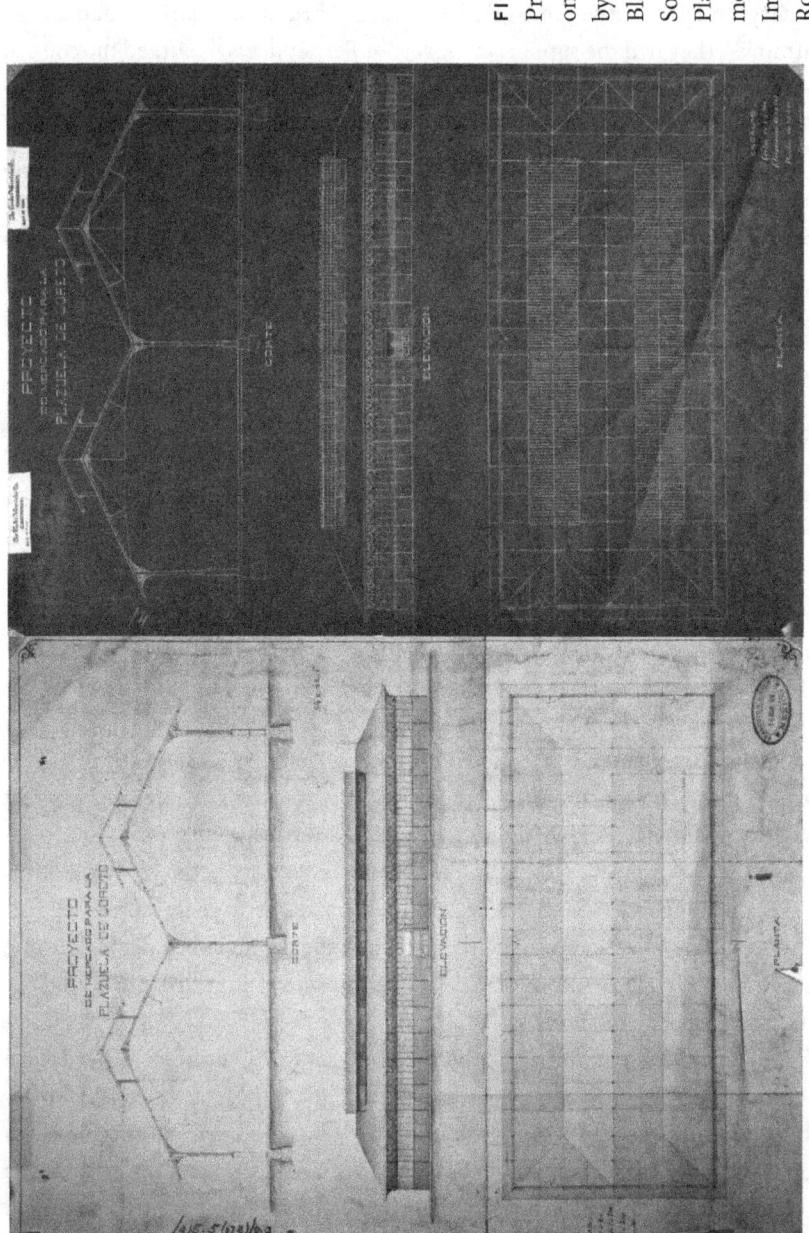

FIGURE 4.
Project for a market on Plaza Loreto by Francisco R. Blanco, 1888.
Source: AHCDMX, Planoteca, planero 1, módulo 3, fajilla 58. Images courtesy of Roberta Vassallo.

Councilors wanted to transform La Merced into "a proper market," complete with shops, a covered viento section, warehouses, an office for the administrator, and a wharf to load and unload the produce brought in through the canals that still crossed the city.[40] Their primary motivation was increased revenue collection: the ayuntamiento hoped to entice well-off merchants, especially those dealing in relatively large quantities, to set up shop in the new, more expensive La Merced while facilitating the fiscalization of viento sales, which would be concentrated there. The council's stated aims also included smoothing the supply of basic goods, improving hygiene and public health, and aesthetically enhancing that part of the city. As work progressed, the local press expressed their delight in the building, which they described as simple but elegant and in good taste.[41]

The city council was so pleased with the favorable newspaper coverage and the expected boost in market fees that the president of the ayuntamiento proclaimed he wished markets commissioner Agustín Róvalo could be made perpetual councilor.[42] Róvalo instead served three years, but—emboldened by his success—he proposed the extension and refurbishment of all existing market halls and the construction of several additional ones.[43] The president of the Republic approved of the council's concerns for revenue, aesthetics, and public health as well as of its ambitious plans of public works for markets, instructing Governor Fernández to follow up. Soon the governor took the lead. Impatient with the pace of change, he wrote to the ayuntamiento on multiple occasions with detailed suggestions, and insisted that outsourcing the works to private industry was preferable to relying on the council's personnel.[44] To encourage the council to follow his advice, he promised to obtain modifications to the city's fiscal laws that would more than triple maximum market fees, and he offered his personal assistance in negotiating the purchase, or perhaps the donation by the national executive, of the necessary real estate.[45]

The governor's interference increasingly strained the relationship between the executive and the city council. The earliest conflict concerned El Volador, the city's main and oldest market. In 1882 the governor complained that the market, with its active trading in foodstuffs, was an unsuitable neighbor for the National Palace. He expected that after the construction of the projected new market halls, El Volador would become redundant and could be shut down.[46] Journalists backed his position, disparaging both El Volador and the council. *El Monitor* read: "This market is in an incredible state of complete abandonment, the garbage and mud make it impassable. What is this

Ayuntamiento thinking?"[47] The governor asked for the site to be turned into a department store specializing in luxury products.

While the ayuntamiento agreed that El Volador needed improvement, it objected to the governor's plans. Councilors employed different strategies to push back. First, they expressed their opposition to the proposed department store by arguing that the laws of the *Reforma* did not allow the council, as a corporation, to own such an establishment.[48] In 1886, in an attempt to keep El Volador open, councilor and markets commissioner José María Rego presented a project to upgrade its infrastructure, with a budget and a plan by the engineer Roberto Gayol. The council anticipated that if these works were carried out, "we will have a market which, if not equal to the cultured capitals of Europe and the United States, will at least not do injustice to the good name of the Ayuntamiento of Mexico."[49]

But President Díaz intervened almost immediately. He made it clear that he expected more drastic measures, causing the council to quickly withdraw its proposition and search for a compromise.[50] The ayuntamiento knew that private interests had an eye on the land on which the market stood, so they considered parceling it and selling the pieces to the highest bidders.[51] They got a reasonable estimate of its value when Francisco R. Blanco negotiated the inclusion of the El Volador plaza and buildings as collateral in the contracts he signed in 1888 to expand and refurbish the new La Merced Market and to build halls for the San Juan and Loreto Markets.[52] After the council fulfilled contractual obligations with Blanco, thus lifting the mortgage on El Volador, another developer, Ignacio F. Alfaro, proposed to buy it to turn it into a ten-story "model building" for private and government offices.[53] *El Tiempo* maintained the pressure, insisting that "it's a scandal that when foreigners visit us and want to learn about our customs they go to our main market . . . to find a filthy pigsty deserving the most severe censure."[54] Only Juvenal, from *El Monitor Republicano*, opposed the dissolution of El Volador. He invoked those very customs and the inconvenience it would cause nearby households who would now have to allow their servants to take longer journeys to procure their daily provisions.[55]

At the center of the controversy over El Volador was a clash over the meaning of public markets and the social and physical boundaries that separated them from street thoroughfare. Municipal markets long had been held primarily *al viento*, wherever the ayuntamiento allowed them: out on the streets, around market halls, by the canals, or in plazas. This approach to markets had reflected the council's fiscal needs and its prudent management of the local moral economy. But the economic prosperity of the 1880s gave the national authorities confidence in their capacity to act on a set of novel ideas about what constituted acceptable commercial spaces and practices. Markets, they believed, should happen indoors. Ayuntamiento members might have agreed personally, but their priorities as councilmen led them to oppose the elimination of sales taking place outside. The ayuntamiento repeatedly disagreed with the governorship over what qualified as proper use of the city streets and markets. In most instances, the president, his ministers, and the local police, as well as the press and the city's property owners, all took the governorship's side.

These disputes had lasting effects on the city's markets and their semantics. The ayuntamiento had always distinguished registered, tax-paying viento vendors from unregulated peddlers. But as far as the executive branch, journalists, and wealthy residents were concerned, all vendors outside of the few existing market halls were *vendedores ambulantes*, a phrase that then became widely used in the 1880s. The halls that Governor Fernández demanded the ayuntamiento build in 1882 were intended to house all vendedores ambulantes who currently impeded the free movement of pedestrians and carriages in the city center. He was not alone. Beginning in the early 1880s the local police, who responded to the orders of the secretary of the interior (or *secretario de gobernación*) received instructions to prevent vendors from setting their stalls on several streets and plazas, even in places where they had been carrying out their trade al viento for years.[56] The press, for its part, unanimously clamored for action against what journalists perceived as ambulantes' detrimental effect on the cleanliness and culture of the city. Downtown property owners complained frequently and harshly about their supposed immorality.[57]

Undoubtedly, the ayuntamiento shared the prejudices of the rest of the Porfirian elite. Market administrators often blamed the poorest traders, who sold from mats on the ground, for the lack of order in the city center and criticized street vendors in general for acting "against the rules of morality." *El Municipio Libre*, the official voice of the council, decried the cluster of stalls formed as an outflow from El Volador Market on Universidad Street, "especially because this street is frequented by the ladies of the National Music Conservatory, who have to tolerate the unseemly language of the vendors."[58] In an attempt to encourage families to visit markets without fear of being offended, councilors passed measures increasing fines and sanctions on vendors

FIGURE 5. *Viento sales on Academia and República de Guatemala Streets*, 1895. Source: William Henry Jackson. The Library of Congress. Digital Collections.

who mistreated their customers.[59] At the same time, market officials worked tirelessly to improve hygiene, prevent stalls from blocking traffic, and to keep the streets that vendors occupied as tidy as possible. What is more, the ayuntamiento's markets commission also made repeated efforts to relocate vendors to specific plazas and alleys where they could be more easily controlled, and by 1887 it launched a "campaign" against unregulated street sales.[60]

But while the city council opposed the activities of untaxed peddlers, it sought to accommodate and protect regulated viento sales. Councilors adamantly asserted: "we will never consent to extending the prohibition [of sales] to doorways and plazas, where the fiscal laws currently in force allow them."[61] As late as 1887 the council responded to the attacks of the press regarding sales on Universidad, Bajos de Portacoeli, and Rejas de Balvanera Streets by arguing they were a source of significant municipal revenue and, in addition, provided subsistence to a great many families.[62] In this way the ayuntamiento upheld its prerogatives to create markets and collect viento fees without police interference, together with its members' ability to perform their moral duties toward the poorest market vendors.[63]

Even as the council defended viento sales in the short term, it espoused the longer-term vision of vendors confined to covered markets. The ayuntamiento believed investment would resolve the tension between fulfilling its rights and duties and modernizing the city. Markets commissioners assumed that the construction of the new halls would create sufficient room for vendors to be "contained" in accordance with the exigencies of "culture and civilization."[64] Councilors expected that the combination of better infrastructure and more stringent controls would also modify vendors' behavior, teaching them to act in accordance with the authorities' new urban mores:

> In effect, the dominant habits of our populace mean that trade in foodstuffs taking place in markets has so far lacked favorable hygienic conditions; this will no longer be the case since they will place their wares in special booths, in the spaces designated for them, benefiting consumers and improving public hygiene, owing to the vigilance that we will exert in the premises, where, according to the common expression, there will be a place for everything, and everything will be in its place.[65]

The ayuntamiento claimed this would be in vendors' best interests. Councilors insisted that markets were dangerous as they stood, and that refurbishments would make them safer for traders by replacing the existing precarious stalls, which so frequently collapsed or caught fire. Equally, if viento vendors accepted the proposed moves, they would no longer have to endure exposure to the wind and weather; besides carrying out their trade more comfortably,

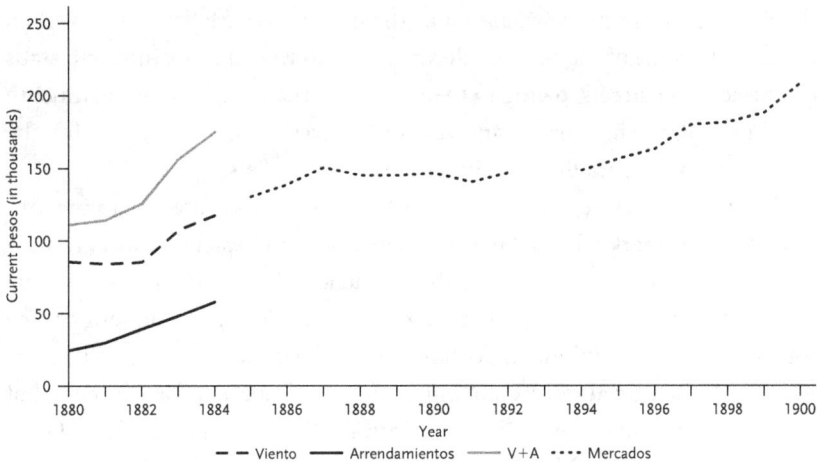

FIGURE 6. Revenues due to markets (current pesos), 1880–1900.
NOTE: Viento and arrendamientos are reported separately up to 1884, while from 1885 data are reported only for "mercados."
SOURCES: *Discurso*, various years 1880–1900; *Municipio Libre*, various dates 10/1/1884–1/6/1893; AHCDM, ACM, RyM, vol. 3740, exp. 1274.

their own health and businesses would benefit from more hygienic conditions."[66] Councilors' compassion was adapting to the capitalist boom sweeping the city.

In this way, the ayuntamiento envisioned the inclusion of proprietary traders into the modern city. The prerequisite was not necessarily social or economic standing but acquiescence to the rules of conduct the authorities considered appropriate for the public of the capital of the Republic. Indeed, councilors made repeated efforts to integrate small-scale vendors into the new halls, so at times having substantial capital or handling large volumes of merchandise could even prove a hindrance. By the mid-1880s, capitalist merchants who occupied the biggest spaces in the existing halls had started to receive the attention of markets commissioners. In 1886 the council denounced the fact that "he who first rented three or four meters now occupies eight or ten, paying only for the original concession. It is time we ended this abuse, so we can make space for more vendors while increasing revenue collection."[67] The following year, when newly appointed markets commissioner F. Mejía surveyed the city's markets, he noticed that El Volador and San Juan Markets housed some extremely large shops. In El Volador he found twelve grocery stores of up to forty square meters each, and in San Juan, butchers' and food stalls comprising up to twenty square meters. Since none of them paid appropriate fees, he decided to raise their charges accordingly, expecting that the financial disincentive would make them give up space that could be then allocated to some of the small-scale vendors who were trading in viento stalls on the adjacent streets, owing to the lack of alternatives.[68] The ayuntamiento sought to balance merchants' and vendors' interests while trying to fulfill the larger goal of reorganizing the city's streets and markets.

The true test came when, in close succession, the ayuntamiento inaugurated five new market halls. First was San Cosme, in September 1888. In June 1889, the city council reported with confidence: "The works in markets arranged by the council are progressing apace. . . . Surely in a month or two we will be able to see these important constructions completed, and then we will feel the beneficial results, not only in terms of aspect and adornment, but equally in terms of hygiene."[69] Soon afterward the council opened San Lucas Market. By early 1890 Blanco's glass and iron halls in Loreto, San Juan, and La Merced were finished and in operation.[70] Their inaugurations became public celebrations of government achievements. When a sixth market, the Mercado Martínez de la Torre, was officially opened a few years later, in Colonia

Guerrero, attending the ceremony were the secretario de gobernación (and President Díaz's father-in-law) Manuel Romero Rubio, the recently appointed governor Pedro Rincón Gallardo, all of the members of the ayuntamiento, and what the *Discursos* characterized as a "great number of notable persons."[71] Local residents expressed their gratitude to the presiding authorities for their "support" and "protection" by offering a "magnificent lunch" followed by fireworks and a dance organized by the richest families of the neighborhood.[72]

The excitement surrounding the new halls did not last. Despite widespread support for the closing down of El Volador, the ayuntamiento hesitated. The council transferred merchants and vendors dealing in foodstuffs away from El Volador and into the new markets,[73] but it remained reluctant to let go of its valuable rents, which were "stable and neither onerous nor objectionable to anyone."[74] In the 1890s the market continued to house ironmongers and toy, shoe, and clothes vendors, even as it began to be referred to as the "ex-Mercado del Volador," or "antiguo Mercado del Volador."[75] Moreover, the members of the ayuntamiento repeatedly resorted to it when compassion required them to relocate vendors no longer tolerated in other areas. During the holiday seasons of November and December 1891, for example, the markets commission decided to allow street vendors, "extremely poor people who seem to subsist all year from what they make in those months," to use El Volador for their trade.[76]

Soon the halls that had held so much promise revealed the ayuntamiento's incapacity to produce the orderly urban environment the Porfirian elite required. Attempts to fill the new markets and eliminate old vending practices faced significant obstacles. Few people seemed interested in renting spaces in the new Loreto Market, inducing the council to pass a resolution ordering wholesalers to move their business there and forbidding them from unloading their produce in La Merced. They were also offered the enticement of a six-month rent waiver as well as permission to sell retail there. With these measures councilors hoped to rationalize wholesale trade and to free up space in the remaining markets for those carrying out their business on the streets and plazas.[77] But within a year, the markets commission reported that their efforts to bring the Loreto Market to life had failed, for which they blamed the opposition of merchants and "old and deeply rooted customs." The members of the commission promised not to rest until these customs were eradicated. "We hope to . . . soon bring the day when the press and neighbors stop complaining."[78]

Many proprietary vendors found they could not afford to rent a stall within the refurbished halls, so the council, following precedent, gave them permission to continue to trade al viento. The persistence of these street sales brought the ayuntamiento the harshest criticisms.[79] After pondering, not without sarcasm, what exactly the purpose of the new expensive constructions was, given that the city streets remained a "ridiculous village *tianguis*," *El Universal* demanded: "Reduce market fees if necessary, but *force, force, force* vendors to disappear from the streets. If their trade is productive, they will necessarily move into one of the existing markets halls."[80] Censure had focused on El Volador in the 1880s, but in the 1890s, the most vitriolic attacks were reserved for La Merced Market, where *El Nacional* complained that "for reasons of economy or neglect . . . vendors have introduced disorder, migrating to the sidewalks and nearby hallways."[81] *El Universal* wondered:

> In that galley called La Merced Market, which in the summer becomes an oven and in the winter an icebox, there is not enough room for all the vendors, so they have scattered on to the streets, forming a labyrinth of stalls, fruits, vegetables, pushing and shoving. . . . In this sea swim the *vendedores ambulantes*, object of the rage of the police. What is this? Should we declare them vagrants? Should we classify them among the microbes? Should we pursue them as criminals? . . . Are their labors legal or not? Should we lock them up? Or could we hang them on a coat rack so they don't get in the way?[82]

In the face of this onslaught, the ayuntamiento had to acknowledge it could not clear the city's streets.[83] Less than a month after *El Universal*'s diatribe, the ayuntamiento surrendered responsibility to the national government, requesting that the governor order the police to compel viento vendors outside of La Merced to relocate inside the hall.[84] Similar actions took place in all other markets. Eventually, in 1900 the ayuntamiento began issuing licenses to vendedores ambulantes, who were allowed to operate as long as they remained outside the city center and did not sell from stationary stalls.[85] Those who were denied these licenses or found the new rules too constraining resisted, as historian Susie Porter puts it, by "the elegantly simple and powerful act" of ignoring municipal regulations.[86] Under orders from the governor and with the acquiescence of the ayuntamiento, both licensed and unlicensed ambulantes were monitored and chronically harassed by the police.

Yet despite the urban renewal efforts of the previous two decades, at the turn of the century street sales continued unabated. By now journalists

FIGURE 7. *Mercado de San Juan with Street Stalls.* The photograph captures the attempt to create a boundary between market hall and street vending. Source: Charles B. Waite. AGN, fondo Instrucción Pública y Bellas Artes; serie Propiedad Artística y Literaria, tema Mercados, inv. núm. 48.

openly blamed the councilors' timidity and ignorance for what they saw as the inadequacy of the city's disorganized markets.[87] In the streets and plazas around La Merced and San Juan, the two busiest markets, there were respectively four hundred stalls and two hundred stalls during the week, and even more on weekends and holidays.[88] In the city at large there remained 2,197 licensed viento vendors and over 1,000 "provisionally" licensed vendedores ambulantes, compared to the 1,175 active shops within the nine existing halls.[89] Perhaps the biggest transformation was that the ayuntamiento no longer accepted those who sold al viento as an integral part of the city's markets. Instead, these vendors were increasingly marginalized, with their commercial practices considered a transitory ill awaiting suppression.[90]

By the early 1900s, the ayuntamiento came to accept the view of street vending held by the national executive, the press, and most of the city's wealthy residents. They all now regarded both ambulante and viento vendors with a sense of fear and disgust motivated in part by concerns over public hygiene, aesthetics and ease of traffic circulation that the historian Mario Barbosa describes as a "horrified gaze."[91] Yet for the Porfirian elite, the ayuntamiento prompted a similar sentiment. Its conspicuous failure to modernize markets and eradicate seemingly unacceptable practices eroded the legitimacy of the ayuntamiento's authority over urban spaces and its role in the lives of Mexico City's residents. Capitalist development and population growth undermined the city's norms and institutions, and what was once custom became a past to be razed and built over anew.

Urban Renewal and the Making of Locatarios

Although the streets of Mexico City remained congested with vendors, the new markets did not stay empty. Municipal records for 1902 show that at least 1,175 vendors and merchants occupied the ayuntamiento's halls as locatarios, or stallholders.[92] Some of them might have been coerced into renting a stall, while others might have done so only because they did not have the means to move to private premises. But most of these locatarios actively chose to base their businesses in the city's public markets because they saw them as a means to improve their economic prospects and render their position in the commercial life of the city more secure. These vendors and merchants became staunch supporters of modernization. In communications with authorities they reflected their willingness, whether sincerely or not, to participate in the construction of a more hygienic, orderly city. At the same time, locatarios also learned to define themselves in contrast to viento vendors and ambulantes, thereby contributing both to the exclusionary redrawing of the boundaries between streets and markets and to the marginalization of all street vendors. Rather than merely being swept up in the changes, locatarios actively took part in the transformation of their markets.

In the early 1880s, when traders negotiated over market fees they still appealed to custom, invoking the fiscal interests of the ayuntamiento and the compassion that councilors and wealthier merchants were obliged to demonstrate to the poorest vendors. A group of locatarios who established themselves in the refurbished La Merced "with the expectation that the profit of their trade would suffice to cover all expenses," soon felt that the rents the council was charging them were too high, with the press backing their claim.[93] When they petitioned that rents be slashed by a quarter, they addressed the council's financial concerns: the ayuntamiento could not remain indifferent to the fact that half of the new shops were empty, "thus losing not just the rents of these empty premises, but even the product of the viento section because, owing to the lack of commercial life in this market . . . in this [section] there are only a few very poor sellers of fruit and three or four grain stalls with the smallest of stocks." These merchants ended their letter exclaiming that they would receive a favorable response as a "grace" (*gracia*), which, in addition to preventing their economic ruin, would "indirectly benefit many poor persons who by honest work manage to provide their families with the necessary sustenance."[94] The missive is suffused with a sense of responsibility for the community they felt part of. Nine weeks later, after the case had been examined by the finance and markets commissions, the council, who also still believed it had a duty to protect poor vendors and their community, decided the claim was fair. Following precedent, the ayuntamiento responded that each individual comerciante should write with details of his or her specific circumstances to renegotiate their rents in accordance.[95]

Over time, though, locatarios strategically began to weave together the language of custom with the rhetoric of modernization, putting special emphasis on the authorities' preoccupations with public health.[96] In 1888, for example, when the ayuntamiento decided to move forward the closing time of markets to three in the afternoon to permit cleaning by municipal employees, a vendor by the name of Maclovio Herrera wrote a letter appealing to President Porfirio Díaz's "notorious generosity," on the day of the "lucky coincidence of his birth anniversary and the commemoration of the motherland's political independence." Herrera opposed the ayuntamiento's resolution on the basis that it did not respect "ancient customs" and because it was disadvantageous for consumers. The change in working hours did not make sense, Herrera went on, from the point of view of "public health," because sanitary conditions were deteriorating as unsold, perishable foodstuffs were kept in storage between the new closing time and five in the morning, when markets reopened.[97] During the following months many others wrote similar petitions, and they worked. By the end of the year the council had modified its resolution, permitting markets to remain open until four in the afternoon during winter months and five in the afternoon in the summer, to vendors' delight.[98]

Two years later, a few months after the inauguration of the twice-revamped La Merced, a group of comerciantes demanded that the council remove the fountain located at the center of the market on grounds of public health and the need to ease circulation. Some vendors, they reported, had turned the area into a washing place, contaminating the water and the ground around the fountain with trash and grease; moreover, the fountain's outflow into the surrounding streets caused traffic congestion and disgust among all those who passed by.[99] While these locatarios might have been truly concerned with circulation and sanitary conditions, by appropriating the discourse of the elite they also sought to differentiate themselves from those they thought no longer belonged in the city's markets.

Many of those who accepted a place in the new halls used their compliance with the authorities' modernizing designs as an instrument to remove unwanted competitors. La Merced butchers, for example, asked the council to expel meat vendors from the viento section of their market because, given the lower fees they paid, they constituted "unjust competition."[100] By the end of 1902, "merchants and neighbors of La Merced" were accusing vendedores ambulantes of not just unfair, but "illegal competition." The list of their charges was impressive: they claimed that ambulantes evaded all taxes and fees, sold their wares at random prices, cheated their consumers with short measures, circulated fake currency, and purposefully covered up for pickpockets. They called them "a serious nuisance for passersby" who have to endure their "cries, obscenities, altercations, and unspeakable behavior."[101] As they pursued their material interests in opposition to viento vendors and ambulantes, market locatarios both supported and helped define the new boundaries between streets and markets.

Locatarios who aligned themselves with the Porfirian elite's urban renewal project still found themselves engaged in conflicts with the city council. When confronted with tighter and more impersonal controls, vendors and merchants in public markets began breaking from tradition by strengthening their collective voices. The case of Eduardo Salazar is telling. On December 5, 1896, he wrote to the president of the ayuntamiento requesting to rent a stall in La Merced that he knew to be empty so that he could establish his trade in clothes.[102] Ten days later, on the recommendation of the markets commission, the council granted his petition.[103] Within a year he moved from petitioning as an individual to writing on behalf of a group of locatarios who successfully opposed the council's proposal to relocate all clothes vendors in their market to the old Volador Market on the grounds that having always paid their fees on time and having already established themselves in La Merced, it would harm their interests to move.[104] By the turn of the century, when the authorities tried to rid markets of all items but foodstuffs and flowers, Salazar and his group again claimed the right to challenge the decision.[105]

The authorities however, continued to rebuff vendors' attempts at collective action. In 1901, Resiquio Anda and a dozen other traders renting external stalls on the northern side of La Merced Market signed a petition to renegotiate rents, lengthen market working hours, and enlarge the space their stalls occupied. The council reassured the governor that "with the exception of Anda and two of his friends, all other locatarios without exception were taken by surprise by those who collected the signatures, because none of them had the will to make such a petition, since they are all satisfied with the hours and spaces assigned to their stalls."[106] The council managed to ignore vendors demands this time, but the seeds for a growing group consciousness had already been planted, and would take root.

By the turn of the twentieth century, as Robert Buffington's close reading of Mexico City's satirical penny press reveals, the laboring classes were often more self-aware, more adaptable, and better attuned to the changing times than their elite counterparts, suggesting the need to revise, and to some extent reverse, top-down interpretations of the "civilizing process."[107] Market vendors certainly fit this mold. Their newfound locatario identity exposed the contradictions of the Porfirian market projects, which attempted to generate modern subjects out of vendors, while rejecting their participation in policy debates. It also called attention to the period's growing social tensions. Locatarios pushed their way into the public sphere thorough collective action, both to resist official decisions that they considered detrimental to their interests and way of life and to exclude all types of street vendors from the city's public markets. At least in this latter regard, they were as implacable as the authorities.

The Undoing of Custom

As the national government encroached on the council's jurisdiction, and as the council accepted its own limitations, locatarios began directing their petitions and complaints to the governor. Fruit vendors in La Merced Market who had been instructed by the ayuntamiento to confine themselves to their designated spaces turned to the governor for support, asking him to order that they be allowed to occupy up to one meter beyond their stalls, as was customary.[108] Within ten days the governor demanded that the council clarify the situation.[109] By helping the governor put the ayuntamiento in the position of having to justify itself, these vendors inadvertently eroded its authority, legitimizing the transfer of responsibility to the executive branch.

The behavior of merchants dealing in grains in La Merced was even more damaging. In 1899 a group of them refused to pay municipal taxes despite almost daily attempts by fee collectors. The market administrator himself lamented: "these recalcitrant [merchants] are not only affecting the council's treasury in their respective contributions . . . but their bad example and subversion have made other locatarios in their line of business stop paying what they have been perfectly happy to do until now."[110] Six months after the council declined their request for an exemption, during which time they contributed nothing to the city's coffers, these grain merchants put forward the argument that having appealed to the governor, his failure to pronounce himself protected them. Confronted with this outrageous negation of its right to collect market fees, there was nothing the council could do but to ask the governor to resolve the matter.[111]

As the national government grew stronger, the city council lost autonomy and executive capacities to federal agencies.[112] And conversely, as the power of the ayuntamiento diminished, that of the president's appointed governor increased. By 1900, the council formally maintained its responsibility for areas such as markets, slaughterhouses, street lighting, and pavements, but the governor ruled over many aspects of city life, a situation that created numerous overlapping jurisdictions. So while the council retained the right to build and run markets, several closely related issues were under the direct control of the governor: the canals used to transport merchandise; municipal employees, including those in charge of cleaning markets and collecting taxes; the police, who increasingly controlled street vendors; the fire department, so necessary as markets stalls frequently went up in flames; and the public health bureaucracy, which by then had the right to inspect markets and require its own independent licenses.

This process of subtracting municipal responsibilities culminated in July 1903, when Mexico City was politically and administratively reorganized and the council stripped of its rents, properties, and all governing functions over the city. By presidential decree the ayuntamiento was reduced to a *cuerpo consultivo*, an advisory board without any executive powers.[113] But changes went much deeper than administrative reform. The city council had been the political arena responsible for making the city a stable community. Good urban governance had since colonial times involved active councilors committed to managing competing interests. With the suppression of the ayuntamiento the city lost the traditional arbiter of its social interactions.

Nowhere was this more evident than in public markets, where the combination of the ayuntamiento's fiscal concerns and the elite's Catholic duty of compassion had delivered customary arrangements that, "since time immemorial," tolerated difference and even disorder. Custom signified a set of municipally sanctioned rules and constraints binding urban residents of every social standing. It provided a shared code for navigating the myriad economic relations between capitalist merchants, proprietary vendors, and their customers. Custom guaranteed that, at first, the council would give priority in the distribution of spaces in the new halls to those already trading in the location,[114] and that it would adjust individual rents so that they "respect the situation of each stall and the type of trade done" by its holder, because "a general rule would help some, but it would hurt the majority."[115] Even after Congress raised maximum daily rents to twenty cents per square meter, custom had kept fees in El Volador at less than two cents.[116] Custom committed the council to paying for commercial infrastructure, forcing it to refuse funds from merchants impatient to introduce water to their markets.[117] Custom taught councilors to accept the overflow of vendors from any given market into adjacent streets. Custom was behind the inclusion as late as 1885 of an article in the markets bylaw requiring ambulatory vendors to deal directly with fee collectors instead of carrying a license.[118] It also allowed market employees to turn a blind eye to situations increasingly considered infractions and obliged the markets commissioner for 1891, despite his conviction that the ayuntamiento did not have the duty to provide vending sites, to accept the presence of the "ridiculous and nauseating stalls" vendors set up during religious holidays because "these extremely poor people seem to survive all year from the sales they make those days."[119] Custom kept consumers visiting El Volador in spite of the harsh criticisms it received.[120] Custom, finally, was paramount in vendors' defense of their rights to make a living in the city.[121]

As capitalism expanded, custom became contested first from without and then from within. The president, his ministers, the press, and businessmen, who had little at stake in traditional market arrangements, took the lead, pitting themselves against the city council and vendors in an effort to overhaul the city's public markets. Yet by the 1890s both the ayuntamiento and many locatarios embraced the new order, advocating for the eradication of deeply rooted customs. While street vendors continued to invoke tradition in the face of mounting repression and marginalization,[122] custom as praxis and discursive weaponry had lost its force. It dissolved in the new faith in progress and in the quest for profit and a modern city. On July 1, 1903, the day the reorganization of Mexico City went into effect, municipal president Fernando Pimentel y Fagoaga declared, "Until yesterday the Ayuntamiento had control over municipal public services, and intervened directly in the functioning and improvement of the capital. Today, a new era begins."[123] Custom would no longer bear the burden of holding this urban community together.

3 Vendors, Workers, or *Pueblo?* 1903–1928

AROUND THREE IN THE AFTERNOON on Friday, August 1, 1924, Mexico City's market vendors and their families gathered on Palacio Legislativo Avenue. The authorities had refused to grant them permission to hold a rally, but they came together nonetheless, marching through the city center to protest an upcoming hike in market fees. The fire department and the police were unable to disperse the crowd, which newspapers put at 2,500 strong.[1] When the protestors reached the municipal palace two hours later, they cried out, "We don't want more taxes! Down with the onerous fees!"[2] While a group of locatario representatives negotiated with market officials, someone shot a gun. The crowd at the Zócalo panicked. Firemen turned hoses on the demonstrators. Vendors advanced toward the palace doors, where a picket of policemen and the municipal guard opened fire. One protester died on the scene while another succumbed to injuries later in the hospital. Many more were wounded.

In the days that followed these events, the media blamed local politicians for the violence while portraying the locatarios as their humble victims. Until this point public demonstrations by market vendors were unheard of, leading the newspaper *El Demócrata* to speculate on the "mystery that begins with the aggressive and violent way a petition becomes a protest march, which gradually takes the shape of a riot."[3] *El País* portrayed vendors as a passive *"pueblo,"* who had been manipulated by ruthless, opportunistic politicians.[4] This chapter shows how off the mark this interpretation was. Contrary to journalists' claims, market vendors were not only politically active but also organized into unions and federations. Vendors had been engaging in different forms of collective action for the past two decades, and by the mid-1920s they were ready to contest the limits of popular politics and force their way into the city's postrevolutionary public sphere.

The arc of vendors' mobilization can be traced back to 1903, when the ayuntamiento, the long-standing arbiter of the city's social interactions, was stripped of its powers. Whereas markets had been a policy priority for the ayuntamiento, market concerns now became dispersed across multiple ministries and councils. The resulting jurisdictional overlaps created power vacuums, administrative chaos, and uncertainty among vendors and government officials alike. In this new institutional context, vendors repeatedly tried but failed to find interlocutors receptive to their needs. When they understood they could no longer rely on individual pleas for protection, vendors began to enunciate their shared grievances and rights. The success of the Maderista uprising in 1911 catalyzed the emergence of new attitudes and expectations among the city's laboring classes. Vendors embraced both the democratizing principles of the Mexican Revolution and the period's proletarian struggles. After a tentative political settlement reinstated the ayuntamiento in 1917, vendors formed organizations that joined workers' confederations. Tragically for vendors, their novel attempts to protect their livelihoods and make their voices heard clashed with postrevolutionary governments' approach to markets, which lagged behind the changing times.

Fragmented Markets, Orphaned Vendors

In January 1903, as the ayuntamiento became an advisory board without clear functions, the governor of the Federal District, Ramón Corral, boasted, "Mexico City has fully entered the path of great material improvement, and needs to remain on that path, resolutely and persistently, because as a capital of a prosperous free Republic, it has the right to appear high among the cultured cities of the world."[5] The capital continued its transformation, acquiring tramways, wide paved streets, public lighting, extravagant public buildings, and elegant residential areas for the upper classes.[6] Urban improvements gained urgency in the last years of the decade, as the cream of the Díaz regime planned the centennial celebrations of the country's independence movement. During September 1910 the capital would be showcased to the world as proof of the government's economic and political success. Mauricio Tenorio argues that the city of the centennial celebrations—with its parades and inaugurations of monuments, official buildings, and public institutions—embodied a set of interrelated ideals of modernity, the nation-state, and cosmopolitanism.[7] Mexico City was required to look beautiful, hygienic, and orderly, and vendors would be expected to conform.

During the last decade of the Porfiriato many affluent families were moving west, away from the old city center, into new exclusive neighborhoods along the Paseo de la Reforma. The main streets and avenues of the center, in turn, had been taken over by financial institutions and high-end commerce as well as by public buildings. The glass and iron market halls the ayuntamiento had built over the previous decades dotted the landscape. It was in these new neighborhoods and these parts of the city center that the government constructed the modern capital of the *centenario*. On the other hand, the laboring classes—including workers, artisans, and small-scale proprietary traders—increasingly tended to live in their own separate neighborhoods to the east and south of the Zócalo, in overcrowded tenements and improvised shacks.[8] Here progress was a more difficult proposition.

Because of the poor conditions of their dwellings, the lower classes turned to the city's public spaces to meet their most basic needs. Without sewers or running water, they relied on public baths and fountains for personal hygiene and laundry. Inadequate or absent toilets meant that urinating and defecating in the streets was not uncommon. For social calls, including sharing a drink with friends and even having sexual intercourse, public places often offered more privacy than the home. Many among the urban poor also turned to public spaces for the less intimate but equally vital pursuits of peddling, begging, and stealing.[9] While all of these behaviors clashed with the privileged classes' notions of what a modern city ought to be, they could to some extent be overlooked when confined to poorer neighborhoods. But when they happened in areas frequented by the upper and middle classes, or, even worse, by foreigners, they elicited disgust and indignation. In response, city authorities sought to enhance control and modify the public habits of the laboring classes. As they built the city of the centenario, they passed countless rules and regulations concerning the proper use of public spaces, their enforcement falling on the police. The concomitant criminalization of everyday life, Pablo Piccato demonstrates, created a "city of suspects."[10] Street vendors were particularly targeted.

The ayuntamiento had attempted to dispense a degree of justice to street vendors as part of its carefully crafted approach to the city's public markets. But Mexico City was now run by a Superior Council of Government (Consejo Superior de Gobierno) that answered to the secretary of the interior and was composed of three presidential appointees: the governor of the Federal District, the general director of Public Works, and the president of the Superior Council of Public Health.[11] Each had his own areas of responsibility, and the management of the city's public markets was dispersed across their various departments. The governor had jurisdiction over festivities and municipal policing. The management of festivities included oversight of the expansion of permitted vending activities during religious and civic holidays; the management of municipal policing gave him the capacity to use force to implement any official decisions or rules pertaining to the use of public spaces. Public Works was put in charge of market construction and repairs as well as of the provision of such key services as lighting and water. Public Health, in turn, had responsibility for the sanitary conditions of markets and street stalls. Complicating matters further, the allocation of stalls and the daily operation of markets fell outside the scope of the Superior Council of Government; as market halls became properties of the federal government and fees and taxes became federal revenue, the secretary of finance and public credit took over their administration. Finally, not wanting to lose out, the secretary of transport and communications demanded the right to preapprove the issuing of permits for all stands on the city's sidewalks.[12] The impact of these overhauls on the city's public markets was dramatic.

Administrators and fee collectors continued to organize the everyday workings of markets but now also had to contend with the growing assertiveness of the Public Health Council which, in July 1904, created a Sanitary Inspection Service and stationed an agent in each of the city's eight largest markets.[13] Since Treasury and Public Health had different mandates, their employees often received contradictory instructions. Fiscal concerns dictated that as many vendors as possible be accommodated in the city's markets, while preoccupations with hygiene demanded the opposite. When the head of the new sanitary service requested that fruit and vegetable vendors in Santa Ana and San Lucas Markets be forbidden from selling their merchandise unless they rented a stall or at least a place at one of the tables provided by the authorities, Francisco Monteverde, general market administrator, declared that this was "absolutely impracticable" because on most days the number of comerciantes in those markets exceeded the available spots.¹⁴ Both departments agreed on the need to provide for better infrastructure at places like Tepito and La Candelaria, which had hosted unruly agglomerations of vendors for twenty years. But whereas Treasury employees reported on deficiencies and suggested improvements, the Public Health Council took it further. It resolved "to ask [the secretariat of] Public Works to provide these provisional markets with appropriate constructions," or if this was not possible, "that they be suppressed due to their inadequacy regarding matters of public health."¹⁵

Unable to carry out their duties on their own, both treasury employees and public health officials increasingly turned for assistance to the police, who soon became a permanent presence in the city's public markets. According to Administrator Monteverde, "countless *ambulantes* invade our markets," so "without the aid of the police, it is impossible to keep them in order."¹⁶ The police were originally assigned to prevent unlicensed peddlers from operating in the markets and to assist in fee collection, but the scope of their duties soon grew to encompass overseeing *cargadores* (porters), preventing the poor from scavenging for edible waste, enforcing rules mandating that vendors keep their stalls clean, and compelling customers not to dispose of garbage on the pavement.¹⁷ When in 1904 the Public Health Council issued new regulations tightening the requirements for selling meat in the city's markets, the president of the council was happy to report that fifteen insalubrious butchers' stalls in the Martínez de la Torre Market had been destroyed with the help of the police.¹⁸ The same fate befell some improvised shops in Tepito, which vendors had been using as dormitories "against all hygienic considerations."¹⁹ As different authorities came to depend on the repressive capabilities of the police, a number of officers were allocated to each market. In contrast to the public health inspectors, who were fixed, the police rotated periodically, making them a more detached and unpredictable threat. The press took notice; denouncing the "notable disorder and lack of cleanliness in La Merced," *La Patria* blamed not Public Health, but the gendarmes posted there for not doing their jobs properly.²⁰

The governor of the Federal District used his control of the police force to intervene in the everyday management of public life. Sometimes he did so on his own initiative and at other times by supporting or opposing the decisions of the Public Health Council or the Secretariat of Finance. While the governor tended to agree with Public Health, his relationship with the Treasury was not always smooth. In February 1907, general markets administrator Miguel A. León wrote a confidential letter to Governor Guillermo Landa y Escandón. He was puzzled by policemen withdrawing permits he had personally issued to vendors in the Plaza de la Constitución. He declared that while he understood that only the governor—in charge of the city's festivities—could extend temporary licenses during Lent, he had issued the permits following all existing regulations. On this occasion the governor decided to order the police to refrain from interfering with the activities of these vendors.[21] Yet in January 1909, in contrast, the governor backed the general police inspector when he complained about market employees who were allowing vendors to continue to operate stalls to the south and west of Iturbide Market even after one of his agents had removed their booths. In this instance the governor rebuked the market administrator on the grounds that these vendors blocked traffic and, owing to their proximity to pack trains and electric trams, were prone to cause accidents.[22]

With responsibility for public markets scattered across different ministries, departments, and offices, vendors struggled to identify the appropriate recipient of their petitions and complaints. At times, the overlap of authorities created a power vacuum. When Ramón Molina together with other *rebocería* vendors requested licenses to set up stalls in the streets of Portacoeli, Rejas de Balvanera, and La Merced, the market administrator declined their petition, referring them to the governor.[23] In turn, the governor refused to state a position, declaring that in matters of street sales, both ambulantes and fixed stalls, it was the market administration that needed to decide.[24] Other times, it led to changing orders and unstable arrangements. In August 1908, a group of clothing vendors were given permission by the governor to establish themselves around the Martínez de la Torre Market, only to be told a few days later by the market administrator that they had to move to La Camelia Street. Within a week, they were allowed to return to the market but were immediately ordered by the governor, who visited the area in the company of the local police inspector, to move to La Camelia Street once more.[25] From the perspective of market vendors, government interventions were too much or too little, but never enough.

Amid such administrative confusion, communications between the city authorities and vendors all but broke down. In August 1904, after much internal discussion, a new bylaw forbade meat sales in public markets. When Public Health officials expelled a group of long-established butchers from

La Merced Market "for being considered harmful to the hygiene and well-being of the market," these vendors—who included María Martínez Viuda de Zamora, Refugio Carranza, and Antonio González—were unable to find a broker who could vouch for them. They "supplicated" to the market administrator, who they claimed was well acquainted with their predicament, to "mediate with his valuable, honest and powerful influence."[26] They requested that Public Works build shops to the south of the market according to public health regulations or, if that were not possible, that the governor grant them permission to construct such shops themselves.[27] Finally, they appealed to the secretary of the interior to get the Public Health resolutions revoked.[28] Nothing worked. On the basis of market inspectors' claims that meat sales in markets were incompatible with public health standards, these locatarios were informed that, by President Díaz's agreement, all their motions had been denied.[29]

The political reorganization of Mexico City meant that market vendors at large found themselves without a valid interlocutor. In late 1910, when locatarios from La Lagunilla Market saw their fees raised after they refused to pay for new stalls, they appealed to Governor Landa y Escandón for the type of compassion that, in the past, the ayuntamiento had felt dutybound to offer:

> We know you are the Protector, the father of those who toil honestly.... You know well that we are poor, and that the situation today in Mexico is such that we already pay too much for food and housing.... As the genuine representative of our Paternal Government, we ask that you not allow us to be extorted and expelled [from this market] because we cannot pay [the fees] or buy elegant stalls.[30]

The governor's response was laconic. In what had become a formulaic retort, he notified them that it was beyond his competency to resolve the matter.[31] By the end of the Porfiriato, the city's vendors faced more than administratively disorganized markets. The authorities had left them orphaned.

Imperialist Threats and Domestic Turmoil

The pressures facing market vendors and the rest of Mexico's laboring classes in the early twentieth century cannot be understood in isolation from the increasingly vexed national politics, nor the international dynamics that influenced them. Mexico's powerful northern neighbor was encroaching on the country. US companies and banks, which grew larger and more resourceful in these years, were investing in the Mexican economy more than ever before. Meanwhile, the US government claimed the right to intervene in the domestic affairs of Latin American nations to quell disorder and guarantee favorable conditions for production and trade for US businesses.[32] The threat of US intervention in response to any display of internal instability exacerbated Mexico's fear of public contest over presidential succession, leading to the reelection of the aging Porfirio Díaz in 1900 and 1904. But keeping the house in order was not enough. To contain the United States, Porfirian elites sought counterweights in Europe. Their attempts at diversifying economic and diplomatic ties, however, coincided with the intensification of Euro-American imperialist rivalries. Conflicts between US and British oil companies in Mexico, coupled with the US government's dissatisfaction with the way the national government managed these conflicts, played no small part in the crisis that would end the Díaz regime.[33]

The same dependent capitalist development that threatened Mexico from without created turmoil within.[34] By the turn of the century a portion of the upper classes had managed to monopolize political power and the most lucrative business opportunities, including profitable deals and connections with foreign capitalists. The less well-connected sectors of the upper and middle classes grew ripe with resentment at being passed over for business opportunities and government posts. In 1907, when droughts and floods combined with a recession in the United States to sour economic conditions in Mexico, the upper and middle classes decided to act on that resentment, trying to install a vice president who could represent their interests. They failed. Soon they threw their weight behind a newly emerged opposition party led by Francisco Madero, who championed electoral democracy and the end of boss rule. When fraud and repression ensured that Díaz would be reinaugurated in December 1910, Maderista reformers revolted under the Plan de San Luis Potosí, unleashing civil war and revolution.

In just six months, armed civilians and a US military deployment on the border managed to drive Díaz into exile. By late 1911, a free election put Madero in office. Had the revolt been limited to the northern states of Sonora and Coahuila where reformist landlords took control without much trouble, the revolution might have ended with his victory. After all, Madero was respectful of Porfirian politicians, bureaucrats and the military, and was readily recognized by the US and European governments. But the previous decades of capitalist expansion had created other cleavages that could not be so easily dismissed. In Chihuahua, where land and capital had become concentrated in the hands of the rich Terrazas family and foreign firms, small businessmen, workers, peasants, and peons had good reasons to keep up the fight.[35] The same was true in Morelos, where capitalist agriculture had encroached on peasant villages' land and resources.[36] In urban centers like Mexico City, and in strategic industries across the country, workers seized the moment and mobilized to demand better pay and conditions.[37] Lacking the support of these groups, the Madero government was toppled in February 1913 by General Victoriano Huerta, who had the backing of elements of the Díaz regime, its army, the Catholic Church and, at the time, of US and European diplomats keen to see the country pacified and to keep business going.

The civil war that followed destroyed the remainders of the old Porfirian regime. Huerta was attacked from several fronts. In the north, former Maderistas temporarily united with new rebels to form the Constitutionalist Army under Venustiano Carranza. Peasants from Morelos, led by Emiliano Zapata, fought Huerta independently, expanding their operations into neighboring central states. Workers in Mexico City and elsewhere continued to organize. Finally, US oil interests, fearful that Huerta was favoring the rival British company El Águila, lobbied hard for US government intervention, leading to the military occupation of the port of Veracruz. By July 1914, Huerta was gone, along with the institutions of the Porfiriato: the federal army, the police, the judiciary, and most of the bureaucracy.

The defeat of Huerta did not, however, bring stability to Mexico. The victorious armies failed to negotiate peace at the Convention of Aguascalientes. They soon split. Former Constitutionalists from Chihuahua, then led by Francisco Villa, allied with the Zapatistas to advance a program of agrarian reform and defend regional and local political autonomy. In the revolutionary struggles that followed, Carranza's Constitutionalists defeated the combined forces of Villistas and Zapatistas. By October 1915, the Constitutionalists had eliminated the possibility of radical, peasant-driven, redistribution of land.[38]

At the end of 1915, foreign powers recognized Carranza as head of state. Yet at the time the Mexican state barely merited the label. Across the country, generals were regionally strong and divided. Armed struggles for land continued, forcing the Constitutionalists to address the agrarian question. Increasingly militant labor organizations required the new authorities to take a position on the relationship between capitalists and workers. Authorities also had to acknowledge Mexican businessmen's aspirations, and find ways to promote their interests. The connections between foreign companies and domestic interests had to be revised. In 1916, thus, in search of legitimacy, and hoping to restore order, Carranza called a constitutional convention. His proposed constitution provided for a stronger presidency with a single four-year term and the establishment of a central bank. Social reform was not his priority. But in response to pressure from General Álvaro Obregón and others, changes went further. The Obregonistas in the convention believed that social and economic reforms were necessary for peace and successfully imposed their vision. They managed to pass a constitution that recognized labor rights to be arbitrated by government-led boards, allowed for expropriation of privately owned land and mandated agrarian reform, and, while foreign powers were entangled in World War I, nationalized subsoil resources so that mining and oil exploitation could take place only through government concessions. In other words, the new constitution proposed the construction of a stronger state with the legal faculty to intervene in the economy and to mediate class conflicts.[39]

Unfortunately, constitutions alone do not make states. Carranza was sworn into office in May 1917, only to be overthrown by an Obregonista faction three years later in what proved to be the last successful revolt of the revolution. Obregón and then Plutarco Elías Calles would complete their presidential terms over 1920–24 and 1924–28 respectively. In cooperation with parts of the labor and agrarian movements, their governments effectively promoted capitalist development for the benefit of business both domestic and foreign. But the standing of the early postrevolutionary regime was precarious. The United States, even more powerful after World War I, faced no foreign counterweights. US oil companies lobbied so hard against the application of the constitution that the threat of military intervention remained credible.[40] Presidential successions were particularly difficult times: Generals revolted in 1923–24 and allegedly plotted to do so again in 1927. In both instances, they were violently crushed. Catholic peasants went to war against the state in 1926 and fought to the death to keep their religion at the center of their way of life.[41] Groups of workers and peasants pursued their class interests independently of the state, organizing strikes and protests despite official repression. Railroad workers led a general strike in early 1927.[42] That year economic crisis hit Mexico, as if in preparation for the coming world depression. Yet, against the odds, despite external threats and continued domestic turmoil, the new state clung on to survival.

No Island Is an Island

Díaz's fall in 1911 did not change the formal management of Mexico City's public markets. If anything, the departure of the old president and his ministers exacerbated the administrative dysfunctionality of the previous decade. When a "cholera invasion" threatened the city that summer, the Public Health Council argued that to prevent the spread of the disease, the city should ensure the cleanliness of markets and improve controls over the quality of foodstuffs. According to the head of the Sanitary Inspection Service, however, the police did not support his inspectors' actions. Locatarios, he added, consistently failed to comply with the regulations that required them to sweep and keep their stalls clean, and market administrators refused to remove vendors who placed their merchandize on the ground. The governor felt incapable of confronting these issues, so he decided to allocate extra funds for Public Works to expand its staff of janitors.[43] Judging by the repeated complaints of Public Health officials, the results were unsatisfactory. Over a year later, one of those complaints prompted the head markets administrator to visit San Cosme Market, whose disorder and lack of cleanliness Public Health had denounced. In this instance, the administrator determined that the "efforts of the sanitary inspector are exaggerated" and decided, against the Public Health Council, that there was no need to forbid vendors from keeping foodstuffs on the ground.[44] Disagreements between the different offices in charge of markets remained the norm.

The new federal authorities' lack of knowledge regarding the functioning of markets might have added to the complications. In October 1911, for example, unaware of the constraints under which markets operated, Treasury officials ordered the extension of opening times from three to six in the afternoon. Several market administrators quickly responded that this would be materially impossible, because after doors closed, locatarios and employees needed at least two hours to tidy up and leave the premises ready for the next day, something they could hardly do after dark, even if they could hire more personnel, given the "absolute lack of lighting" in all of the halls.[45]

Despite the challenges, vendors continued to reach out for official support and, as before, their petitions frequently involved requests for help in managing competition among themselves. In July 1911, clothing vendors with stalls outside of La Merced pleaded with the governor for "justice" when they asked for a reduction in the fees of forty cents per day that they paid for the right to set up their shops there. They explained that, in the face of the commercial crisis that had begun to engulf the city as a result of the ongoing political uncertainty, they only sold a fourth of what they used to sell, and that at lower prices.[46] The same week, Zenón Gómez and other small-scale fruit vendors from the same plaza wrote to the governor taking the argument further. They insisted that "there was little or no fiscal justice" in what they were being charged compared to the locatarios with better and larger booths within the market hall who, they claimed, paid significantly less. The fruit vendors also objected to what they perceived as unequal police protection, because although inspectors made sure unlicensed peddlers did not intercept customers within the hall or around its gates, ambulantes carried out their business unhindered on the side of the market where they had their stalls.[47] The dismissal they got from the Maderista governor was no more satisfactory than the one they would have received from late Porfirian officials.[48]

But while the early revolutionary authorities' approach to public markets did not differ from their Porfirian predecessors', the upheavals of the 1910s soon brought a series of transformations to the political expectations and social norms of Mexico City's residents. As John Lear and Ariel Rodríguez Kuri have shown, the revolution generated new behaviors and demands, especially among workers, which in turn led to novel ways of interpellating the authorities.[49] Such a narrative of change propelled from below matches the experiences of the city's market vendors: Despite the disappointments with the Maderista government, the revolution gave vendors a new set of political principles to appeal to when communicating with the authorities. Some deployed these principles to attack officials who disrupted their businesses, as when a group of locatarios from La Merced wrote to the governor of the Federal District to denounce their administrator. His "arbitrary and abusive behavior," they wrote, ranged from unjustified detentions and merchandise confiscations to "lifting women's petticoats to see if they were hiding goods" for which they were not paying taxes. In a blunt attempt to capture the spirit of the times, they continued: "Being as you are, a patriot and a democrat, [you should] safeguard our poor interests, so we request that you change the administrator for one who is a friend of the people and not their tyrant."[50]

Others were more sophisticated. Butchers Manuel Rojas, Mariano Madrigal, and Simón Rodríguez led a group of vendors who wrote to President Madero shortly after his inauguration in December 1911 to solicit permission to return to the city's public markets. They explained that they had already attempted to advance their case during the interim government of Francisco León de la Barra on the grounds of the promises Madero had made in his 1910 Plan of San Luis Potosí. But León de la Barra's secretary of the interior had responded that it would be illegal to grant their petition under the existing meat sales bylaw dating from August 14, 1904.[51] Now, they requested that Madero order the necessary modifications to the bylaw, because "while it is true that those regulations exist, it is not less true where their origins lie."[52] They argued that the basis of the law was inconsistent with revolutionary values:

> It is well-known that upon the establishment of the Compañía de Carnes Refrigeradas El Popo, a decree was promulgated forbidding meat sales in markets with the intention of protecting its monopoly by apparent legal formulas. . . . Being an irrefutable fact that meat sales are subject to a monopoly that hurts not only small-scale vendors but the public itself, it should be combated until it disappears; and being a real fact that the Plan San Luis pledged to end all monopolies, it results an irrefutable consequence as clear as the noonday sun that the current government has the duty to combat by all available means a monopoly that is the tyranny of the strong over the weak, of capital over labor.[53]

These butchers wrote with high expectations for the recent political transition. The Plan of San Luis Potosí had called citizens to arms by denouncing electoral fraud and the concentration of power in the hands of the Porfirian elite, but it mentioned neither economic monopolies nor the relationship between capital and labor. Yet the vendors reinterpreted it as a social document that gave meaning to their grievances. In other words, as early as January 1912, vendors construed the political changes operating in the country as a possible defense of their standing in the local economy. Their reference to the "tyranny of capital over labor" signaled a pathbreaking proposition.

Soon after the first revolutionary government was sworn in, market vendors began to identify themselves as "labor", in opposition to "capital," despite the fact that, as proprietary traders, they did not sell their labor power to capitalists in return for a wage. While the terms did not accurately reflect vendors' place in the urban economy or their social relations of production, their use may have alluded to a sense of community built around affective, cultural, and material affinities. After all, many vendors had wage workers in their families and kinship groups, or they alternated themselves between industrial work and small-scale proprietary trading. Even where they did not share such intimacy with workers, they lived in the same neighborhoods, socialized with them, and, just like them, struggled to make a living.

What is more, vendors' identification with labor reflected the changes that were taking place in the city's industrial relations. Class tensions had escalated on Díaz's ousting. In July 1911, after the Mexico Tramways Company fired the organizers of a petition demanding a wage increase, better contractual terms regarding fines and firings, and compensation for injuries, two thousand streetcar workers went on strike. Five months later, textile workers walked off their jobs over issues of pay and hours, with the conflict spreading to several mills in the Federal District and other textile centers across the country. Under pressure from the companies, politicians stepped in to mediate. In December 1911, President Madero created a Labor Department, with the stated purpose of harmonizing relationships between capital and labor.[54]

Vendors saw in this institutional development an opportunity to renew their own relationship with the authorities. From the point of view of the butchers who wrote to the president, association with industrial workers promised to open alternative channels of communication with the Maderista government. Yet their access to, and ability to move, the authorities remained limited in this period. After making some inquiries, the district governor agreed with general markets administrator M. Romero Ibánez to reject the butchers' petition to return to the city's markets on the grounds that "it was made to the exclusive benefit of one group of vendors, to the detriment of another, and to the disadvantage of the public, which would be harmed by being sold in worse hygienic conditions, and without any discount in price, the same meats that it now purchases in the currently authorized shops."[55] The authorities went on to explicitly reject the accusations of El Popo's monopolistic practices, and they ignored the rest of what the vendors had to say.

After Madero's assassination, the situation for comerciantes deteriorated further. Under President Huerta the city began to experience a growing militarization.[56] At the same time, officials attempted to tighten control over public markets. In July 1913, the secretary of interior summoned the members of the Consejo Superior de Gobierno of the Federal District—the district governor, the director of Public Works, and the president of the Public Health Council—and the Treasury official responsible for local taxation to discuss the state of the city's two main markets, La Merced and San Juan. The secretary of the interior was appalled by the way vendors displayed and sold fish, offal, and game. "In both markets the most repugnant thing is the extraordinary lack of cleanliness and the notable amounts of excrement, trash, dirty waters, decomposing matters, all of which are in horrible promiscuity with elements used as foods." In the secretary's view conditions were such that "it seems that no sanitary authorities exist, nor people concerned for public well-being."[57]

Mere weeks after the meeting, in August 1913, Huerta signed an accord for yet another organizational shake-up. This accord gave the governor discretion over which specific goods could be sold in each market, while indicating that he should give priority to stalls selling goods "not ordinarily sold in [other] shops or private establishments," particularly *tiendas de abarrotes* and butchers.[58] Meat vendors would have to wait for better times to return to the city's markets. What is more, the governor soon ordered the removal from La Merced Market of "all stalls dealing in prepared foods, because of the inconvenience they cause for transit and for the market's cleanliness, the awful conditions in which foodstuffs are seasoned, and because they present a miserable sight that is absolutely incompatible with the culture of this capital."[59] He also tried to expel from Martínez de la Torre Market the vendors who sold vegetables on the market's central tables as well as those who sold flavored ices, prepared foods, blankets, embroideries, and flowers in the streets surrounding San Juan Market.

The new government's hasty efforts to sanitize and reorder markets failed to build consensus among the different officials in charge, so the governor's instructions were not fully implemented. The market administrator objected that this time, unlike on previous occasions, no plans had been made to relocate the removed vendors.[60] In January 1914 the secretary of interior demanded to know what measures had been taken by the Treasury to compensate for the loss of revenue implied by the removal of "additional stalls" in Martínez de la Torre and San Juan Markets. In response, the secretary of finance made the remarkable acknowledgment that "such measures consisted in allowing the aforementioned stalls to remain," that is, declining to enforce the order to remove them.[61] Unsuccessful as the governor's attempts at stricter regulation were, they nevertheless increased the already vast distance that separated vendors from the authorities.

Among all the upheavals of the revolution, the war between Carranza's Constitucionalista and Zapata and Villa's Convencionista forces hit Mexico City the hardest. Between the fall of Huerta in August 1914 and the final

Carrancista recovery of the capital in August 1915, the capital city was occupied and evacuated six times. The population endured dismal material conditions. With little to no gold or silver backing and no significant constraints on printing money, the multiple paper currencies issued by the parties at war depreciated rapidly, as inflation spiked. Recurrent banning of enemy currency by the alternating occupying forces, compounded by currency speculation by private individuals and military men, aggravated the monetary crisis. In addition the disruption of transportation systems and, to some unknown extent, production, led to shortages of raw materials and foodstuffs, hobbling industry and feeding the inflationary spiral. Finally, hoarding of available foodstuffs and unprecedented levels of monopolistic practices by local merchants only worsened matters.[62] Inflation estimates are unreliable for this year, but they suggest up to a fifteenfold price increase for basic goods.[63]

Hunger and typhoid took hold of the city.[64] Consumer protest marches, supplications to the authorities and merchants, and, when everything else failed, food riots became facts of everyday life.[65] On June 25, 1915, for example, groups of impoverished women and children stormed thirty stores and five markets. One woman was shot by a store employee who opened fire on the crowd, and two hundred other women were arrested.[66] According to witnesses and contemporary journalists, such actions were mostly desperate, irrational affairs. The historian John Lear suggests, however, that they were a gendered response to the political crisis and the breakdown of the local moral economy, as women defended family and community under what they perceived as unusually unjust circumstances.[67] Market vendors now had to cope with the desperation of their customers in addition to limited supply and the authorities' neglect.

In response to the crisis of 1915 the Constitucionalistas set up an emergency food supply system run by five actors who were not always on the best of terms. In charge, writes historian Rodríguez Kuri, were the occupying army's provost and the ayuntamiento, which had been temporarily re-empowered for this purpose.[68] They were supported by, or at least tried to coordinate the actions of, the city's existing institutions of public welfare, private charities, and organized merchants. From August 1915, when Constitutionalist forces regained definitive control of the capital, the efforts to normalize the provision of basic goods fell primarily to Colonel Ignacio C. Enríquez, whom Carranza appointed as president of the city council. By June 1916, the ayuntamiento directly administered at least twenty-seven stores that sold beans, sugar, rice, salt, butter, flour, soap, and charcoal as well as twenty-nine distributing meat, ten dealing in fish, and seven selling clothes and footwear.[69] Even though public markets were the city's most visible retail outlets, they were conspicuously absent from this emergency system. This was perhaps the result of the more than a decade long disarticulation of the relationship between locatarios and the authorities, and the ongoing crisis in the management of markets.

Despite the creation of this emergency supply system, inflation continued unabated, and with it, conflicts over real wages. Workers in Mexico City responded by forming and expanding their own organizations. The anarcho-syndicalist Casa del Obrero had catalyzed a unionization drive after its foundation in September 1912, and by mid-1914 it included teachers, carpenters, shoemakers, printers, textile workers, and streetcar workers. Unionized workers went on strike in defense of the purchasing power of their wages and to protest against layoffs and reductions in hours. In every case the authorities sought collaboration with those individuals and groups in the labor movement who could restrain workers' collective demands, attempting to sanction official channels for containment of class conflict. Eventually the Casa del Obrero chose to negotiate to protect their affiliates' jobs, forming a pact with Colonel Enríquez and other Carrancistas to recruit the Red Battalions in January 1915. But not all workers took this stance. Electrical workers, whose Sindicato Mexicano de Electricistas was the most powerful union in the city, rejected any such alliance and went on strike three times in 1915 alone.[70]

Class struggle peaked in the spring and summer of 1916. In May, secretary of finance Luis Cabrera announced the issuing of *infalsificables*, a paper currency meant to replace all previous Constitutionalist bills. When later that month the newly formed Federation of Workers' Unions of the Federal District shut down the city in demand that wages be pegged to a gold standard, General Benjamín Hill, Obregón's ally and military commander of the plaza, mediated a settlement between labor and business representatives that forced workers to accept pay in infalsificables instead. As the bills depreciated, tensions mounted, leading to a general strike supported by 86,000 workers on July 31. The revolutionary government did not hesitate; on the third day the city was declared under martial law, and the strike committee was arrested and court-martialed.

Workers' militancy and the responses it elicited changed the course of Mexico's political economy. While the failure of the general strike and the repression that followed were a setback for the labor movement, struggles over pay, hours, and conditions soon resumed. The state that emerged in 1917 could not ignore workers' assertiveness and strength. The new constitution recognized rights to a minimum wage, an eight-hour day, and a weekly day of rest, together with the freedom to unionize and the right to strike in order to renegotiate terms of employment. By the same token, however, capitalists' pressure on the authorities to generate profitable conditions for their operations led to a set of constitutional constraints on these same workers' rights. Unions would require governmental recognition; official rulings would declare whether strikes were legal or illegal; and mandatory arbitration by tripartite boards composed of labor, capital, and government representatives would determine the outcome of strikes. The Federal District was among the first jurisdictions to pass labor laws and resolutions to implement the constitution's mandates. The authorities' role as mediators of conflicts between workers and capitalists was thus institutionalized, and it was in this new context that vendors resumed their efforts to improve their lot.

"The People, Machine-Gunned by Political Interests"

Fourteen years after President Porfirio Díaz stripped the Ayuntamiento de la Ciudad de México of all executive power, the 1917 Constitution ratified under Carranza restored its control of its urban properties, economic activities, and fiscal resources. Once again an elected body controlled the city's public markets. But the differences were stark. While a group of men closely aligned with the national executive had dominated the ayuntamiento in the decade prior to 1903, the council now turned into a battlefield of disparate, though intersecting, political and social struggles.

From the beginning, the resurrected ayuntamiento was rife with factional disputes. Different factions of self-declared Carranza supporters improvised political parties to compete against one another for seats on the council. The same was true during Obregón's and Calles's terms thereafter. Presidential successions were particularly tumultuous times, as groups behind opposing aspirants measured their forces in the capital. In late 1919 and early 1920, Carrancistas, Obregonistas, and the supporters of General Pablo González fought hard over control of the ayuntamiento; conflicts between Callistas and those who backed General de la Huerta shaped municipal life in 1923; and as Obregón pursued his reelection in 1927, his allies in the city did all they could to crush his opponents on the council.[71]

These power struggles helped transform the ayuntamiento into the epicenter of local labor politics during this period. As political incentives changed and power began to concentrate once again in Mexico City, the labor movement splintered. In the capital, the most important division was between the unions that chose to fight capitalists as independently from the state as possible and those that combined social struggles with the pursuit of positions of power within the government. The CGT (Confederación General de Trabajadores, or General Confederation of Workers), formed in February 1921, favored the first strategy, including direct action.[72] The CROM (Confederación Regional Obrera Mexicana, or Mexican Regional Labor Confederation) espoused the second, which its leaders called *acción multiple*.[73] The CROM's political arm, the PLM (Partido Laborista Mexicano, or Mexican Laborist Party), supported Obregón against Carranza in 1920. In return, one of its leaders, Red Battalion veteran General Celestino Gasca, was appointed district governor, a position he kept until 1923. In 1924 the PLM held the majority of seats in the Ayuntamiento de la Ciudad de México. In alliance with President Calles, from January 1925 to July 1928, its dominance of Mexico City's council was absolute. Though the CROM never controlled both the council and the governorship—Governors Ramón Ross (October 1923–June 1926, intermittently) and Francisco Serrano (June 1926–June 1927) consistently supported groups that openly opposed it—it used whatever power these offices afforded its leaders to fight not only against employers but also against the CGT. At stake was the CROM's ability to control workers' representation in the capital.[74]

Both the factional disputes between Carrancista, Obregonista, and Callista groups, and the clashes between the CROM and the CGT bore heavily on vendors' ability to navigate the city's reconfigured public sphere. Markets, like other public services under the control of the contested ayuntamiento, became a locus of chronic conflict, even during years of relative political peace. For example, two rival Obregonista factions claimed to have won the December 1920 ayuntamiento elections and proceeded to establish their own separate councils, one under the Partido Cooperativista banner and the other under the banner of the Partido Liberal Constitucionalista (PLC). Physical clashes ensued when both councils tried to charge fees and taxes to market vendors in January 1921, forcing then Secretary of Interior Plutarco Elías Calles to intervene and close down the Cooperativista council.[75] From outside the ayuntamiento, the Cooperativistas continued to undermine their opponents by complaining about their handling of markets. In May 1922,

Cooperativista organizer Ramón Medina addressed Secretary Calles to denounce the ineptitude of market officials, who often delayed the issuing of licenses and were prone to taking bribes. He explicitly held the council's president, Miguel Alonzo Romero, and its secretary, Abraham González, responsible for "materially strangling" vendors. "There is no *Municipio Libre*, this is free theft, free plundering by the so-called *Peleceanos* [the members of the PLC]."[76] Alonzo Romero was quick to respond. Later that month, he wrote to President Obregón to assert that the accusations against him were due to his own attempts to purge the council's market administration of corrupt elements.[77]

By this time, Mexico City's public market infrastructure had fallen into a state of disarray. During the first decade of the twentieth century the population of the capital had grown by 36 percent, and between 1910 and 1920 by another 31 percent.[78] But market hall construction failed to keep up. So as the number of residents making a living by means of petty trading increased, there was no way for peddlers to find stalls to carry out their trade. La Lagunilla Market, inaugurated in 1904, was the last hall of the Porfiriato; during the early years of the revolution the city managed to build the Juárez Market in 1912 and an annex to Santa Catarina Market in 1913.[79] These were far from sufficient. After the ayuntamiento regained control in 1917, its officials accommodated the overflow in areas contiguous with existing halls, in "exterior" stalls in adjacent streets and plazas, or in clusters of al viento stalls in those parts of the city still lacking a market building.[80] In March 1919 the council's markets commission reported that 70 percent of the revenue stemming from *rastros y mercados* came from fixed stalls outside of market halls.[81] By June 1924, the ayuntamiento was distributing approximately 10,000 vendor licenses each month, while citywide market hall capacity did not exceed 1,200 stalls.[82] In other words, the boundaries between public thoroughfare and markets had been blurred again.

While political competition brought instability and violence to the city, it created the space for vendors to highlight the official neglect of public market infrastructure and to redefine the terms of their engagement with the authorities. In the past they had sought to do this individually, or in ad hoc groups, but now, like so many workers and proprietary producers and traders around them, they did so by forming unions.[83] These unions were organized within and around individual halls, or on specific streets where vendors set their stalls, and many of them joined together to form federations that would,

FIGURE 8. La Lagunilla Market, 1922. Source: AGN, Instrucción Pública y Bellas Artes, Propiedad Artística, C.I.F., PAL/8176, Inventario 3.

in turn, affiliate with labor confederations. Vendors were thus able to articulate a collective defense of the shared interests of their groups and place specific demands on local government. In June 1923, for example, the Sindicato de Comerciantes del Exterior del Mercado de San Juan wrote to Obregón to express its members' support for the decision to close down gambling dens in markets and other parts of the city. "Mr. President, we beg you to accept our sincere vote of gratitude, and we also beg you . . . to do everything in your power so these establishments might never reopen."[84]

In a similar vein, in May 1922 the leadership of the Federación de Sindicatos de Comerciantes del Exterior de los Mercados del Distrito Federal (FSC) penned a letter to Municipal President Romero Alonzo to commend his decision to remove corrupt market employees. Moreover, following an agreement reached by a "general assembly" of union representatives, the FSC requested a meeting with the council to discuss how vendors could best contribute to the improvement and cleanliness of markets.

> In spite of the scores of unjustified criticisms we receive in the press, which Machiavellianly claim that we are the enemies of progress . . . we want the satisfaction to be first to point out the eyesore that markets have become; . . . in

the past the Ayuntamiento would not deign to listen to us . . . and always considered us mere pack animals, only acceptable for the yields of our labors, without seeing us as an integral part of Society, and hence with the right to take part in the concert of free men.[85]

When they met with Romero Alonzo the following month, one of the points the FSC brought up was the situation of their compañeros in San Lucas Market, whom the ayuntamiento was trying to relocate. In the absence of municipally provided stalls they had had to improvise their own, which led to complaints against their poor quality and lack of hygiene and to police attempts to remove them. Instead, the FSC proposed that the ayuntamiento build a new set of booths in the same location. A month later, they repeated their concerns in a letter to President Obregón. They considered that their suggestions were "reasonable" because the proposed booths "strictly followed public health regulations," would generate revenue for the council and, given their requested location, "would not hinder traffic."[86]

Unions could find common cause with the ayuntamiento when it came to public hygiene, morals, and infrastructure, but their attempts to negotiate fiscal charges were more contentious.[87] Because market fees and tax levels affected the entire vendor population, locatarios across different markets mobilized together in what, for vendors, were new heights of collective action. When submitting petitions in writing did not achieve the results they demanded, vendor organizations could now threaten to take to the streets. And on August 1, 1924, they did. After markets closed, groups of locatarios marched toward the municipal palace to protest a resolution due to go into effect that day, which they claimed would double the amount they paid in fees and taxes. On streets they had long occupied with their stalls, they now walked with explicit political purpose.

It was a dangerous time for municipal politicking. The previous December's local elections had taken place in the midst of the delahuertista rebellion, which several Cooperativista Ayuntamiento members, including former municipal president Jorge Prieto Laurens, had openly supported. After the rebellion failed, the Cooperativista councilors who were supposed to return for the second half of their two-year terms had gone into hiding, fearing arrest or worse. Three groups made up the rest of the ayuntamiento: the Laboristas of the PLM were in the majority, with fifteen seats; the Partido Cívico Progresista (PCP) held seven, including the presidency; and the Liberal Constitutionalists (PLC) had only three.[88] In March 1924, the Laboristas had presented an initiative to remove ayuntamiento president Marcos E. Raya, of the PCP. After Calles was elected president of Mexico in July, the Laboristas and the CROM on the ayuntamiento took advantage of the downtime during the transition to advance their agenda. By summer 1924, vendors had found themselves in the middle of an ongoing political battle between the PLM and the PCP.

Having been unable to convince this fractious and fractured ayuntamiento to change their plans to raise fees, vendors' unions decided to take action. On Friday August 1, 1924, after three in the afternoon, as many as 2,500 vendors and their families gathered near the statue of Carlos IV on Palacio Legislativo Avenue and marched together through the city center in defiance of the authorities' refusal to grant them permission to hold a rally.[89] Displaying banners proclaiming, "We are hungry and thirsty for justice" and "La Lagunilla vendors protest against the injustice of the council," they demanded that the amounts they paid for their stalls not be increased.[90] The fire department and the police tried in vain to break up the demonstration. When crowds of vendors arrived near the municipal palace shortly after five in the afternoon, President Raya agreed to meet with a group of locatario representatives. Yet he promptly excused himself, leaving them to discuss the situation with councilor Ramón Velarde, chair of the markets commission, and Pedro Galicia Rodríguez, head of the markets department.

While negotiations were taking place, someone shot a firearm. Panic and confusion ensued, aggravated by the action of the firemen, who turned hoses on the demonstrators. The demonstration advanced toward the palace doors, where a line of policemen and the municipal guard opened fire. By six in the evening, the Red Cross and the White Cross were tending to the wounded. One protester was dead and twelve were injured, one of whom later passed away in the hospital. The journalists covering the story believed that many others had been hurt, but had fled the Plaza de la Constitución without medical assistance.

Laborista councilor Federico Rocha immediately accused Enrique Cota, a former PCP ayuntamiento employee who had been Raya's *agente confidencial* during the earlier months of the year, of having fired the gun that brought on the panic and had him arrested. That evening, soon after the Zócalo was vacated, fourteen members of the ayuntamiento's Laborista block released a statement condemning the government's response to the protest. They compared the shooting of the locatarios with November 1922's water riots, for which they had blamed then municipal president Alonzo Romero.[91] The parallel suggested, implicitly but obviously, that President Raya was to blame for the violence. The Laboristas demanded that both the Municipal Guard and Enrique Cota be punished.[92] In the days that followed, the press publicized these accusations and others. While the Laboristas insisted that it was President Raya who had ordered the violence against the vendors, Cota and Raya accused the Laboristas of attempting a coup against the PCP. According to Agent Cota, when the demonstrators approached the municipal palace, Councilor Rocha had shouted, "¡*Ahora muchachos!* . . . ¡*Muerte al Cívico Progresista!*"[93] In Cota's version of the story, the municipal guard shot at the crowd only after this intervention, when it was forced to defend itself. President Raya agreed, repeatedly declaring that he had not ordered the open fire, but that the guards had no choice in the face of his political enemies' attempts "to create public alarm."[94] He had the support of PCP and PLC councilmen who published a letter denying that Raya had any responsibility for the shooting of the locatarios and calling for an investigation of the events.[95]

Both sides' stories, as well as media coverage, portrayed vendors as passive victims who bore no responsibility for the deaths and injuries. While such an angle demonstrated a degree of sympathy with the laboring classes, it simultaneously denied vendors' unions any real political agency. An editorial in *El Demócrata* three days after the demonstration read: "Who provoked the shooting? Who brought the locatarios tumultuously to the Municipal Palace's doors?"[96] In a matter of days journalists answered with a consensus: opportunistic members of the PLM, they wrote, had caused the confrontations in order to force Raya to resign. The media reduced vendors to the nondescript "*pueblo*," which had been "machine-gunned by political interests."[97] In the opinion of the press, vendors had not freely chosen to march to the Zócalo as a deliberate political act; instead, their demonstration was the product of Laborista manipulations. According to *El País*, "The agents of a sinister gang cheated the humble market vendors with the biggest perfidy. . . . For all we know and have seen, the rally was not organized by market vendors but by a group of politicians."[98] The *Excélsior* reached a similar conclusion: "Low political passions, which in these times of declining social values have reached inconceivable levels, were responsible for last Friday's bloody incidents. . . . The *locatarios* unconsciously found themselves mixed up in this mess."[99] So much for a revolutionary public sphere.

Vendors did not remain silent. In the aftermath of the demonstration, they filled their markets with black paper flags in sign of mourning and

FIGURE 9. Vendors' demonstration makes the headlines, and even the cartoon section of the main newspapers. Source: Hemeroteca, Biblioteca Lerdo de Tejada.

organized a public burial for the dead. They also gave journalists their own accounts of the events of August 1. Although they did not contradict the view that the PLM was responsible for the violent turn of the demonstration, vendors pointed to a different, but intersecting, set of conflicts. From their hospital beds, Angel Gómez and four other wounded locatarios declared they had willingly attended a peaceful demonstration to protest against higher taxes. They recalled, however, that as they were arriving at the Zócalo they had been joined by a group of agitators who immediately started stoning the municipal guard.[100]

The FSC corroborated their claims. According to its secretary general, Pedro D. Nájera, their organization had organized the locatarios' demonstration following an agreement by the vendor unions from twelve different public markets: La Merced, La Lagunilla, San Cosme, San Juan, El Volador, San Lucas, Juárez, Mixcoac, Tacubaya, Tacuba, La Dalia, and Nonoalco.[101] When their protest march reached the Palacio Municipal, however, they found a group with banners of their rival, the Unión de Comerciantes del Exterior de los Mercados (UC). At that point, three of the UC leaders, Pascual Paz, Samuel Polanco, and Dámaso F. Díaz, communicated to vendors that they had already arranged for a meeting with councilman Velarde, from the markets commission. While they were forced to negotiate together, the members of FSC had no sympathy for the UC's leadership. They insisted that its three bosses were only trying "to give themselves importance and to obtain a representation they do not have." In fact, they claimed that the UC existed only in its leaders' "atrophied brains."[102] Nájera declared that the leaders of the UC, all of them employees of the ayuntamiento's markets department, had incited violence not only with the purpose of discrediting the FSC but also of undermining President Raya and influencing municipal appointments. UC leader Samuel Polanco did not deny his attempts to remove the head of the markets department, Galicia Rodríguez. Writing in the city's newspapers that the UC's intention was to defend "the people" against the taxes he was about to impose, he insisted that Galicia Rodríguez "suffers from the grave and unforgivable fault of not knowing absolutely anything about public markets."[103] The FSC responded in an open letter condemning the UC's maneuvers.[104]

The hostility between these two vendor organizations, the FSC and the UC, needs to be understood within ongoing conflicts in the broader labor movement. Whereas the Federación de Sindicatos de Comerciantes del Exterior de los Mercados del Distrito Federal was affiliated with the nominally anarcho-syndicalist CGT, the Unión de Comerciantes del Exterior de los Mercados belonged to the CROM.[105] In all probability, in August 1924, vendors had become entangled in the confrontation between the CROM and the CGT, which had been escalating as the CROM fought to expand its power within the labor movement and encroach on the CGT's membership. Thus the media's denunciation of the role of local politics in the tragedy was probably correct, even if journalists failed to recognize vendors' conscious participation in the events.

On August 30, 1924, *El Demócrata* published a short article announcing that the city council had decided to cancel the increase in rates on the locatarios. It also reported that in return for the goodwill displayed by the authorities, the FSC had committed to move hundreds of its members' stalls to the new market halls that the ayuntamiento was planning to build.[106] The article, however, did not dwell on the reasons why vendors got what they had wanted. Was it due to the publicity around their demonstration and the outcry caused by its violent repression, or had the upheavals in the ayuntamiento simply made it politically incapable of going forward with the new market fees and taxes it had approved behind closed doors? Was it a victory for the FSC, or had the Laboristas pushed for it to show vendors what the CROM could deliver? The answer probably involved all of the above.

The violent turn of their demonstration showed vendors the risks of accepting the mediation of labor confederations in their negotiations with the authorities. In November 1924, the UC's leader, Dámaso Díaz, "greeted and welcomed" President-elect Calles in the name of the city's *comerciantes del exterior de los mercados*, or vendors with stalls outside of, but administratively connected with, existing market halls.[107] A month later, the PLM took over the city council. As long as the CROMistas dominated the council and enjoyed Calles's support, the CGT-affiliated FSC had a hard time defending the interests of vendors. In August 1925, the FSC denounced the PLM-appointed head of the markets department, Fernando Escamilla, for taking advantage of his position to force vendors to join CROM-affiliated unions. Calles curtly responded that their "exhaustive document" had been forwarded to PLM municipal president Arturo de Saracho; by referring this complaint against a PLM member to the PLM itself, he effectively dismissed it.[108] Facing such a hostile environment, it is not surprising that several vendor organizations migrated to the CROM.[109]

Still, some market vendors found the association with the CROM problematic and therefore tried to detach themselves from their organizations. On May 11, 1926, forty-eight vendors of *gorditas* from Guadalupe Hidalgo wrote to the secretary of gobernación and the district governor to request protection against Benito Arredondo, secretary general of the CROM's Unión de Locatarios del Mercado Hidalgo y Comerciantes en Pequeño, from which they had resigned en masse. They declared that they had joined the union in July 1924, to "defend our interests and those of our compañeros, which were being harmed by the then current municipal authorities, and to create a means of mutual defense against whoever might try to hurt us." Soon, however, they realized that in the name of "the social struggle" they were in fact participating in political maneuvers to overthrow the local ayuntamiento. The situation became intolerable when, after a "friend of the laboring classes" took over the council, Arredondo began using his support to "establish preferences and tyrannies . . . to the point of extorting us and imposing punishments harsher than those of a foreman in times of capitalists' domination . . . becoming the scourge of the proletariat of Guadalupe Hidalgo."[110] The vendors declared that Arredondo, with the assistance of the municipal president and the local police, had forced them to abandon their stalls, both to take revenge and to coerce them back into the union. The secretario de gobernación and the governor sided with the vendors and returned them their stalls. But the CROM's Unión de Locatarios del Mercado Hidalgo would not let the matter rest. A year later, with the Cristero rebellion in full swing, they tried to retake their places in the market by accusing several of the vendors who had participated in the complaints of being religious fanatics and enemies of the government.[111]

Conflicts also arose when vendors' interests clashed with those of wage workers. In 1923, the constitutional right to a weekly day of rest was implemented in the Federal District, requiring the closing down of public markets and commercial houses on Sundays along with the district's factories. This placed vendors in a difficult position, as Sundays were when consumer traffic was highest and they made their best sales. Capitalist owners of commercial establishments were lobbying hard to have the law changed so that they could open their shops on Sundays, leaving them free to choose their employees' day off. Vendors faced a dilemma. Should they act according to their material interests and side with the capitalists? Or should they, in solidarity with those who belonged to the same confederations as they did, support a measure that workers were fighting for, even though it would reduce vendors' incomes? The Centro Cosmopolita de Dependientes de Comercio, which represented commercial employees and had been pushing for the decree, predicted and feared the former would happen. In November 1923, it warned Governor Ramón Ross that "market locatarios had publicly threatened with a protest demonstration against the [Sunday rest] decree." The Centro Cosmopolita was "prepared, if not to prevent it [the demonstration], to organize another one, as numerous or larger."[112]

Instead of openly confronting workers, though, vendor unions decided to petition for exemptions. So while in a letter to President Obregón the FSC celebrated the measure in favor of "workers and employees [obreros y dependientes de patrones]," it requested that market vendors be allowed to sell on Sundays, because as "unemployed workers," they counted on that day's trading to alleviate their families' critical situation. Conflating workers' grievances with vendors', they wrote:

> If industrialists close down factories or reduce the number of workers or their hours, if workshops cut down on employees, or the government imposes

higher municipal contributions, while the "agiotistas," those insatiable octopuses from whom we obtain our working capital, increase their margins, all of this makes the situation of the proletariat more afflictive, and to make matters worse comes the decree of Sunday rest, which completes our misery.[113]

Soon, however, proprietary vendors' unions began to back their demands by enunciating their class differences from the same proletariat. In the name of "more than ten thousand families of market vendors," who "provide workers with their basic needs at lower prices," the UC requested that public markets remain open on Sundays because, "unlike industrial workers, day laborers and domestic servants . . . in our business we carry out all functions, and we give ourselves the necessary rest our bodies require."[114]

When vendors questioned their identification with wage workers, self-interest sometimes trumped solidarity. In 1927, market vendors from San Ángel wrote to President Calles to ask him to put a stop to a railroad strike that, having obtained the support of large numbers of workers in that municipality, was putting them out of business.[115] The relations of production that proprietary vendors were engaged in, with their creditors, suppliers, and customers, differed in fundamental ways from those experienced by workers with their employers, implying a distinct, and sometimes conflicting, set of material interests. Vendors' organizations were beginning to recognize this. In February 1928, still under the auspices of the CROM's Federación de Sindicatos Obreros del D.F., vendors gathered in a second yearly convention of *comerciantes en pequeño* of the Federal District, where they created a Departamento de Protección al Pequeño Comerciante to promote vendors' interests and to coordinate their relationship with the authorities.[116] While this departamento does not seem to have amounted to much, it came at the tail end of a decade of organizational experimentation that would come in handy for market vendors later that year, when the political map of Mexico City was again redrawn.

Revolutionized Locatarios, Unreformed Markets

By 1930 Mexico City's population surpassed one million people, triple what it had been at the start of the century.[117] Because of the rise in both consumer demand and the number of people seeking a living in the capital, the number of proprietary vendors had increased dramatically. But in the midst of growing inequality and political tumult, market hall construction failed to keep up.[118] As a result, the overflow of stalls had to be accommodated in surrounding areas, with the number of locatarios selling in adjacent streets and plazas far exceeding those within the existing purpose-built halls. As one Public Works official put it, all of the city's existing public markets had expanded by "invading the surrounding streets with stalls."[119]

The old Porfirian characterization of these markets, including the horror elicited by their perceived backwardness, survived the departure of President Díaz and the constitutional proclamation of a new state in 1917. With the ayuntamiento reinstated, in February 1918 Cooperativista councilor Prieto Laurens condemned El Volador Market as nothing but a gathering of *rateros*. "Foreigners wonder, how is it possible that Mexican authorities tolerate this, just a few steps away from the elegant National and Municipal Palaces?"[120] A year later, another Cooperativista councilor, Ramón Riveroll, referred to the market formed in the streets surrounding El Volador as "a true flaunting of rags and filth . . . a true plague."[121] In March 1925, Vicente Lombardo Toledano, who was then a Laborista Party councilor, claimed that "big markets should tend to disappear. . . . They do not exist anymore in other parts of the world." He denounced Mexico City's markets as "nothing but a reminder of the traditional indigenous 'tianguis' that present all the most undesirable conditions of unhealthiness and discomfort."[122]

Market vendors themselves as well as urban developers embraced such views whenever it suited them. When Cándido de la Fuente and 106 other traders of secondhand clothes and ironworks protested against their relocation to the Plazuela de Allende, among the reasons they listed was that the new location was unsuitable for a market because it was unhygienic and full of thieves.[123] Equally, one J. Wiechers justified his proposal to sell a plot of land to the ayuntamiento for the construction of a new hall in Santa María de la Ribera on the grounds that the existing improvised markets in that colonia were "not only against rules of hygiene, but . . . such agglomerations hinder traffic and present an unpleasant sight, inappropriate for a city such as this capital."[124]

While official and private attitudes toward markets remained unaltered, market vendors were among those whom Luis González y González calls the *revolucionados*, common men and women who during the civil wars of the 1910s found novel areas of political interlocution and new ideological justifications to legitimize their demands.[125] This chapter has demonstrated, however, that to understand the transformations in locatarios' relationships with the authorities, we need to insert them into a longer time frame: the changes taking place in public markets had started before, and continued beyond, the decade of political and military upheaval. In particular, the government's neglect of market vendors, and the creativity of vendors' responses to this neglect, cut through the standard periodization of the revolution, highlighting continuities between the emasculation of the ayuntamiento in 1903 and its final abolition in the crisis of 1928. In the late Porfiriato, the social tensions brought about by the expansion of capitalism and the modification of local political structures—most significantly the removal of all executive powers from the city council—had already begun to reshape proprietary vendors' political stances. Because the state lost the ability, or at least surrendered the obligation, to respond to their needs, market vendors were forced to sharpen their claims to their rights. After 1911, as they learned a new political vocabulary, their grievances fostered collective action among class-based groups. By the time the city council regained its full governing faculties in 1917, locatarios were ready to organize unions to articulate their demands, which they expressed through an identification with wage workers and their struggles. For better or worse this association would not last, in part because of the level of violence of labor politics in this period, but also because proprietary traders' social relations of production and role in the local economy differed in important ways from those of workers. What would last, however, was vendors' mobilization within a civil society that slowly but permanently transformed the city's politics.

4 Political Experimentation in a Time of Crises, 1929–1945

DURING THE GREAT DEPRESSION, Mexico City witnessed a period of intense political and economic experimentation. In 1929, the federal government created the Consejo Consultivo, a corporatist body designed to supplant the labor movement as the intermediary between the state and the urban popular classes in Mexico City. Yet managing the local political economy proved harder than the government expected. The multiple class conflicts that vendors were engaged in constrained their efforts. The old Porfirian market halls were overwhelmed by population growth, leading to a proliferation of street stalls that became, once again, a major source of tension. Wealthy capitalist merchants clashed with small-scale proprietary vendors over regulations of minimum prices and the use of public spaces. Large industrialists, property owners, and urban planners joined merchants in opposing all types of street vending, while vendors, workers, and the head of the markets office tried to distinguish between its acceptable and unacceptable forms. Competition among vendors themselves further complicated negotiations. Mired in these overlapping, entangled disputes, the authorities constructed careful compromises that, in the end, they were unable to implement. Successive governments struggled to handle an increasingly divided vendor movement.

Starting in 1932, economic recovery brought political stability to the capital, allowing the Department of the Federal District, now fully in charge of the city, to pour resources into public markets. Driven by demands from vendors, construction companies, and other interested parties, the government kick-started a redevelopment program in yet another attempt to move vendors off the city's streets and into purpose-built facilities. But, as their Porfirian predecessors had learned at the end of the nineteenth century, building market halls was not enough to reshape how vendors used public spaces. Even the flagship Abelardo Rodríguez Market remained undersubscribed because the Department of the Federal District failed to manage the competition between street vendors and market vendors. Without effective mechanisms to solve the ensuing conflicts among their organizations, vendors' commitment to relocate to the new hall remained tentative, and all deals were prone to falling apart. By late 1936, the situation had deteriorated as a result of mounting inflation. President Lázaro Cárdenas imposed price controls on everyday necessities in an attempt to protect the purchasing power of wages and appease industrial workers. Unsurprisingly, the prospects of a reduction of their profit margins only worsened proprietary traders' relations with the state. But alienating the city's vendors was risky. Large numbers of locatarios supported Juan Andreu Almazán, the challenger to Cárdenas's chosen successor, Manuel Ávila Camacho, in the controversial presidential election of 1940. After Ávila Camacho succeeded in the national election, the new administration decided it was time to gain greater control over vendor organizations. To do so, the state would have to build up its institutional capabilities.

The Consejo Consultivo, an Experiment in "Democracia Funcional"

In 1929 the world entered its greatest capitalist crisis to date. Crashes had occurred before, but in scope, scale, and persistence, the Great Depression had no precedent. As the globe's most powerful economies collapsed and turned protectionist, international trade and investment dried up. For Mexico, the worst years were 1929 to 1932, when real GDP fell by over 17 percent. The external sector was the most heavily affected, with the value of Mexican exports tumbling to a third of their precrash level by 1932. The ensuing pressure on the peso forced Mexico to drop the gold standard.[1]

Political uncertainty compounded these economic conditions. The Cristero rebellion, a response to President Calles's attempts to implement secularist and anticlerical constitutional provisions, had become increasingly violent, spreading to thirteen states by 1928.[2] That July, a Catholic militant assassinated President-elect Obregón.³ Interim president Emilio Portes Gil was tasked with carrying out a fresh election but faced a threatening climate. Calles and his allies, desperate for an orderly transition, created the Partido Nacional Revolucionario (PNR, or National Revolutionary Party) in early March 1929.⁴ Obregonista general José Gonzalo Escobar attempted a coup, with a third of army officers behind him, but failed to gain control.⁵ With the urban middle classes supporting an opposition candidate in the 1930 election, former education minister José Vasconcelos, the PNR resorted to fraud and violence to secure the victory of Pascual Ortiz Rubio.⁶ It was not enough. Ortiz Rubio resigned in September 1932, and the new party had to content itself with governing through a provisional president, Abelardo Rodríguez, for two more years.

Crisis, however, begot opportunities. As the purchasing power of whatever was left of Mexican exports plunged, imports became expensive, creating incentives for entrepreneurs in the country to invest in the production of consumer and intermediate goods. Businessmen were soon resorting to politics, and in particular to their influence on economic policy, to push for currency controls, differential exchange rates, and specific tariffs that would stifle any remaining foreign competition. These improvised policies of import substitution reignited growth and helped the development of domestic industries.⁷ The government also stepped up direct support for business. In 1933, the public financing agency Nacional Financiera was created to help struggling banks and to channel public funds into commercial agriculture and real estate development. What is more, the federal government invested in new infrastructure, particularly in irrigation and road works. Construction firms with access to public contracts became highly profitable ventures. In this context, real GDP grew by 20 percent between 1934 and 1937, while industrial production grew ever more rapidly.⁸

In Mexico City, the political tumult prompted the federal government to tighten control over local affairs. In the wake of the political crisis caused by Obregón's assassination, Calles and his allies decided to abolish Mexico City's ayuntamiento for good.⁹ After the necessary, though speedy, congressional debates, on December 31, 1928, provisional president Emilio Portes Gil signed the Ley Orgánica del Distrito Federal y Territorios Federales, merging the municipalities of Mexico, Tacuba, Tacubaya, and Mixcoac into a Departamento Central to be administered by a presidentially appointed Jefe del Departamento Central, soon to be renamed Jefe del Departamento del Distrito

Federal.[10] This reorganization eliminated the capital's electoral competition at the municipal level. It also ended four years of command of the city council by the Partido Laborista Mexicano, the political arm of the Confederación Regional Obrera Mexicana (CROM), whose leaders were mistakenly suspected (maybe purposefully so) of having instigated Obregón's murder. The Callistas were intent on countering dissent, and disbanding the ayuntamiento allowed them to do so.[11]

The CROM had agglutinated a significant fraction of the new civil society that the Mexican Revolution had ushered in, bringing together so many unions and associations that, by early 1929, it could claim to represent 160,000 of Mexico City's economically active residents out of a population of over a million. In addition to manual and clerical workers, the CROM also included proprietary traders and owners of small workshops as well as peasants, neighborhood activists, and tenants.[12] For a decade it had acted as an intermediary between its affiliated organizations and the municipal and national authorities, using the city council as a venue for negotiation. The suppression of the council sought to overturn this configuration of local power, simultaneously undermining the CROM and buttressing the position of the national government in the capital. The CROM would remain active, but, facing public attack, it ceased to be the main umbrella under which different urban groups tried to advance their interests.

Mexico City's civil society, however, could not be ignored. In January 1929, the federal government created the Consejo Consultivo del Departamento Central, which the sociologist Diane Davis explains was an alternative institutional mechanism for the city's organized groups to express their grievances and demands.[13] Though it did not have executive or legislative powers, the Consejo Consultivo obtained the mandate to collaborate with the jefe del departamento in the management of the city.[14] Convening at least bimonthly, it was to be composed of thirteen councilors chosen by the president from organizations representing diverse interests, the so-called *fuerzas vivas de la ciudad*. Eight councilors would come from groups that had been active within the CROM in the late 1920s: three from workers' unions and five more from associations of small-scale vendors, small-scale industrialists, peasants, public employees (including teachers), and tenants (*colonos* and *inquilinos*), respectively.[15] Capitalist merchants were in turn represented by a delegate from the local chamber of commerce, large industrialists by a delegate from the chamber of industry, and the remaining three councilors represented, respectively, professionals (mostly architects and engineers), property owners, and mothers' associations.[16] To the extent that formal political participation remained possible at the local level, it became the prerogative of these well-defined interest groups. During its inaugural meeting, the first jefe del departamento, seasoned class conciliator José Manuel Puig Casauranc, celebrated the consejo as "an original experiment" in "functional democracy."[17]

The creation of the Consejo Consultivo constituted an early, rather timid effort to diffuse tensions specific to Mexico City's increasingly complex socioeconomic structure. According to Mexico's first industrial census, in 1930, there were 3,473 manufacturing enterprises in the Federal District, half of which were small concerns, with five employees or fewer. In contrast, there were only sixty-nine firms with over one hundred workers.[18] Figures for commercial establishments are harder to come by, as the first commercial census was not taken until 1940. Population figures indicate, however, that in 1930 there were at least 60,697 people in the capital whose stated occupation was in commerce.[19] Some worked in elegant department stores such as El Puerto de Veracruz or El Palacio de Hierro, but the vast majority were proprietary vendors. At least 20,000 carried licenses issued by the district's markets department.[20] Calles and his allies hoped the Consejo Consultivo would be an arena for the representation of these diverse urban groups and social classes, a more orderly platform for the promotion of their interests than the turbulent politics that the former ayuntamiento had offered. Because the public's interests were often contradictory, the consejo was also an attempt to reconcile competing claims over resources and governmental support. The goal was not simply to regulate and channel political forces but to thereby pacify them.

The institutional innovation of the consejo contributed to the differentiation between workers and proprietary producers and traders. Labor delegates brought grievances against capitalists to the consejo, but workers and capitalists had other, more effective channels to negotiate their differences, such as conciliation and arbitration boards and the judicial system.[21] The consejo was therefore of secondary importance to these classes in their dealings with one another. Instead, its discussions were dominated by disputes that pitted small-scale, proprietary producers and traders against large-scale industrialists and capitalist merchants. These groups not only competed for customers but also had conflicting views over urban regulations and, in particular, those pertaining to the use of the city's public spaces. As the consejo was required to preapprove new bylaws and sanction modifications to the many existing ones, both sides sought to engage it against the other every time it suited them.

Soon after the consejo began to operate, for example, small-scale producers and traders of charcoal submitted a request that the government set minimum prices to prevent large-scale producers and merchants from undercutting them by selling below cost. The Jefe de reglamentos, one Mr. Haro, observed that small proprietors, who had between two hundred and three hundred pesos of working capital, could not resist this competition for more than a couple of days and were forced to sell their stalls to "*malos comerciantes*," who in some cases had seized up to thirty "*casillas*" in the same marketplace already. "The government has the duty to protect the interests of the public," Mr. Haro stated, "that is indisputable; but should this consideration be extended to the obligation to protect small businesses?"[22] He left it to the consejo to ponder the issue, but not before warning councilors that if they did not take action, monopolies would soon corner the charcoal market and dictate prices at whim.

While government regulations could potentially protect proprietary producers and traders, they often reinforced the dominance of larger capitalist enterprises, as was the case with the city's bread industry. Historian Robert Weis has shown how, starting in 1929, owners of the largest bakeries in Mexico City systematically obtained the authorities' support against competition by independent producers, typically family enterprises, and petty retailers, in return for agreeing to increase pay and improve conditions for unionized workers.[23] In the name of preventing the formation of monopolies and of securing the city's supply of bread, the departamento passed a *reglamento* mandating that no *fábricas de pan* could be located within tenements or apartments, forbade the opening of a bakery within five hundred meters of an existing one, set a minimum price, and created a corps of honorary inspectors who would help the authorities enforce the new bylaw.[24]

The small producers and traders affected by the *reglamento del pan* construed the Consejo Consultivo, inaugurated just after the rule had passed, as a forum for their grievances. In September 1930 the consejo discussed the possibility of amending the reglamento. A representative of the Liga de la Pequeña Propiedad, which represented independent bakers, objected that the distance requirements between bakeries were too restrictive, being even greater than those for cantinas. The reglamento, moreover, was in practice only applied to small-scale producers, because capitalists consistently obtained injunctive orders, or *amparos*, from the courts, allowing them to circumvent it. Furthermore, the Liga complained that minimum prices were only selectively respected, and that given that the supposedly honorary inspectors were in reality paid by the Unión de Proprietarios de Panaderías, the association of the city's most powerful bakery owners, "they protect only the interests of this group, while they victimize independent individuals."[25] The small-scale bakers succeeded in convincing the consejo to temporarily modify the reglamento to address their objections.

In the early 1930s the proliferation of street stalls regained its historic role as a major source of conflict in the city. The *Revista de Obras Públicas* drew attention to the city's need for a new round of planning and investment in additional market space. Because previous municipal authorities had failed to provide purpose-built halls, architect Francisco Bulman explained, the old Porfirian markets had expanded by "invading surrounding streets" with myriad stalls, which, besides being "foul-smelling and unhygienic, give the public thoroughfare a disagreeable appearance, and leave a bad impression on the tourists who visit us; they also hide the facades of beautiful houses, and force pedestrians to walk at the center of the streets."[26] With the number of automobiles increasing every year, the danger of traffic accidents was becoming a focal point of debates over commercial uses of the city streets.[27] What is more, Bulman believed, because many colonias lacked most public services, every street was a potential market. As a cautionary tale against past authorities' lack of foresight, he reflected on the experience of Colonia Peralvillo, where a vendor had obtained a permit to establish a stall on Beethoven Street from the old ayuntamiento. When other vendors had sought to follow his precedent, it was impossible to refuse them licenses, and the street "became populated by locatarios." First they built booths that could be considered "semi-ambulantes," and little by little their radius of action grew, until the street was completely full. At that moment, the Departamento de Salubridad had demanded improvements in hygiene, which led to the locatarios' request for help from the ayuntamiento, which they obtained, resulting in "the more or less good condition, to the extent it was possible, of their stalls, leaving the street of Beethoven transformed into the market of the same name."[28]

Capitalist merchants joined the fray. Their main business association, the Cámara de Comercio de la Ciudad de México (Chamber of Commerce of Mexico City), had used the newly launched consejo as a platform to launch an attack on street commerce in the spring of 1929. The cámara's representative, Rodrigo Montes de Oca, presented a project for a new reglamento on street sales in downtown areas that would, he claimed, improve traffic circulation. His ultimate goal, however, was to eradicate what he considered disadvantageous competition from street-stall owners, many of whom, he protested, had enough capital to rent private premises and whose rent-free businesses had an unfair advantage.[29] The proposal was supported by Mr. Lajous, the representative of large-scale industrialists, who argued that "all those who have set stalls on the streets, on the pavements, and outside market halls . . . must be made to pay the same taxes as [established] merchants, and to respect the same working hours."[30]

The Cámara de Comercio encountered opposition right from the start. With the excuse that Montes de Oca and Lajous had called the traders in question ambulantes, the departamento's jefe de mercados tried to limit the scope of the debate and forthcoming reglamento to encompass only itinerant peddlers and especially those who sold goods in installments door-to-door.[31] It seems likely that he was motivated by the fact that, unlike the owners of stalls, these traders were beyond the departamento's control. The representative of small-scale vendors, Emigdio Hidalgo Catalán, agreed on this more restrictive, and more literal, definition of the term *ambulante* and with the support of the labor representatives managed to postpone a resolution.

In May 1930, Montes de Oca, who had been reappointed to the Consejo Consultivo, restated the need for a reglamento de ambulantes. By then the new representative of small-scale commerce, Pedro Villegas, seemed prepared to reach a compromise that at least in the short run would appeal to large-scale merchants as well as to many among his much more fluid constituency. Accepting the chamber of commerce's position, he was willing to support a reduction in the size of street stalls, and of the number of licenses issued, in order to protect vendors within market halls and small-scale merchants in private shops from competition by other independent proprietary traders. Instead of stating this openly, however, he produced a scapegoat, directing attention to foreign vendors who, according to him, had taken over the streets flanking the city's markets. As they had already accumulated enough capital, he conceded, they could be forced to move to private accommodations "so that the stalls they now occupy become available for use by Mexicans, so that the conflict becomes one between Mexicans."[32] Montes de Oca concurred that foreigners were a threat to large and small commerce alike.

Others urged caution. Labor councilor Antonio Díaz Lombardo insisted that, given the economic crisis that engulfed the city, no rushed decisions be made. He proposed that the national authorities be consulted first, and that then more effort be put into reconciling the needs of the "*comerciantes en pequeño*, who have the right to live," with the demands of the "*comercio grande*, who is confronting difficult circumstances."[33] The government was also wary of the merchants' advances. PNR operator Crisóforo Ibáñez, acting as president of the Consejo Consultivo in his capacity as secretary of the Departamento del Distrito Federal, reminded councilors that the city was experiencing high unemployment, and with so many people going hungry they should refrain from embarking on any type of "anti-social work."[34] The only alternative that appealed to all parties was for the government to build new halls to relocate vendors, but unfortunately the departamento's finances were in no position to support such expenditures. Instead, they sought to manage the competing needs of stakeholders who were all suffering from the Depression in different ways.

When Lamberto Hernández became jefe del departamento on October 1930, he picked up where his predecessor had left off. In his first meeting with the Consejo Consultivo, Hernández discussed the "very delicate subject of *comercio ambulante*, because if it is true that traders give downtown areas a pretty disagreeable aspect, it is no less true that we must be tolerant of the poor's need to make a living."[35] Recalling the consejo's earlier nationalist concerns, he announced that, inspired by "patriotic sentiments," the president had given orders to the secretary of interior to carry out an investigation to determine whether the "foreign elements" who were "killing our *pequeños comerciantes*" had obtained the necessary permission for commercial activities upon arrival in the country.[36] Soon, chief of intelligence services Pablo Meneses found himself reporting on the immigration status and economic activities of "a large number of Russians, Czechoslovakians, Poles" accused of invading the streets of Jesús María and the surroundings of San Juan Market.[37] For its part, the departamento commissioned its own survey of foreign vendors to determine whether they had enough resources to relocate from their stalls on the city's streets to private premises.[38] A small-scale comerciante by the name of Dionisio Coria wrote to the departamento in the name of "the Mexican Family," decrying Chinese, Syro-Lebanese, and Jewish "blood-suckers" who had supposedly taken over the stalls outside of La Lagunilla Market.[39] His letter was circulated for commentary through the departamento's offices.

By early 1931, after almost two years of negotiations, the Consejo Consultivo was ready to propose a *reglamento del comercio semi-fijo y ambulante* that promised something to every one of its members.[40] "Semi-fixed" street stalls could remain, but only as long as their owners had a total working capital of less than three hundred pesos and no means to rent a private shop.[41] This would reduce competition with established merchants large and small as well as with market vendors, while benefiting landlords. Stalls in downtown areas also had to shrink in size, a measure that appealed to bus owners and drivers who favored smoother traffic flow, and to the architects represented in the consejo, who had begun to lobby for the burgeoning tourism industry. "Ambulatory" vendors would now face tighter constraints, but those with long-standing licenses were temporarily exempted, together with those selling "objects of the lowest value," as requested by labor representatives worried that many among them were unemployed workers.[42] President Pascual Ortiz Rubio put the new policy into effect by signing a decree in March. A month later, in the context of heightened xenophobia fanned by the local press, foreign vendors were forced to give up their stalls in the city's markets.[43]

The consensus that was so hard to achieve was all too easy to undermine. By December 1931, discussions in the Consejo Consultivo were already suggesting that the reglamento had only been selectively enforced. Small-scale industry representative Armando Salcedo stated that it was shameful how *puestos semi-fijos* continued to block the streets surrounding La Lagunilla Market. Montes de Oca, still representing the Chamber of Commerce, cited an article in *El Universal* lambasting the invasion of central streets by vendors and proposed that the consejo request that the police chief take stronger measures to enforce the provisions of the reglamento. He was outraged that tennis shoes were being sold on Tacuba Street. Even the representative of small-scale commerce, Gonzalo Velarde, agreed that "the city itself has turned into a market," though he insisted that vendors should not be disturbed until appropriate market halls became available.[44] Labor councilor Elías Hurtado, responding to pressures from the Alianza de Comerciantes en Pequeño del Primer Cuadro and the Unión de Resistencia de Comerciantes Semifijos y Ambulantes, soon began a campaign to change the reglamento. Speaking before the consejo, he argued:

> There are so many traders competing with each other that this is truly a mess. I am against those who compete with serious commerce, those who take to the streets with embroideries or shoes, merchandise in hand, without paying

real contributions or rents. . . . Trade that is not in basic items should be banished from the streets. But commerce in primary products, products of immediate consumption, I think we have to tolerate.[45]

In February 1932, with the departamento under a new jefe, Vicente Estrada Cajigal, the consejo agreed to modifications to the bylaw to allow ambulantes to sell basic goods and the products of small domestic workshops in downtown areas.[46]

Ultimately, the Consejo Consultivo was unable to make its painstakingly crafted compromises work. Montes de Oca decried the continued presence of street vendors and asked the consejo to demand that the jefe del departamento enforce the reglamento. Velarde, the representative of small-scale commerce, jumped in. Tensions among street vendors were rising. He acknowledged that, despite agreement that there would be no more than three hundred licensed itinerant vendors in the city center, "unfortunately, due to the maneuvers of their organizations," the number of authorized ambulantes had grown to eight hundred. In fact, according to a departamento official who attended the consejo discussions, these organized vendors were "the first to complain" about the chaotic state of downtown streets. Velarde estimated that, in addition, there were seven hundred to 1,200 unauthorized peddlers. He proposed that the groups concerned with the enforcement of the reglamento name honorary inspectors to review all existing licenses in conjunction with the relevant authorities.[47] The Cámara de Comercio and organized ambulantes were not the only ones upset by the growing numbers of street vendors. Market vendors were alienated too. In October 1932, the locatarios from Álvaro Obregón Market declared a strike to protest the competition they suffered from vendors in adjacent streets; they abandoned their stalls and refused to pay taxes. Locatarios at three markets in Tacubaya followed suit.[48]

Conflicts over street vending revealed the limits of the Consejo Consultivo. Its founders had assumed the existence of coherent interest groups, united behind, or at least holding positions consistent with, their organizations' official representatives. But small-scale vendors proved that conflict was more widespread and, most importantly, more fine-grained. Proprietary traders were in permanent competition with one another for customers and commercial spaces, leading to chronic clashes among themselves and between their organizations. Such fragmentation made it difficult, if not impossible, for vendors to construct a collective identity around their shared social relations of production, including with their suppliers and creditors. Individual organizations could only hope to make local, short-term deals with sections of other classes or the government. These deals, when expedient, included attempts to undermine, or even eliminate, rival vendor organizations.

Recognizing the harm this was causing them, in May 1932 twenty-six legally recognized organizations of small-scale vendors came together to form the Federación Nacional de Comerciantes e Industriales Mexicanos en Pequeño. José Escamilla, secretary general of one of the founding unions, proclaimed the need to

> unify the criteria of the different elements of each market, putting an end to the antagonism that currently rules, and that only leads to rivalries. It is notorious enough that today each market has between four and six organizations, all with the same objectives, but they are only good at clashing with each other, generating hatred, selfishness.[49]

As part of the solution to their disunity and to highlight the commonalities in their economic lives, later that year the federación petitioned the Consejo Consultivo for the creation of a state-funded Banco Refaccionario del Pequeño Comerciante de los Mercados del Distrito Federal. They argued that such a bank "would bring many benefits for the organization of small-scale vendors . . . and free them from the clutches of greedy lenders [*agiotistas*]."[50] Vendor representatives remarked:

> We firmly believe that our only salvation is our unity, and that the formation of cooperatives for consumption, credit and production [financed by a Bank of Small Commerce] would alleviate the heavy burdens of the usurer and the intermediary, that is, the *bodeguero*, who do not leave us enough margin to live; they are our main enemies.[51]

Vendor organizations had emerged in the course of the Mexican Revolution to confront the official neglect their rank and file had been suffering since the Porfirian authorities suppressed the ayuntamiento. Fifteen years later these organizations were ready to demand institutional innovations and new levels of state intervention in the local economy to improve their material well-being and help them cement their class identities.

In early January 1933, labor councilor Elías Hurtado reminded his colleagues that "the consejo cannot and must not engage in politics, except for the high politics that benefits the classes here represented. Here no class prevails; all is harmonized for the sake of the common good."⁵² But this vision could not survive the inter- and intraclass conflicts that drove the city's politics. As the economy began to recover, large industrialists and merchants, property owners, bankers, architects, and civil engineers urged the government to redirect urban development and policy-making discussions away from the consejo and into other venues. They succeeded. Mere weeks after Hurtado's exhortation, the Ley de Planificación y Zonificación del Distrito Federal⁵³ created a Comisión de Planificación where only these groups would be represented to the exclusion of the rest. The consejo had been unable to contain the demands of the multiplicity of actors who took part in the city's economic life. Its resulting loss of power left proprietary producers and vendors without effective channels for participation, paving the way for renewed political and social unrest in the city.⁵⁴ While it continued to exist for decades, for all practical purposes by 1933 the consejo was a truncated experiment.

One City, Many Markets

In December 1932, President Abelardo Rodríguez appointed politician and entrepreneur Aarón Sáenz as Jefe del Departamento del Distrito Federal.⁵⁵ His two-and-a-half-year-long tenure represented a period of relative political stability at the local level,⁵⁶ which, coupled with economic recovery, left lasting marks on the cityscape. Historian Patrice Olsen describes how under Sáenz's leadership private- and public-sector actors joined forces to reignite the process of urban development.⁵⁷ Developers built new colonias along with hotels and office and commercial buildings, partly financed by the recently created public credit agency Nacional Financiera.⁵⁸ Higher revenues and the newly formed Banco Nacional Hipotecario Urbano y de Obras Públicas allowed the Departamento del Distrito to embark on a series of public works.⁵⁹ The departamento erected monuments to the revolution and to General Obregón, updated and completed the old Porfirian project for the Palace of Fine Arts, and paved and widened numerous streets. In response to growing outspoken demands for public services, it also expanded public lighting and water-distribution networks; built primary, secondary, and technical schools with capacity for tens of thousands of pupils; finalized two subsidized workers' housing projects; and, a week before Lázaro Cárdenas assumed the presidency, inaugurated a new, multifaceted commercial facility, the Abelardo Rodríguez Market.⁶⁰

Sáenz received both criticism and applause for these works. His detractors in the press were quick to point out that he personally stood to profit from this ambitious urban overhaul, as the Compañía de Fomento y Urbanización, the construction and paving company he owned in partnership with Calles, secured the period's largest contracts.[61] Not surprisingly, departamento officials supported Sáenz, commending his building program as having "no precedent, either in its nature, the importance of the works, or in the services it provides to the city."[62] The Consejo Consultivo in turn decided to pay "a humble homage" to Sáenz for his "magnificent work."[63] In a session specially arranged for the purpose, small-scale vendors' representative José Luis Fernández took the floor to extol how "in your capable hands, guided by the intelligence of a modern man, the complicated administrative machinery, so necessary for the well-being of the collectivity, has resembled the perfect mechanism of a clockmaster." Labor councilor Rosendo Salazar's proclamation was even more fulsome. Celebrating the government's pursuit of "distributive justice," he thanked Sáenz on behalf of all residents, and in particular of workers. He congratulated him for the Centro Escolar Revolución and the departamento's housing projects, which "give the urban proletariat greater trust in revolutionary regimes." He called the Abelardo Rodríguez Market a work of "huge importance." He concluded by pronouncing Sáenz's labors as "unique, firm, great, and positively revolutionary, in the high and pure sense of the word."[64]

The reorganization and building of public markets was central to the period's urban renewal efforts, and for good reason. Vendor groups had been lobbying for a market construction program for years. In March 1930, locatarios who had been instructed to vacate El Volador Market asked to be allowed to move to Mixcalco, urging the government to redevelop the market there.[65] On another occasion the PNR committee for the Federal District wrote to the Consejo Consultivo to support a vendors' initiative calling for the construction of a market on the Canal de Jamaica and the general improvement of the area.[66] Often, vendor support for market projects stemmed from rivalries among stallholders within and around market halls. Two weeks after the first meeting of the Consejo Consultivo, the Unión de Comerciantes del Mercado de la Lagunilla requested that the 200,000 pesos budgeted for market improvements in 1929 be invested in enlarging their market. The Unión de Comerciantes hoped such an extension would allow the departamento to incorporate more vendors into the covered areas of La Lagunilla, where they would pay the same fees as those already inside the market, thus reducing their unfair advantage. Small-scale vendors' representative Emigdio Hidalgo Catalán remarked that he had a meeting with these vendors, who were "very enthusiastic . . . and willing to cooperate with their own funds so long as the departamento takes their petitions into account."⁶⁷ They were not successful. Three years later, in February 1932, another group of La Lagunilla vendors submitted a similar petition requesting the reorganization of their market, "because due to the installation of cloth and notions stalls on Honduras Street, the eastern part of the market has died, while the northern side has been completely deserted."⁶⁸ Otherwise, they warned the consejo, they would have to take to the streets to find customers.

Architect Muñoz García of the Department of Public Works also supported a program of market development, in part because he too wanted to see vendors move indoors. Making references to the need to improve traffic conditions, hygiene, and the appearance of the public thoroughfare, he urged the departamento to stop treating the city streets as viable commercial spaces. While he acknowledged that markets were an indispensable public service, he insisted that the government ought to renounce the revenues generated by street stalls.⁶⁹ The departamento, he argued, should build new halls for the use of "vendors of few resources. . . . Today, this stands in accordance with the social ideal of helping those who can hardly help themselves."⁷⁰ But unlike the petitioning vendors, Muñoz García proposed to leave to private initiative the construction of "commercial centers in the proximity of markets, to offer small-scale commerce appropriate locales."⁷¹ All but the poorest vendors, he continued, should be forced to rent such private premises. He was explicit about whose interests he was advocating. Echoing the chamber of commerce's position in the Consejo Consultivo, Muñoz García explained that his plan would reduce "disloyal" competition to established merchants and "benefit property owners" who "day after day, see their [rental] properties vacated owing to unequal competition" by street stalls. To finish, he declared: "Let's revolutionize! Let's rectify our criteria, modify our laws, so that the ideal of modern life becomes a reality in our cities!"⁷² Muñoz García and other Public Works officials considered buttressing the expansion of capitalism to be the overriding obligation of progressive politics.

Pushed by these converging interests, Sáenz publicly recognized the imperative of market reform. At the end of 1933 he described "the market problem" as "one of the most urgent, serious, and difficult to resolve." By his estimates, the city counted on forty markets, "which are barely sufficient to serve half of the population residing in the capital of the Republic. This demands

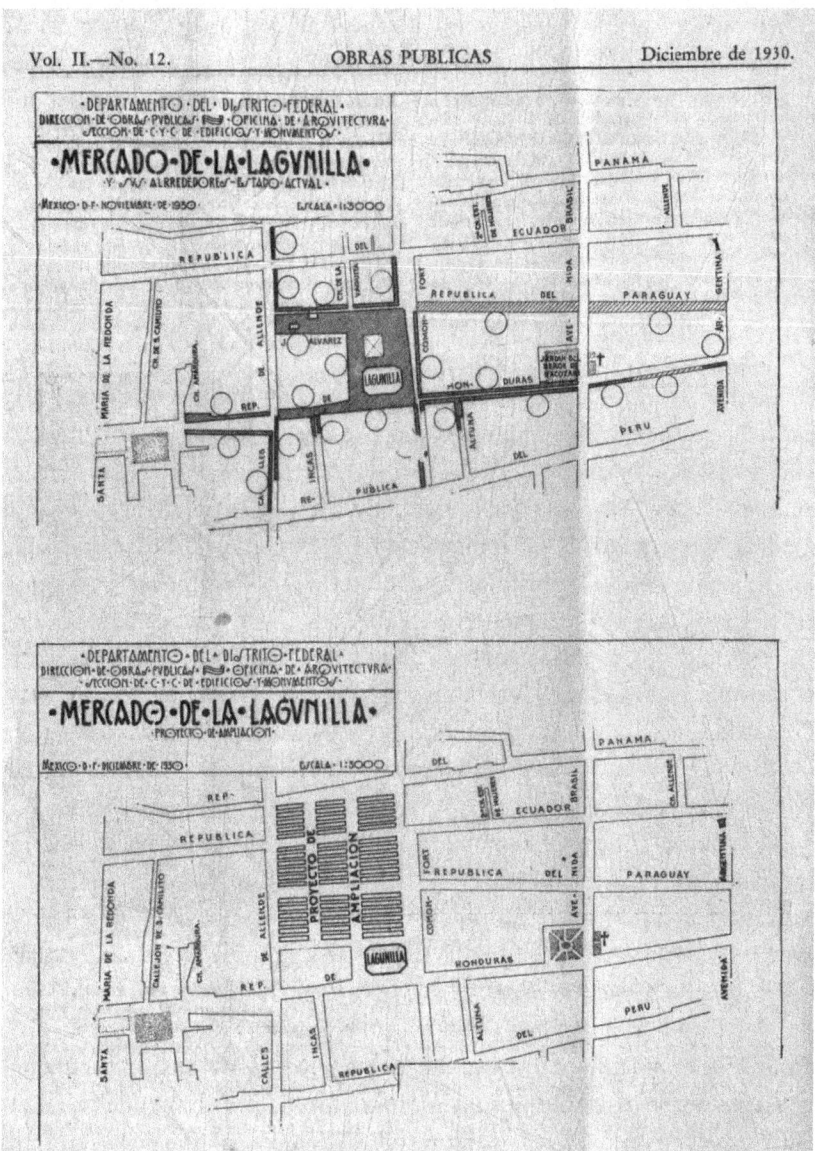

FIGURE 10. La Lagunilla Market, 1930. The top panel shows the streets surrounding the Porfirian hall occupied by market stalls. The lower panel shows a plan proposing the consolidation of these stalls in a new building adjacent to the existing hall. Source: Revista Obras Públicas 2, no. 12, December 1930, 272. Reproduction courtesy of the University of New Mexico's Center for Southwest Research and Special Collections.

either the construction of new market halls in proportion to population growth, or the improvement of existing ones, in order to increase their capacity and their efficiency."⁷³ Sáenz thus launched his campaign to transform the city's ever-growing street markets into sanitary and orderly indoors facilities. He got off to a good start. That year he was able to report the construction of the Melchor Ocampo Market as well as the extension of the Morelos Market in Colonia Tacuba.⁷⁴

In addition, the departamento signed a pilot contract with a private investor, María Luisa Reyes Espíndola de Cal y Mayor, for the construction and administration of a market in Colonia del Valle.⁷⁵ As with markets built by the government, the execution of the plans for this hall combined coercion and enticement. The contract stipulated that the departamento would enforce a kilometer-wide "market protection zone," within which all licenses for fixed and semifixed stalls would be revoked. At the same time, to make moving to the market more attractive, it committed the concessionary to setting aside five thousand pesos for small loans to locatarios—from which she no doubt expected to make a profit. The representative of *madres de familia* to the Consejo Consultivo, Sra. Quezada de Martínez Garza, requested that the authorities ensure that the market owner also provide a day care facility for the children of the locatarios, "a social service so indispensable in the times we live in." The owner would contribute the room, and either the Department of Public Health or Protección a la Infancia would supply the necessary personnel.⁷⁶

Once again, differences among market vendors themselves produced resistance to the project. In January 1934, vendors in the Unión de Comerciantes Semifijos en el Mercado Insurgentes, finding themselves in the new market protection zone, were informed that they had to close down and remove their stalls within a matter of weeks. In response the union's secretary, José Mendoza, wrote to President Rodríguez to request his intervention against "such arbitrariness, because they are not to blame for the smallness of the market hall, and the fact that the signatories do not fit in it."⁷⁷ Common practice dictated that the president's office forward the complaint to the departamento. A month later, the secretary general of the departamento, José Benítez, was compelled to address the vendors' accusations that the local government had based its decision on "trivial considerations" and was responding to "influences far removed from the people."⁷⁸

Benítez's reply to the Unión de Comerciantes Semifijos indicates the many groups with interests at stake in any market redevelopment project. It also shows the extent to which markets policy was reactive rather than planned and that it responded to pressures from these groups. "For some time," he explained, "the Departamento has been receiving complaints about the stalls around the Insurgentes Market." Some complaints concerned isolated instances of alcohol sales at night, when there was little control. Others came from merchants with stores near the market who protested that the "invasion" of the sidewalks in front of their establishments by vendors hurt their interests. Furthermore, the chief of police had requested that the stalls be removed to improve the flow of traffic around the intersection of Chapultepec and Insurgentes Avenues. Finally, the secretario de economía nacional had intervened following a complaint by the managers of Hotel Genève that vendors' presence on the streets was detrimental to tourism, "an industry that the government has been giving support to in the belief that it would greatly benefit the country." Benítez concluded, "thus you should be able to accept that the departamento has enough reasons of public interest, even if in this case the members of your union might incidentally suffer." Still, he offered vendors two extra months and invited them to discuss the situation further in the hope that many of them would follow the example of most of the locatarios inside the Insurgentes Market hall, who not long ago had been in their position.[79]

Having contracted out the market at Colonia del Valle, the departamento directed most of its own funds and attention to the construction of the Abelardo Rodríguez Market. Located within a few blocks northeast of the Zócalo, it was designed by Muñoz García to provide the neighborhood around Venezuela Street with a state-of-the-art "modern and sanitary" commercial structure, improving traffic circulation and valorizing the area's properties. This marketplace would form part of a larger complex offering social and cultural services, among them a civil registry, a day care center for vendors' children and a theater, the Teatro del Pueblo.[80] While the hall was projected to include only 335 stalls, the multipurpose site was much larger, the size of a quadruple block that included a colonial era Jesuit school, much of which was preserved as historic patrimony. The buildings juxtaposed newly constructed modernist and art deco interiors with the school's sixteenth-century cloisters, all combined under stark, neocolonial facades. The Abelardo Rodríguez Market was inaugurated with great fanfare on November 24, 1934, with President Abelardo Rodríguez and President-elect Lázaro Cárdenas attending the celebrations.[81]

Under the supervision of Diego Rivera, a group of ten Mexican and foreign artists were commissioned to produce murals to decorate the walls and ceilings around the market entrances, hallways, and patios. The works, which in the end covered 1,523 square meters, were completed by 1936. Most of the murals aligned with the Departamento del Distrito's original commission to emphasize the importance of public health and nutrition.[82] Ramón Alva Guadarrama's *The Production of Charcoal* and Marion Greenwood's *Foodstuffs and Their Distribution along the Viga Canal*, both located near entrances, depict public markets as the country's vital link between the artists' imagined modern mestizo city and the traditional, indigenous countryside. Farther into the market, however, the murals take a more radical turn.[83] Marion Greenwood's vast *The Industrialization of the Countryside*, which merges into her sister Grace's *Mining*, and Pablo O'Higgins's *Workers' Struggle against Monopolies*, expose the manifold tensions between capitalist progress, commercial intermediation, and exploitation. A critical internationalist narrative emerges, one rallying workers, vendors, and peasants to unite against the period's interrelated global threats of imperialism, fascism, and war. This was, as the original title of Isamu Noguchi's monumental wall sculpture on the top floor indicates, "History as Seen From Mexico in 1936."[84] At the time the market was showcased as one of the most important urban renovation projects of the decade. Historian Ageeth Sluis describes it as "a microcosm of revolutionary reform."[85]

For all its progressive elements and apparent benefits, the Abelardo Rodríguez Market did not make economic sense to vendors. With the support of the Federación de Comerciantes e Industriales Mexicanos en Pequeño, a group of street vendors who described themselves as *comerciantes ambulantes del Mercado Melchor Ocampo*, refused to take up stalls within the new market hall, despite the concerted efforts of the market administrator, fee collectors, and the police. They argued that neither their capital nor the volume of their sales were sufficient to pay the fees. Still, "to avoid difficulties, they [were] willing to wear the mandatory uniform, carry their respective licenses, and remain within assigned spaces."[86] Another group of locatarios from La Merced and San Lucas Markets protested that they had already spent money preparing for the traditional holiday fair, the *romería de navidad*, at their respective markets, but the departamento was forcing them to relocate to the Abelardo Rodríguez for the occasion.[87] A few months later, congressman José María Dávila wrote to the president on behalf of a group of comerciantes from the Unión de Locatarios de Puestos Aislados de la Ciudad de México with stalls on the streets of Del Carmen and República de Colombia, requesting a repeal of the order that they relocate to the new market.[88]

The president's office recommended a postponement of the relocation,[89] but Secretary Benítez objected, noting that "it is not possible to allow the existence of stalls in those streets . . . because it would render worthless the substantial expenses incurred to house the area's small-scale vendors."[90]

Above all, vendor organizations complained that the Abelardo Rodríguez Market lacked sufficient consumer traffic. The Federación Nacional de Comerciantes e Industriales en Pequeño, which had encouraged its associates to establish their stores there and had taken one of the largest units as its offices, complained in April 1935 that "commercial movement is nil."[91] Donasiano Lascano, president of the Unión de Comerciantes del D.F., agreed and refused to move his organization's haberdashers to the Abelardo Rodríguez despite the authorities' exhortations, because "there is absolutely no demand there."[92] But the issues were more complex. The government's failure to persuade vendors to occupy the new market revealed its inability to confront a highly mobilized but fragmented vendors' movement. The fact that many vendor organizations belonged to the Federación Nacional de Comerciantes e Industriales en Pequeño, which was nominally affiliated with the PNR, should have facilitated negotiations. But with multiple organizations representing vendors within each market, party officials found it hard to distinguish among them in order to form the alliances required to legitimize its urban policies. It only took a large enough group of vendors deciding to remain on the surrounding streets to undermine the decision of any other group of vendors to enter the Abelardo Rodríguez Market.

Both local and national politics were highly divisive in these years, and as vendors fought for their livelihoods, they became entangled in political maneuvers for power on larger terrains. Lázaro Cárdenas assumed the presidency in December 1934, facing a country run by Callista military commanders and governors. Until then a loyal Callista himself, he took action immediately, replacing operational commanders with his own men and intervening in state elections.[93] In some states this was not enough to displace unwanted governors, forcing him to seek new alliances. In Coahuila, for example, political control was achieved only after a massive agrarian reform in the cotton producing area of La Laguna gained him the support of the 30,000 new *ejidatarios*.[94] Land redistribution, however, did not take place in a vacuum. In La Laguna as in other parts of the country, it was the result of both political calculations and continual mobilizations of peasants, rural workers, and peons.[95] Without their mobilization, the ejido sector would not have grown to represent 41.8 percent of the total population working in agriculture, and 47 percent of all cultivated land.[96]

As the economy grew, industrial workers regained a militancy that had been subdued by the economic crisis. Railroad, mining and metal, and petroleum workers formed powerful national unions, often under Communist leadership, in 1933, 1934, and 1935. Across the country the number of strikes spiked. In June 1935 Calles publicly condemned the new unionism as treason to the national interest and a generator of economic chaos.[97] Under attack by Callistas and capitalists, in February 1936 these unions came together to form the Confederación de Trabajadores Mexicanos (Confederation of Mexican Workers, CTM). The CTM threw its support behind Cárdenas in accordance with the Communist International's antifascist Popular Front strategy.[98] The president reciprocated, backing their strikes, which again grew in number in 1936 and 1937.[99] In Nuevo León Cárdenas managed to get a palatable governor elected only after threatening Monterrey's most powerful capitalists with expropriation.[100]

Cárdenas's efforts to shore up control extended to Mexico City and its vendors. In June 1935, he asked Sáenz, along with the rest of the national cabinet, to resign, appointing Cosme Hinojosa to the position of Jefe del Departamento del Distrito Federal. The president also made his own brother, Alberto Cárdenas, the new jefe de mercados.[101] Market oversight soon became more punitive. That summer, a group of vendors who had been selling vegetables in Mixcalco Market and its adjacent streets for twelve years were forced to abandon their stalls. The departamento gave them a tough choice. They had to either give up trading or take up space in the new Abelardo Rodríguez Market, even though they insisted they could not afford to do so.[102] They complained that the newly appointed jefe de mercados disregarded the existence of a court order (*amparo*) in their favor.[103] Forty vendors who decided to remain in their stalls alleged that the police and Salubridad officials routinely harassed them.[104] As the conflict escalated, Ángel Arana, secretary general of the Comerciantes en Pequeño del Mercado Mixcalco sought the president's intervention: "Your brother, Mr. Lieutenant Colonel Cárdenas, refuses to listen to us. We do not want to cause you troubles, having always supported you. We beg you to name another person to take care of our conflict, so justice can be done. Our families today went without bread."[105] The union also decried the daily imprisonment of vendors at an improvised detention center within the Abelardo Rodríguez Market itself. Speaking for the Departamento del Distrito, Antonio Villalobos explained to the president that the vendors so detained were "recidivist ambulantes" picked up from "forbidden zones," who were kept at the market for only the time required to forward them to the appropriate authorities.[106] While artists were still hard at work crafting the market's extraordinary murals, the president's brother was using the site as a jail.

These coercive practices proving ineffective, the Cardenista government soon recognized that it needed to increase its administrative capacity over vendor affairs. Until then, there were no specific provisions for dealing with the type of conflicts between organizations that hindered any market redevelopment project. As late as April 1934, the Consejo Consultivo had responded to a complaint by the Unión Femenina de Comerciantes y Madres de Familia del Mercado de la Lagunilla against a rival female vendor organization by stating that it could not intervene in personal or interunion matters, which ought to be resolved independently by the organizations involved.[107] This hands-off attitude had to change. In August 1935, after an organization of "mothers of La Lagunilla" invited Councilor Sra. Tapia de Gómez to visit their market, she returned in shock: "I observed things impossible to tolerate, and the Consejo needs to take action . . . to find a way to improve the conditions of this market, because . . . pavilions were built for certain types of vendors, but then others arrive with money to purchase those places, and these vendors have to move out of the market."[108] This pattern was replicated in the rest of the city's markets: poorer locatarios, many of them women, were being displaced by vendors with more means.[109]

By mid-1936, Jefe del Departamento Cosme Hinojosa had created two new offices within the markets department. The first was a statistics office, because, he explained, "economic and social imperatives demand precise knowledge of all the elements that coalesce around the expansion of markets." This office was immediately given the task of mapping the city's markets, including the different *zonas de mercado*, the clusters of street stalls that fell under the control of particular market administrators.[110] The second was the Oficina de Agrupaciones y Asuntos Sindicales, established "to attend to the numerous conflicts that arise daily between locatarios or their organizations, as a result of the application of bylaws and other decisions by the markets department."[111] According to the new offices, between September 1936 and September 1937 the number of licensed stalls in the city barely grew, from 17,782 to 17,934. But there was a lot of movement: 5,070 new licenses had been granted and 4,918 revoked. This means that on average thirty-eight stalls were

FIGURE 11. Union of Female Vendors of La Lagunilla Market and Adjacent Streets, and Other Markets. Source: Mediateca INAH, Colección Archivo Casasola, 1934–1940.

renegotiated on any given day, producing ample room for clashes among vendors and between vendors and the state.[112]

The road to more effective management of the vendor movement would be rocky. If a combination of closer links between the state and vendor organizations and repression had become essential to governing the city's markets, it also risked fostering oppositional sentiments, as events at the Martínez de la Torre Market illustrate. In August 1935, Guillermo Blancarte of the Federación Mexicana del Trabajo denounced rival union leaders who, with the support of their market administrator, "by threats and blows try to sow terror among our compañeros." The complaint extended to the entire markets department, which had also intervened against this federation, evicting member vendors from their stalls on the market annex on Mosqueta Street.[113] Similarly, less than a year later the president of the Unión Mexicana de Comerciantes en Pequeño del Martínez de la Torre protested against Alberto

Cárdenas's decision to revoke a license from a compañera, "favoring enemies" instead.[114] Vendor representative Agapito Cifuentes remarked, "What a contrast, Mr. President, you extend your hand to the poor while your brother contradicts your ideology."[115]

Inflation Management and Contested Elections

In history, as in life, problems rarely displace each other. They accumulate. As the Mexican government developed closer connections with the city's vendor movement, disputes among their organizations became more violent, generating discontent among the rank and file. To make matters worse, the late 1930s witnessed a surge in inflation, which prompted the Cárdenas administration to intervene in urban markets for basic goods following demands by workers and capitalists. Vendors were thus further alienated by price controls and direct state participation in retail activities. By the end of the decade, in the midst of a contested presidential race, the government was suspicious of the political allegiances of proprietary traders, whose interests had been subjugated to those of groups that carried more political weight. With a right-wing opposition emboldened by the rise of fascism around the world, vendors in the capital were perceived as a high-risk group.

In 1936, as the cost of living in the Federal District rose and the purchasing power of wages declined, workers began to mobilize.[116] That March, Fidel Velázquez and Rodolfo Piña Soria, in the name of the Federación Regional de Obreros y Campesinos del D.F., requested presidential intervention so that "authorities regulate the price of commodities, because the current situation renders nugatory both the minimum wage and the payment of the seventh day."[117] The Sindicato Mexicano de Electricistas made a similar demand in December, for "the formation of a Central Committee for Price Regulation."[118] The Confederación de Trabajadores Mexicanos (CTM) amplified the message. Committed to Popular Frontism, it was careful neither to criticize the government nor to confront capitalists and focused instead on "hoarding" merchants. By 1937 the CTM was leading a wave of demonstrations and proclamations against the high prices of basic foodstuffs. The government initially responded encouragingly: wary of the political cost of conflicts over higher wages, it set up price controls and sought to blame inflation on ruthless middlemen and retailers. A propaganda campaign against "speculators" responsible for "starving the population" ensued.[119]

Such actions put small-scale vendors in a difficult situation. If wholesalers did not respect official prices, it was impossible for retailers to do so. Once they paid their suppliers and creditors, and the rent or fees for their commercial establishment, they needed to add a margin in order to make a living. But wholesalers were out of the public eye. Since consumers bought from vendors, it was vendors who were chronically denounced and fined for infringements. In response they tried to defend themselves by shifting the public focus and decrying the abuses committed by their suppliers. In June 1937, for example, small-scale vendors from the Federación de Comerciantes e Industriales en Pequeño attacked the Asociación Nacional de Almacenistas Comerciantes de Víveres y Similares, which represented the city's most powerful wholesalers, in the national press.[120] Yet vendors had little traction. Because they sold in public spaces, they faced both consumers' anger and government attempts at price controls.

At the same time, Cárdenas's government intensified its efforts to control the vendor movement. Early 1938 witnessed a new round of violent episodes involving the police and local politicians in the Martínez de la Torre Market. In January, Ángel Fraga Ferreira on behalf of the Juventudes Izquierdistas de México condemned "harassment" by the police and the Markets Department as "they unjustly imprisoned more than twenty families."[121] His appeal for presidential support seemed to have gone unheard. Tensions also spiked between the market's different vendor organizations. From the same market, on April 2, Altagracia Hernández of the Liga Revolucionaria de Comerciantes en Pequeño del Mercado Martínez de la Torre wrote to President Cárdenas to inform him that earlier that day, a group of comerciantes led by "professional politician" Luis R. Velasco had assaulted the liga's secretary general Genaro Mijangos at the corner of Moctezuma and Zarco. Velasco was a member of the Consejo Consultivo that year and had been involved in the creation of the Federación de Comerciantes e Industriales en Pequeño earlier in the decade. The clash between the two groups of comerciantes ended, Hernández reported, with dead and wounded on both sides and with Mijangos hurt and in jail. "Markets authorities, far from offering us guarantees, have been extorting us, and Velasco's group, encouraged by the attitude of lower officials, has not shown any restraint in throwing itself at us, leading to this mess, which has already produced orphans and anguish."[122] She demanded justice, but her chances of obtaining a positive response were negligible: The federal government was occupied with more urgent matters.

The previous month, March 1938, Cárdenas—pressed between mobilized workers and recalcitrant foreign oil companies refusing to respect Mexican law—had nationalized the oil industry. In anticipation of a difficult presidential race in 1940, he had also formed a new party, the Partido de la Revolución Mexicana (Party of the Mexican Revolution, PRM). Through the PRM he painstakingly forged a pact among all major agrarian, labor, and government employees' organizations, the military, and what was beginning to be referred to as the popular sector, mainly the new Mexico City–based Federación de Sindicatos de Trabajadores al Servicio del Estado (Federation of Unions of State Employees).[123] Unlike the PNR, which had been created to coordinate a political transition among political elites, the PRM had all the makings of a corporatist organization. The PRM was informally backed by segments of the capitalist class with interests in finance, manufacturing, and construction, which had expanded thanks to the government's progrowth economic policies.

The creation of the PRM and the alliances on which it was based deepened vendors' exclusion from political life. They found themselves squeezed by the government's need to placate workers' demands for affordable food and other everyday necessities. As part of the government's efforts to contain inflation, especially in major urban centers, Cárdenas oversaw the formation of the Comité Regulador del Mercado de las Subsistencias.[124] The State Food Agency started out by selling to the very wholesalers the government was otherwise vilifying, but after receiving much criticism it began to supply grains to authorized retail merchants in the larger cities. These merchants obtained subsidized products, and in return committed to reselling them at official prices. By June, Mexico City, the largest consumer market in the country, had twenty-two authorized retailers, nine in La Merced Market alone.[125] This lowered prices for some consumers but increased pressure on the many proprietary vendors who lacked access to the subsidized goods.

Soon after, in October 1938, a commission of presidential advisers raised concerns about this new approach to food policy. They argued that the committee's actions had been too limited to actually create effective competition. Most small-scale vendors still had to buy from wholesalers who had no incentive to lower their prices. What is more, a policy of price controls, the commissioned warned, would create a "dangerous territory because it will require the deployment of an army of inspectors, which . . . will burden small-scale vendors with bribes, not lowering prices in the slightest," and will most certainly lead to resentment among the many proletarian elements who own small commercial businesses and have bought at high prices, a resentment that will diminish their support for the Revolution, and make them side with large commerce, following it in any fascist intent that it might share with other reactionary sectors, especially when elections approach.[126]

The same advisers reiterated this concern less than three months later in a report on the political situation in the city. They warned of the possibility that the committee's "revolutionary" intervention in basic goods markets could beget a "reaction" determined to agitate public opinion against the government. Due to the failure of price controls and the limited effects of subsidizing a small number of retailers, they recommended establishing outlets to sell cheaply and directly to the public. But they cautioned that even this measure, necessary as it was, entailed serious political risks as it would displace a large number of small-scale vendors. The commission warned, "Among such groups of small producers and traders is where in other countries fascism has recruited its infantry."[127]

In these divisive times, relations between proprietary vendors and the state reached an all-time low. In August 1939, for example, the Consejo Consultivo declared the Alianza de Comerciantes en Pequeño del Mercado Hidalgo "in open rebellion against the departamento."[128] The group had rebuffed attempts to carry out a census of their stalls. They had also refused to relocate to allow concessioner María Servín de Peralta to carry out works in their market, requesting that the contract for the running of the market be given to them instead. When the Consejo Consultivo informed them that it was not possible to rescind the existing concession, they went to the courts, seeking an amparo, which was denied. Still, they would not move, despite repeated efforts by the police to make them.[129] By the end of 1939, there were twenty-five official stores in the Federal District, selling subsidized grains, sugar, lard, and milk at prices that undercut what vendors were able to offer.[130]

Frustrated market vendors, writes Diane Davis, were among the groups that, lacking effective mechanisms to contest Cardenista urban policies, threw their support behind opposition presidential candidate General Juan Andreu Almazán.[131] His alliance with the CROM's historic leader Luis N. Morones attracted many vendor unions that had been, or still were, affiliated with his confederation, and which had been pushed aside by the PRM leadership.[132] Moreover, the intelligence services' fear of an *almazanista* fifth column within the government bureaucracy might not have been unfounded, and there are some indications that Almazanista sympathizers were attempting to influence small-scale vendors' political behavior.¹³³ Councilor Paz de López alerted the Consejo Consultivo that within the police "there are several inspectors, among them one Mr. Pimienta, that are making downtown vendors sign for an almazanista party before they can obtain their licenses."¹³⁴ Almazán inaugurated his campaign for the presidency with a massive rally in Mexico City on August 28, 1939.¹³⁵ Market vendors stood behind him.

Mexico's conservative opposition movements had been growing for several years. General Saturnino Cedillo had revolted—although he was quickly crushed—in April 1938. Disgruntled Catholic middle classes had joined the fascist Sinarquista movement, which mushroomed in the Bajío countryside to claim half a million followers by early in the next decade.¹³⁶ Monterrey industrialists funded the creation of the Partido Acción Nacional (Party of National Action) in September 1939.¹³⁷ In 1940, Almazán's campaign gathered enough momentum that it would take the full weight of the Cardenista machine, and considerable violence and ballot box rigging, to elect Cárdenas's chosen successor, PRM compromise candidate and former secretary of defense Manuel Ávila Camacho to the presidency.¹³⁸ In all probability the PRM was defeated in Mexico City where, as in Guadalajara and Monterrey, the urban middle classes and myriads of proprietary producers and traders, excluded as they were from the governments' economic and political priorities, had openly supported Almazán.¹³⁹ Few doubted that, no matter what official figures said, President Ávila Camacho had not carried the capital on election day.

Forgotten by the Revolution

When Ávila Camacho assumed the presidency in December 1940, war was raging in Europe and an Axis victory looked not altogether unlikely. His administration played the international situation well.¹⁴⁰ In November 1941, in the midst of arrangements for hemispheric cooperation against the fascist threat, Mexican officials reached an agreement with the Roosevelt administration to settle all pending oil and property claims.¹⁴¹ They signed a commercial treaty in December 1942, a year after the United States had entered the war, allowing bilateral trade and US investment in Mexico to boom.¹⁴²

Domestically, Ávila Camacho took advantage of the international crisis to demand national unity.¹⁴³ As the president led the country into a "battle for production," the CTM and the newly formed progovernment business organization Cámara Nacional de Industrias de Transformación (National Chamber of Transformation Industries, CANACINTRA) agreed to the suppression of strikes and the rapid arbitration of disputes.[144] Between 1940 and 1944 GDP grew by an average of 6 percent per year.[145] At the same time, inflation was rampant and wages were falling behind; industrial real wages in Mexico City fell by 45 percent between 1940 and 1946, which in the context of economic growth suggests income polarization.[146] In spite of the best efforts of the labor bureaucracy, rank-and-file agitation could not be contained and the number of strikes shot up during the last three years of the war.[147] Spontaneous food riots and hunger marches also multiplied.[148] Public markets became, once again, outlets of class conflict.

The federal government had been closely monitoring vendors' politics, for though Almazán lost his political standing after the 1940 election, the forces that had rallied behind him did not go away. Intelligence services spied on vendors as part of their tracking of opposition groups, which now included former Almazanista groups and Communist organizers.[149] At the same time, encouraged by the gobierno del distrito, the new administration decided it was time to respond to vendors' long-standing demand for a dedicated bank for locatarios. In December 1941, Ávila Camacho initiated the necessary legislation in Congress, explaining that the bank would protect vendors from "usury rates that, apart from reducing the just profits they have the right to, necessarily inflate the price of the merchandise they offer the public."[150] The Banco del Pequeño Comercio del Distrito Federal was officially formed in the summer of 1943.[151] Within two years it would boast of having branches in twenty-five markets and more than 37,000 completed operations. It would also praise itself for having been instrumental in the organization of credit unions, through which vendors made collective purchases, obtaining better terms from their suppliers.[152]

More broadly, the PRM leadership scrambled to build up strength among dissident urban middle-class and self-employed proprietary groups.[153] In September 1942, the party sponsored the formation of the Federación de Ligas del Sector Popular del Distrito Federal. The secretary general of the Federal District remarked that the new organization would help redress "the neglect that elements of the popular sector have suffered, [which] created the conditions for some leaders of the right to disorient the people."[154] Jesús Bautista, founder of the Federación de Comerciantes e Industriales en Pequeño, joined its executive committee. The following February, the party followed up with the creation of the Confederación Nacional de Organizaciones Populares (National Confederation of Popular Organizations, CNOP), which promised to defend the class interests of its members.[155] The CNOP incorporated organizations of professionals, state employees, small-business owners, proprietary vendors, and other self-employed groups as well as *colonos* and youth and women groups. Bautista was its the first small-scale vendors' delegate for the Federal District.[156] CNOP representatives soon became the largest bloc in Congress.[157]

A new phase of party restructuring and institution building had begun, and organized vendors seized the opportunities this provided to advance their interests. A few months after the creation of the CNOP, on the letterhead of the PRM's Comité Central Ejecutivo del D.F, the Sindicato de Comerciantes en Pequeño del Interior y Exterior del Mercado de La Merced y Calles Adyacentes penned a list of grievances, which included planned increases in market fees; abuses by wholesalers, which made vendors "practically commission-only employees"; and the "exorbitant interest rates" vendors were still paying to private lenders. They believed they remained "one of the forgotten groups of the benefits of the Mexican Revolution."[158] The state had made significant progress in the management of the city's mobilized but fragmented vendor movement, but much remained to be done.

5 Vendors' Developmentalism, 1945–1966

THE YEARS AFTER WORLD WAR II saw major economic and political transformations across Mexico, with Mexico City at the center of the country's developmentalism, or *desarrollismo*. The economy grew and industrialized, driven by a state that provided support to capitalists and invested heavily in infrastructure. To ensure workers' acquiescence to minimal wage rises, the government attempted to guarantee the availability of relatively cheap basic goods, fixing prices of everyday necessities and promoting direct sales from both large- and small-scale agricultural producers. Just as in the late 1930s, market vendors felt squeezed. They resented having to compete for customers with these producers as well as with capitalist merchants and government stores offering subsidized foodstuffs. At the same time, substantial migration and population growth led to an increasing number of peddlers, who also clashed with established vendors over sales and trading spots. It took significant compromise and creativity by government officials and vendor organizations to resolve the tensions that played out in the streets and markets of the capital.

The state reshaped the vendor movement with both inducements and repression. The new Partido Revolucionario Institucional (Institutional Revolutionary Party, PRI), created in 1946, incorporated the popular classes through the Confederación Nacional de Organizaciones Populares (National Confederation of Popular Organizations, CNOP). Using and extending the new institutions, state actors eliminated certain vendor organizations and promoted others according to political and personal imperatives. In return, vendors were able to use the PRI to promote their interests as retailers, arguing for improved market infrastructure and social services, protection from competition, and arbitration in distributional struggles. Building on their organizational experience from the previous three decades, vendors took part in national election campaigns, fought to elect sympathetic congressmen, and strengthened their civil associations to better negotiate with the Federal District's government. Like industrialists and urban developers, vendors requested more, not less, state intervention—but on their own terms. The combination of economic growth, public investment, and a robust but cooperative vendor movement allowed politicians and vendor leaders to negotiate a successful program of urban renewal. This is how the city built 160 markets with a capacity for over 50,000 stalls. Organized vendors found their place in what has come to be known as the "Mexican miracle," embracing a way of life that promised they too could join the growing urban middle class. Yet urban renewal rested on the exclusionary distinction between locatarios and ambulantes, which would ultimately undermine their gains.

Hecho en México

World War II left Mexican politicians and men of capital in an ambivalent position. Cooperation with the Allied war effort had boosted the economy by inflows of foreign capital and high demand in the United States for Mexican exports, not only of raw materials but also of manufactured goods.[1] It had also elevated the political standing of Mexico in the international arena. In July 1944, the country presented a self-confident image at the Bretton Woods Conference, where finance minister Eduardo Suárez chaired one of the three commissions in charge of designing the financial institutions that would oversee the global economy for decades to come.[2] In these respects, the future seemed bright.

At the same time, there were reasons to be wary. The United States emerged from World War II an unrivaled industrial and military superpower. Mexico's external sector had become ever more dependent on US markets: by the end of the war more than 80 percent of its foreign trade was with the United States.[3] In addition, Mexican industrial growth relied on US financial and technical assistance. So when in the spring of 1945 the United States disclosed its postwar economic plan for the hemisphere, at Chapultepec Palace of all places,

Mexican elites were in for a shock. The so-called Clayton Plan proposed that Latin American countries abandon any aspirations to industrialize and instead refocus their economies on the exports of primary products, in the hope that European reconstruction would absorb any increased production. Latin American governments were expected to dismantle protectionist policies, embrace free trade, and facilitate the movement of foreign capital in and out of their countries.[4] As the Cold War began to unfold, anything less than full compliance would be dubbed socialism.[5]

But Mexico had changed. Thanks to the trade disruptions and probusiness policies of the Great Depression and World War II, Mexican firms were now producing larger volumes of consumer goods and industrial inputs.[6] Capitalists in light industries were the first to object to the Clayton Plan. CANACINTRA (the National Chamber of Transformation Industries), which represented mainly small- and medium-sized firms in the Mexico City area, was the most vociferous critic of the plan, citing the economic burden of renewed foreign competition. Organized labor, led by the CTM (or Confederation of Mexican Workers), agreed with the capitalists' objections, pointing to the negative impact open trade would have on employment and wages.[7] In isolation, the protestations of CANACINTRA and the CTM would not have sufficed to challenge the US postwar settlement. The broader protectionist consensus that emerged stemmed from a combination of mounting trade deficits and the realization that US grants and loans would not be forthcoming on the scale necessary to fund Mexico's development. When Miguel Alemán assumed the presidency in December 1946, he pledged to continue on the path to industrialization.[8]

With international reserves dwindling fast, macroeconomic constraints left the new administration little option but to implement trade controls and raise tariffs in 1947, and to follow up in July 1948 with a devaluation of the peso. Thus sheltered from competition, manufacturing industries continued to grow, now at an average annual rate of 7.6 percent between 1949 and 1958, more than a percentage point faster than overall GDP.[9] But the belief that the government should be directly involved in the country's industrialization went beyond support for protectionist measures. The developmentalist dictum of import-substitution soon grew into a national ideology. In the name of progress, modernization, and growth, the state openly promoted capital accumulation. Contrary to assertions by some US and domestic opponents, government intervention in the economy did not displace private enterprise, as demonstrated by the period's high rates of private investment.[10] Rather, economic policy made these enterprises more profitable, especially for those businesses that commanded official favors including tax exemptions, cheap credits, preferential access to import permits and foreign currency, guaranteed purchase contracts, and land grants. The influence of the CEPAL (the UN's Economic Commission for Latin America) notwithstanding, import-substitution policies did not stem from a philosophical position or follow a systematic program, *pace* the Banco de México's Bureau of Industrial Research. There is ample evidence of the particularistic, discretionary nature of state actions.[11]

Despite the government's nationalistic rhetoric promoting economic independence, and even occasional expressions of anti-imperialism, economic policy did not block or discourage the inflow of foreign capital. External pressures were quickly accommodated within Mexico's state capitalism, and US investment in manufacturing expanded dramatically during both the Alemán administration (1946–52) and the Ruiz Cortines administration (1952–58). Available data suggest that together with the largest of Mexican firms, multinational corporations benefited disproportionately from developmentalist policies.[12]

The government promoted capitalist agriculture just as avidly as it did industrialization. Public funds were poured into rural areas in the form of subsidies and infrastructure works, particularly irrigation. Large agribusinesses were the primary beneficiaries. And while about 40 percent of agricultural subsidies targeted the production of cheap food for urban centers, exporters received the lion's share of support. Here too the nationality of the company was not the guiding principle. In La Laguna region, for example, one of the firms profiting most from state-financed water-management projects was none other than Clayton's cotton business, Anderson, Clayton & Co.[13]

While the key decisions of economic policy behind developmentalism were made in the corridors and offices of ministers and presidents, in negotiation with men of capital and their advisors, sustained capital accumulation also required the acquiescence of organized civil society. It was to this end that the leadership of the PRM reorganized and renamed the official party, creating the Partido Revolucionario Institucional (PRI) in 1946. Where the PRM had counted on the CTM and the CNC to obtain the support of the labor and peasant movements, the recently formed Confederación Nacional de Organizaciones Populares (CNOP) provided the PRI with the institutional mechanisms necessary to engage with different sections of the urban middle and popular classes, whose numbers were growing fastest due to population growth and migration. Paramount among them were market vendors. By incorporating vendors together with government employees, small industrialists, and the organized residents of Mexico City's inner and outer slums—the old *vecindades* and the growing *colonias paracaidistas*—the CNOP mobilized support in congressional and presidential elections in large metropolitan areas, most importantly in the capital.[14] As a result, the PRI was able to balance and coordinate Mexico's diverse and often clashing interests within a progrowth compact. But the formal and informal networks the PRI created went beyond the unequal exchange of votes for resources and favors. They also served as channels both for civil society demands and for state agencies to deliver social programs, expanding the links between state and society.[15]

Still, the politics of developmentalism remained conflictual. The left had been under attack even before the beginning of the Cold War, and by the late 1940s, under US guidance, unions and governmental offices had been successfully purged of Communists.[16] Whereas Communist-free unions were tolerated, and when necessary rewarded, independent militant actions were swiftly suppressed; the same went for peasant organizations and their protests.[17] Inside and outside official politics repression was rampant,[18] and denunciations of electoral fraud were systematically met with violence.[19] However, given the degree of contestation and popular participation, the pragmatism of the political leadership, and the many "holes" in the PRI, the system could plausibly be described as no more than "softly authoritarian."[20]

Supported by these strategies for containing social conflict, developmentalism worked. Between 1946 and 1966 real per capita GDP rose on average 3.1 percent per year.[21] Industry grew as a share of the economy, and by 1960 workers were enjoying sustained real wage increases.[22] Social expenditures and public education expanded.[23] Public works across the country acted as effective propaganda for the party.[24] Despite the violence and repression that plagued Mexican politics, state-promoted capitalist expansion cemented the perception that the pursuit of social justice was best served by appealing to official patronage. Politicians at the top of their game were capable of discerning which group's demands to attend to in order to ensure governability, and which could be ignored without serious consequences. In a country where the state controlled less than 10 percent of GDP, this was no small feat.[25] Vendor leaders, for their part, learned how to navigate the era's politics in order to get themselves a place at the table.

Vendors and the Cost of Living

The developmentalist drive was nowhere stronger than in Mexico City. A combination of protectionism, investment in public services, and direct industrial promotion transformed the capital and its environs. Manufacturing output grew in real terms from 2.2 billion pesos in 1940 to 7.3 billion pesos in 1950, and 13.5 billion pesos in 1960. As a share of national production, this represented an increase from 32 to 46 percent.[26] By 1955, Mexico City already produced more than half of the country's matches, cigarettes, soaps and detergents, pharmaceuticals, wheels and tires, and auto assembly parts.[27] Industrial employment increased dramatically, rising from 89,000 workers in 1940 to 407,000 in 1960. As a result, Mexico City's share of the country's manufacturing labor force climbed from 24.6 to 46 percent.[28] Meanwhile, and partly due to the higher labor demand, the city's population expanded from 1.5 million in 1940 to 2.2 million in 1950, and 2.8 million in 1960. The Federal District's population, in turn, grew from 1.8 million in 1940 to 3.1 million in 1950, and to a staggering 4.9 million in 1960.[29]

With rapid economic expansion came high inflation, a trend that did not bode well for market vendors. The prices they charged as retailers of basic goods were the most visible element of the cost of living. In the second half of the 1940s organized workers demanded higher wages to cope with rising costs, but what they were granted by industrialists, with the support of the government, did not keep up with inflation. Unions therefore appealed to the government to reduce the prices they paid for basic goods. In response, following the pattern developed by the Cárdenas administration, the government intervened directly in the provision of everyday necessities. To complement inadequate nominal wage gains, Enrique Ochoa has shown, the government offered price controls and food subsidies. It also created a new State Food Agency, the CEIMSA, that would become a primary vehicle for managing industrial relations.[30] Needless to say, vendors had much to lose from government intervention in the city's supply network.

Inflation management gained even more political urgency in the aftermath of the 1948 devaluation of the peso. In late July, intelligence service agents from the Dirección General de Investigaciones Políticas y Sociales (General Directorate of Political and Social Investigations, DGIPS) began to make daily visits to the city's markets to gather information on the evolution of the prices of basic goods, observe consumers moods, and record related political comments. After each visit, DGIPS agents submitted written reports to their superiors, which were then summarized into a single memorandum that, marked as confidential, was forwarded to the secretary of the interior.[31] According to the memo of July 22, 1948, for example, agents visited the markets of San Juan, La Merced, La Lagunilla, Tepito, Hidalgo, Martínez de la Torre, San Cosme, Santa Julia, Tacubaya, Tacuba, Vallejo, and Guadalupe Hidalgo, where they witnessed "tough bargaining, and exchanges of harsh words and insults" between vendors and their customers. The memo also related interminable attacks on the government, noting that the most vituperated officials in this case were the secretaries of finance and national economy, and, above all, the head of the Department of the Federal District, Fernando Casas Alemán. Many vendors and market-goers believed he was personally profiting from the situation. The memo ended on a worrying note, expressing fears that "people were losing respect for the high office" of the presidency and stating that people were talking of "taking violent measures."[32]

Over the next few days, intelligence agents reported further price hikes along with rumors of forthcoming demands for higher wages and possible strikes.[33] By July 30, they conveyed a general sense of alarm: "Prices have not continued to go up, but discontent has not gone away.... The atmosphere in general is charged with pessimism.... There is incessant propaganda urging workers to take a more assertive stance, even if it came to confronting the government."[34] On August 4, the railway workers' union began to discuss the organization of a "monster demonstration against the high cost of living."[35] Five days later another memo relayed two tendencies within the labor movement: "One that insists on maintaining discipline and order to face the situation in cooperation with the government, and another one that at all costs wants wage increases, and if refused, plans to resort to strikes." Most railroad workers, trolley workers, cinematographers, and electricians supported the strategy to demand wage increases.[36] On August 14, their unions took a page in *El Universal* to invite "the working class, all the progressive and revolutionary organizations, non-unionized workers, the people of the Federal District and the Republic at large" to a demonstration a week hence. While taking pains to express that the demonstration was not against Alemán's "democratic regime," the organizers opposed key aspects of his economic policy, such as its terms of relation with the United States and its management of wage demands.[37]

The Alemán administration quickly took action to contain the growing discontent, not by increasing wages but by lowering the cost of essential goods. The Departamento del Distrito announced the tightening of price controls, while the State Food Agency declared it would increase its supply of subsidized goods to the city. In addition, the federal government launched the much-publicized "*mercados agrícolas*," where producers would sell directly to the public in order to circumvent intermediaries and thus, in theory, achieve lower retail prices.[38] In tune with Alemán's developmentalist support for agribusiness, the government attempted to guarantee supply to the new markets by working with large capitalist agriculturalists, represented by the Asociación Nacional de Cosecheros de Cereales y Productos Alimenticios (National Association of Cereal and Foodstuff Producers, ANC). The ANC had been created the previous year with presidential backing as an umbrella organization for 620 producer groups. Given the opportunities offered by the fight against the high cost of living, the ANC now moved to, as it put it, "break the monopoly" of the city's largest wholesale merchants.[39] The invitation to sell in the mercados agrícolas was also extended to smaller agricultural producers, and both the Confederación Nacional de la Pequeña Propiedad Agrícola, and the Confederación Nacional Campesina (National Campesino Confederation, CNC) accepted it gladly. These organizations also appreciated the chance to enter the city's supply network and soon started to boast of their collaboration with the official campaign against inflation in their correspondence with the authorities.[40]

Intelligence agents described the "very good impression caused by the determination of the government to watch over prices and the other measures in favor of lowering the cost of living."[41] In particular, "the opening of the [first] *mercado agrícola* in the Colonia del Valle has created optimism. People from all social classes are attending it to make their purchases."[42] The city's press corroborated this perception.[43] By August 16, *Excélsior* declared the success of the market, which was so crowded that by ten in the morning it was hard to walk around it; the entire stock of vegetables, grains, poultry, bread, milk, and other products sold only too rapidly.[44] *El Universal* agreed, explaining that the reason was that prices there were 25 percent lower than elsewhere. In an editorial it further remarked that "it would be desirable that other [such] markets were built with the same impetus. Every zone of the Federal District needs one."[45] The following day, *El Nacional* announced that two more mercados agrícolas were due to be inaugurated the following Saturday, the very day of the workers' planned demonstration against the high cost of living.[46]

Whereas workers and consumers appeared pleased, vendors were not. As retail outlets, the mercados agrícolas represented direct competition with the city's public markets. Already on August 18, intelligence agents interviewed locatarios of the Lázaro Cárdenas Market, which was located near the first mercado agrícola in Colonia del Valle, who complained about the loss of clientele. The agents noted that these vendors were planning an assembly to discuss their new challenges and to decide on how to best approach a forthcoming meeting with Casas Alemán, the head of the Department of the Federal District.[47]

Organized vendors soon engaged the press to publicize their grievances and defend their place in the city's commercial structure. In an article in *Excélsior*, the Federación Nacional de Comerciantes e Industriales en Pequeño argued that, instead of creating new retail outlets, government efforts to reduce the cost of living should focus on providing vendors with subsidized goods that they could then sell on at the official prices. They proposed the establishment of two big distribution centers on the outskirts of the city and a network of smaller depots in the proximity of each of the Federal District's forty-two markets, where they could buy cheap merchandise.[48] Short of that, they requested to be allowed to purchase from the mercados agrícolas in order to resell in the city's public markets, "with the solemn promise to obtain [only] a fair profit."[49] The government took note.

Government intervention strained the already difficult relations between wholesalers and vendors. By the late 1940s, La Merced neighborhood, home to the city's largest food merchants, functioned as a supply depot and distribution center.[50] Locatarios from all over the Federal District purchased stock at La Merced warehouses and shops. In as much as vendors' incomes depended on the prices they paid their suppliers, conflict between them was systemic. Now, according to *La Prensa*, the Federal District's commission for the enforcement of price controls sought to reduce prices by collaborating with large-scale merchants and repressing retailers.[51] Were price controls to work, someone's profits had to give, and wholesalers had an advantage: it was far easier for the government to enforce controls on retail sales.

The politicization of the cost of living threatened to turn structural tensions between wholesalers and market vendors into a public confrontation. A group of locatarios told *Excélsior* that they blamed the high cost of living on "the six-hundred warehousemen [*bodegueros*] of La Merced, who hoard fruit, vegetables and to a lesser extent, grains and seeds, and the four hundred dry goods storekeepers [*almacenistas de abarrotes*] who hoard seeds and grains in large quantities." What is more, they accused these merchants of encroaching on the new *mercado agrícola* with the help of local officials.⁵² *El Popular* also reported vendors' complaints that "it is the same speculators [*coyotes*] from La Merced, exploiters [*comerciantes hambreadores*] such as the brothers Julio and Abraham Vera, the Moranchels, and the Rossettes who control the new *mercado* in the Colonia del Valle."⁵³ According to *Excélsior* the producers from the ANC shared this view. The secretary of that organization was quoted calling these merchants "a cancer that was starting to take hold of the mercado agrícola."⁵⁴

The vendors who talked to the press maintained that the government's failure to protect their interests was "causing serious agitation among seventy thousand locatarios who are willing to attend the demonstration and gathering of the twenty-first,"⁵⁵ which *El Popular* insisted was "for the implementation of effective measures against the high cost of living" and "a fight to the death against speculators, hoarders, those enriching themselves by the misery of the people."⁵⁶ The nature of the planned demonstration became a matter of dispute. The unions organizing it took a page in *Excélsior* to state, against accusations from the CTM and business leaders, that it was "neither Communist, Catholic, nor Masonic, but of Mexicans against the high cost of living."⁵⁷ Still, the apparent paradox of vendors demonstrating alongside workers against the prices they were themselves charging did not go unnoticed. *La Prensa* reported that the Confederación Patronal de La República Mexicana considered the participation of the locatarios as evidence of extremism because it was against their interests to limit their own profits.⁵⁸

Available sources do not reveal whether vendors attended the demonstration, which according to intelligence agents had a substantial though not huge turnout of seven to eight thousand, probably a purposeful underestimation. Vendors' grievances, however, were well represented at the rally. A banner denounced the power of the large wholesalers, proclaiming, "the government of the Republic resides in La Merced."⁵⁹ In one of the speeches the agents recorded, Adán Nieto, on behalf of the miners' union, declared that "the people, like myself, ask what causes the increase in the cost of living, and we respond that it is caused by corrupt politicians, the usual exploiters [*hambreadores*], and bad officials." Acknowledging the government's efforts to control prices, this speaker lamented that "unfortunately in Mexico the law only punishes poor meat vendors instead of the real hoarders, the influential, or the *amigazos* of the president." He also referred to the mercados agrícolas as those "little markets . . . that resolve nothing, that are only a palliative," arguing that "the problem of the cost of living could only be solved by eliminating all monopolies and hoarders, as well as by cutting the nails of cronies and enriched politicians."[60]

The government could not remain indifferent to the concerns of market vendors and attempted to reassure them that it did not intend to displace them from the city's supply chains. The very day of the demonstration, *La Prensa* announced the decision to devote the soon-to-be inaugurated mercado agrícola of Jamaica exclusively to sales to locatarios. The State Food Agency vowed to open stores in other public markets as well, to supply subsidized products to the locatarios so they could resell them at "fair prices."[61] The secretary of agriculture met with various groups of vendors to discuss how they could work together to reduce prices.[62] Following these meetings, he negotiated an agreement between the large producers of the ANC and the Federación Nacional de Comerciantes e Industriales Mexicanos en Pequeño to "supply them directly, and eliminate intermediaries." The ANC approvingly described the Federación de Comerciantes as a natural ally in their own campaign to push out local intermediaries, because this organization represented the majority of the locatarios and small-scale vendors of the markets of the Federal District.[63] The goal was for vendors to be able to sell at the same price as the mercados agrícolas. The press celebrated the agreement, with the *Excélsior* anticipating "the general collapse of prices in the [Federal] District's sixty markets" and applauding "the locatarios' cooperation in this great crusade."[64]

Despite official efforts, vendors continued to resent the competition from the mercados agrícolas. If we are to trust journalists, the mercado agrícola in the Colonia ex-Hipódromo de Peralvillo attracted thirty thousand customers on a typical morning, while the one in the Colonia del Valle had twenty thousand visitors.[65] In early September the federación addressed President Alemán to make their objections explicit. "Loyal as we are," its leadership had decided to "speak frankly" of what they saw as the wrong turn that the campaign against the cost of living was taking. In particular, the mercados agrícolas were causing vendors "material harm because due to the disproportionate free publicity received by these markets, both by the press and the radio, the consuming public does not attend the other markets, where fifty thousand comerciantes [and] heads of households are suffering the consequences." Most importantly, the federación explained that vendors found themselves at a disadvantage because while they had to pay market fees and incurred transport costs to move the merchandize from wholesale depots, the mercados agrícolas were exempted from all taxes and had their goods delivered directly by producers. Moreover, these markets were generating conflict among vendors themselves, for as the federación told Alemán, a "few chosen ones have found places in them to set up stalls and make a profit." The federación leadership worried about the political implications of the "disorientation" that this inequity among vendors would create, warning the president that the new markets were "undermining to some extent the confidence placed in you." More than a caution, this seemed like a veiled threat. Vendor leaders insisted that Alemán act promptly, to "realize the plan to supply the people by means of small-scale traders."[66]

The leaders of the Federación de Comerciantes were not alone in expressing vendors' dissatisfaction with the way the mercados agrícolas were being run. The independent Unión de Pequeños Comerciantes del Mercado Río Blanco, for example, claimed that 90 percent of those selling goods in the mercado agrícola Francisco Sarabia were comerciantes from other city markets, rather than producers, as they should have been; intelligence agents soon confirmed that the Uniones de Comerciantes del Mercado Martínez de la Torre y La Merced were operating in this market.[67] The government was also aware that La Merced wholesalers were maneuvering to maintain control over food distribution in the city. Both the ANC and the CNC-affiliated Union Nacional de Transportes Ejidales insisted that the new markets were not fulfilling their role because they had fallen in the hands of "the large-scale merchants of La Merced."[68] A commission in charge of monitoring controlled goods concluded that the charges were true, and that the mercados agrícolas were staffed by "those who are fronting for known hoarders [*acaparadores*]," and by "old-time locatarios of ordinary markets."[69]

The national government needed to look proactive in the fight against inflation, but these conflicts were more than it had bargained for. On October 30, 1948, the *Diario Oficial* published a presidential decree putting all markets, including the mercados agrícolas, under the purview of the Departamento del Distrito Federal, thus devolving the problem to the local authorities. Unsurprisingly, this tipped the balance in favor of well-entrenched local interests and would do little to ameliorate the reported problems.

The transfer of jurisdiction took place in March 1949. Small producers from the CNC immediately saw their access to the mercados agrícolas curtailed and complained to the president about the treatment that they were receiving from the new head of the markets department, one Mr. Rojas. A group of ejidatarios trying to sell their goods at the mercado agrícola Santa Anita accused Rojas of "representing the economic interests of monopolistic merchants, for he has attacked [our] markets, violently, closing down stalls, threatening us with jail time, imposing fines, and ordering policemen to assault us." They were indignant, writing that "we believe this is not the way to repay our efforts to collaborate with the government."[70] In a similar letter to Alemán, "campesinos" from San Nicolás Buenos Aires y Ciudad Cerdán, Puebla, "politely request constitutional guarantees for our compañeros . . . who cooperate with your campaign to lower the cost of living." They protested that if they were to lose access to the mercados agrícolas, they would be left with no option but to sell to La Merced wholesalers.[71] Eventually the large producers of the ANC joined their protests. In a letter to Alemán they blamed the continued dominance of La Merced wholesalers on the Departamento del Distrito, claiming that the problems with these markets started the moment the department's officials assigned administrators who, instead of assisting producers, "surrendered [them], in fact, to intermediaries and professional merchants."[72]

In November 1949, intelligence agents again recorded widespread discontent around what they characterized as the "great anarchy" in retail prices all over the city.[73] The press mourned the failure of the mercados agrícolas. *Excélsior* recalled their origins and early success and discussed the need to "clean or purge them."[74] In a more pessimistic editorial, *Novedades* wondered: "Should we admit that it's impossible to give the people less expensive foodstuffs?"[75] Alemán would once again promise to enforce price controls, punish offending vendors and merchants, and supply the city with subsidized products.[76] The complex web of overlapping and conflicting interests involved in providing everyday necessities to Mexico City's residents, however, made these promises hard to keep.

Growing City, Growing Challenges

The failure of the mercados agrícolas removed an important source of vendor discontent but did little to improve their prospects in *desarrollista* Mexico. State intervention in supply chains continued unabated, and the government expanded the operation of CEIMSA stores throughout the 1950s. To make things worse, market vendors faced mounting private sector competition. A

FIGURE 12. SUMESA supermarket in Colonia Roma. In Spanish the acronym for Super Mercados Sociedad Anónima reads as "your table." Source: Mediateca INAH, Colección Archivo Casasola, ca. 1961.

group of Monterrey-based bankers formed Super Mercados S.A., or SUMESA, to introduce the "modern technique" of "American-style self-service stores" to Mexico. They believed this would be a more efficient system than the existing labor-intensive network of small stores and "traditional markets."[77] The National Chamber of Commerce (Cámara Nacional de Comercio, CANACO) supported SUMESA's "serious and evolutionary commerce" and characterized vendors' practices, by contrast, as backward. CANACO harangued the government to take all necessary measures to ensure that "all of that energy spent on small-scale trading should be employed in agricultural production and in industries, allowing commercial interests to become decent enterprises that yield true profits."[78] Still, it would take decades for supermarkets to realize SUMESA's plans to replace public markets as furnishers of the tables of urban residents, starting with the most affluent among them.

Vendors were more immediately threatened by growing competition among their own ranks. The expansion of manufacturing and other capitalist sectors was insufficient to absorb Mexico City's growing working population, so the vast majority of residents had to find other ways of making a living.[79] Many of them flocked to proprietary trading in its many forms, due to its flexibility and low barriers to entry. In 1945, the chamber of commerce put the number of small-scale vendors in the city at 70,000.[80] Of those, it claimed, only 2 percent based themselves inside market halls. The rest plied their "poor and primitive" trade in fixed, semifixed, and portable stalls around markets and on the streets more generally. In the standard diatribe against these vendors, CANACO accused them of posing a risk to public health by selling poor quality, contaminated, or adulterated products and giving the city a deplorable appearance. The Federación Nacional de Comerciantes e Industriales Mexicanos en Pequeño, for its part, denounced the "peasants that come to the city to fail" and informed the press that it intended to request "the Department of [the Federal] District's protection against the disadvantageous competition from a floating mass of more than one hundred thousand maladjusted workers, who one day are garbage pickers or porters, and the next [day] penny-vendors of fruit and trinkets."[81] The federación's prejudices aside, rural migrants were only part of the story;[82] natural population growth implied a young population, with many children taking to peddling to provide for themselves, or to contribute to their family's income.[83]

Regardless of vendors' origins or ages, their growing numbers made government officials uneasy, for they overwhelmed the city's already deficient market infrastructure and laid bare the Department of the Federal District's financial limitations. In January 1947, the director of public works attended a meeting of the department's advisory board, the Consejo Consultivo, to discuss the works program for Mexico City proposed by the head of the Federal District, Casas Alemán. His account was sobering. He acknowledged that all urban services required attention, but, he explained with regret, the department lacked the resources to tackle them. One "of the most serious problems of the city is the absence of humane markets," he said, but "the whole public works budget of several years would not be enough" to solve it. While he estimated that the city needed ten large and 250 small markets, no funds had been allocated to market construction in that year's plans.[84]

After hearing this account, the Consejo Consultivo asked the head of the Markets Office, Iñigo Noriega, for further information and for a report on his management of the city's public markets. Three months later, Noriega informed the consejo that he could not say how many vendors there were in the capital's forty-two markets because most trade took place in *zonas de mercados*, or market areas—in many cases the streets adjacent to market halls—where vendors set up their stalls with the authorization of local officials.[85] He had ordered all administrators to take a census of the zonas de mercado under their responsibility, but the task was proving difficult.[86] In anticipation of the results of his inquiry, however, he had requested the printing of 45,000 extra licenses, which, if issued, would bring the total to 85,000 for the Federal District as a whole. Noriega had also instructed market administrators to survey the material state of each market and to create a list of repairs needed. He had received only a few replies, but he was aware of the urgency of the works. Most halls were over forty years old and in poor condition. Drainages had collapsed. Pavements and metal structures were in disarray. Several markets lacked lighting and water. "It's a true catastrophe," he concluded.[87] Desarrollismo had yet to reach the city's markets.

Organized vendors agreed it was high time the government stepped up its efforts. They blamed the combination of inadequate public investment and growing vendor numbers for the mounting conflict among their rank and file. Jesús Bautista, who had been secretary general of the Federación Nacional de Comerciantes e Industriales Mexicanos en Pequeño since its founding, gave a newspaper interview in September 1949 drawing attention to the issues affecting the vendors of La Villa de Guadalupe. Bautista complained that vendors were once again facing pressure to reduce the size of their stalls, noting that each time they had done so in the past, the space freed up had been given to new arrivals. Instead of resolving disputes, the practice only made them more frequent, so that "today the matter has taken the proportion of a class problem." He believed the resulting violence among vendors would subside only once the authorities built "a large and modern market" with enough capacity for all the vendors operating in the area.[88]

Clashes among vendors were daily occurrences in the city's zonas de mercados. In June 1949, Jesús Guzmán Olmos wrote to President Alemán on behalf of the seven hundred families that composed the Union of Small-Scale Vendors of La Lagunilla Market, the second largest in the city. Stalls around the Porfirian market hall had spilled on to the streets of Honduras, Peru, Juan Álvarez, Paraguay, Allende, and República de Chile, the plaza and streets of Comonfort, the alleys de La Vaquita, Altuna, Incas, and beyond.[89] Guzmán Olmos wanted Honduras Street cleared: The vendors in his union had vacated that very street more than a decade earlier on condition that the area would be protected. Now, they asked that permits for stalls on Honduras Street be revoked, and that the police patrol the area.[90] Because these locatarios believed their long-standing agreement with the authorities had been broken, they were preparing to abandon the market hall and retake the streets. He feared there was nothing vendor leaders like himself could do to prevent this. Guzmán Olmos had been actively lobbying, unsuccessfully, for improvements to La Lagunilla Market for months.[91] But this time he framed his remarks as representative of the city's vendors at large: "We consider it's time the Government of the Departamento del Distrito Federal create a program to protect public markets, and to put a check on street vending, because avenues of the largest city of the Republic look like Arab souks, while market halls find themselves half-empty."[92]

Vendors had been making similar demands for decades, but now they were received with a new urgency. The city authorities recognized that if they were to guarantee the supply of everyday necessities at prices workers could afford, public markets were due for an overhaul. Political operators also understood that they needed the backing of organized vendors if the PRI wanted elections in the capital to run smoothly. In an increasingly crowded, competitive city, vendors intensified their collective claims for an active state able to mediate their conflicts and deliver the public services that would allow them to make a better living. This time, the government agreed—with the expectation that offering vendors what they wanted would enable greater political control over markets.

Political Operators Take the Lead

The case of the Banco del Pequeño Comercio illustrates how an agency meant to provide a service to vendors opened avenues for political operators to use patronage and exclusion to extend the reach of the PRI in the capital, as well as to further their personal ambitions. In May 1950, Jesús Bautista wrote once again to President Alemán on behalf of the National Federation of Small-Scale Vendors and Industrialists.[93] He described how the federación, ever since its formation in 1932, had lobbied for the creation of a public bank to serve its members. After the Banco del Pequeño Comercio was formed in 1943, the federación's members had worked to support it. When the bank was almost dissolved in 1948, Bautista and other vendor leaders had met with Alemán and obtained the three million pesos in public funds needed to save it. But in December 1948, a new law modified the statutes of the bank: from then on, instead of lending to individual vendors, the bank would work with credit associations based in specific markets.[94] In March 1949, the personnel of the bank was reshuffled, and Guillermo Martínez Domínguez became the head of the Office for the Promotion and Organization of Credit Associations. "From that day, Mr. Martínez Domínguez has used all means available to him," Bautista wrote, "to systematically develop a web of hostilities, hatred, intrigues, and slander against this Federation, its affiliated organizations, and even against the small-scale vendors whose only crime is to be members of this Federation."[95]

For fourteen months, Bautista insisted, Martínez Domínguez had denied credit to the members of his federación. Despite Bautista's repeated complaints, nobody had corrected this irregularity. He also accused Martínez Domínguez of paying one Macario Lucero a large amount of money to herd in outside vendors, or *"comerciantes paracaidistas,"* to displace federación members from the markets of San Juan, Bugambilia, and Lago Garda. Martínez Domínguez, Bautista continued, "is not only going to bankrupt the bank, but he is widening the enormous division within small commerce in the Federal District, instead of attempting to harmonize and unify it."[96]

The federación was not alone in its denunciation of Martínez Domínguez. Juan de Dios Bojórquez, director general of the bank by presidential appointment, and in theory, Martínez Domínguez's boss, had his own objections. In March 1950, within three months of having taken up his position at the bank, Bojórquez wrote to secretary of hacienda Ramón Beteta that he was considering resigning over problems with his subordinate. Bojórquez accused Martínez Domínguez of forming the new credit associations to benefit people who responded to him, to whom he appeared as a "protector or leader," giving them money without safeguarding the interests of the bank.[97] Bautista corroborated this objection in another letter to President Alemán, sent in April, alleging that Martínez Domínguez had been using bank funds "to create groups to support his own ambitions."[98]

The representatives of Martínez Domínguez's credit associations refused to take the blame for the precarious financial situation of the bank. The same day that Director General Bojórquez wrote to Secretary Beteta, these representatives wrote to President Alemán condemning the chaos that, they argued, Bojórquez himself had created. They claimed he broke the law, refused to listen to them, paralyzed the operations of the bank, and spent its money in absurd ways.[99] Both Martínez Domínguez and Bojórquez stayed at their jobs, but a year later, in February 1951, the credit associations were back on the offensive, attacking Bojórquez for irregularities, including moving the bank's offices to an overpriced property owned by his son. The leaders of the credit unions threatened to "cause a public scandal of large proportions, since each and every one of our five thousand compañeros would be a voice in the public plazas against the immoral behavior we are denouncing." Furthermore, they warned, panic would prevail and payments to the bank would be suspended, forcing it into immediate insolvency. "We don't want to lose this patrimony you have given us. We will fight to preserve it. But we are at a dead-end whose only exit is your personal intervention, and we trust you fully."[100]

Bojórquez wrote to Alemán again later that month. Having failed to put a stop to Martínez Domínguez's maneuvers, he was preparing to leave the bank and wanted to put his objections on record. From the beginning of its operations, the director general recounted, the bank had functioned with political aims. During its first six years, it had been under the control of the Federación Nacional de Comerciantes e Industriales Mexicanos en Pequeño, which had almost ruined the institution, leaving it with bad debts for 650,000 pesos. At the end of 1948, following the change of its statutes, the bank itself began forming credit associations, setting up around forty of them across an equal number of markets. In Bojórquez's opinion, these ended up being worse than the federación. Credit began flowing exclusively to the members of these associations, and after a year and a half of this policy, they had bad debts of around 300,000 pesos. "The leaders, and even the members [of the associations], have got it in their heads that they are the owners of the Bank, and they are ready to cause scandals and demand rights, when in fact they are only its debtors and sole beneficiaries."[101] His parting recommendation was to reorganize the bank to avoid dealing with vendor organizations altogether; it would be better, he said, for the bank to treat vendors purely as individual subjects of credit.[102]

Bojórquez saw the bank as just a bank and vendors as its customers. He had failed to comprehend that this approach was inadequate in the new political landscape, for two reasons: first, even the small profits generated by municipal markets had become political concerns; second, dealing with vendors meant dealing with vendor organizations. Guillermo Martínez Domínguez, on the other hand, had spotted the political potential of the bank. He used it to undermine the federación and to create his own group of loyal vendor leaders, against the priorities of his boss and possibly at the expense of the bank itself. He understood how to use the institution of the bank and the resources it commanded to bring a part of the vendor movement under his control. We do not know to what extent Martínez's manipulations of the vendor movement had been sanctioned in advance by the PRI leadership, but he appears to have been rewarded. Against the protestations of Bojórquez and the federación, and to the delight of the representatives of the credit associations he had sponsored, in March 1951 Martínez Domínguez was made the new director of the bank.[103]

From early 1952, the new head of the markets office, Gonzalo Peña Manterola, would extend this form of political management to the vendor movement throughout the Federal District, helping the PRI to institutionalize vendor politics. Following the same strategy as Martínez Domínguez, Peña Manterola began attacking the federación as soon as he was appointed, quickly drawing the anger of its leaders. In April 1952, Jesús Bautista's replacement as the federación's secretary general, Francisco Ruvalcaba, denounced Peña Manterola for his "policy of division and hostility toward this National Federation and its member organizations." The federación produced a detailed memo insisting that Peña Manterola "openly protects elements that have no representation whatsoever," and accused him of "harassing our members with the purpose of dividing our organization." The document cited the case of the Mercado 1° de Mayo, which was empty because ambulantes under Peña Manterola's protection had surrounded the premises, poaching customers and impeding access to the hall. The city's head of markets, the memo maintained, had organized these vendors to further his own political agenda. The federación believed the same dynamic was taking place in the zona de mercado of La Dalia, and on Honduras Street in La Lagunilla. In addition, in the markets of Beethoven and La Merced, Peña Manterola had removed vendors to make room for paving work, but once the works were completed, he refused to allow those from the federación to retake their places, giving them instead to other vendors. The memo ended with a plea that it not be forwarded to the head of the Federal District, Peña Manterola's boss, because that would only feed the vicious circle.[104]

Ruvalcaba was confident that his organization's party connections gave him some leverage, as presidential and congressional elections were scheduled for July that year. By the early 1950s, the popular sector had gained importance within the party, giving the federación the hope that it could sway market policy. He requested that President Alemán replace Peña Manterola as the only solution to the upheaval his actions had caused in the city's markets, reminding Alemán that the federación had been an active member of the CNOP from its creation in 1943, and that its leadership had always operated in agreement with the PRI's Central Committee. Ruvalcaba reiterated his assurance of vendors' collective support. But the gambit did not pay off. Peña Manterola played the new game of political patronage and control too effectively for the federación to be able to oust him. He would remain head of markets, joining the new administration under President Adolfo Ruiz Cortines's appointed head of the Department of the Federal District Ernesto P. Uruchurtu. Together, they would radically transform Mexico City's markets, and with them, the political landscape of the capital.

Ernesto P. Uruchurtu, Peddler of Dreams

Uruchurtu took over the Department of the Federal District in early December 1952, promising to tackle the city's service and infrastructural deficiencies. The city's finances were a shambles, so his first task was to increase tax collection. In his inaugural speech, Uruchurtu asked residents to become "exigent contributors." If they wanted their demands met, they had to be willing to pay their taxes.[105] It worked. Thanks to a combination of economic growth, an expanded tax base, and better administration, the Federal District's real revenues doubled between 1953 and 1959, dramatically improving its capacity to perform public works, to the delight of construction companies.[106] This allowed Uruchurtu to fulfill his much-publicized commitment to control flooding, increase the supply of clean water, pave streets, reorganize traffic circulation, expand garbage collection services, and build markets to house tens of thousands of vendors. Famously, he would also build over one hundred fountains and plant thousands of trees and flowers, especially gladiolas. From the beginning, Uruchurtu demonstrated a deep awareness of the anxieties of a growing city. He would do his best to project a positive image of this latest iteration of the city's dash for modernity.[107]

During the Uruchurtu years, argues the sociologist John Cross, a combination of market construction, clientelism, and repression helped the city government bring vendors under tighter control while strengthening both vendor organizations and their leaders vis-à-vis the rank and file.[108] While this is no doubt true, the process was more nuanced and protracted than this suggests. Vendors had been actively seeking political support for a program of market expansion, in particular one that would suppress their competitors, for over twenty years. State actors had been experimenting with different institutional solutions to vendors' quest for proprietary progress for just as long. Moreover, these political maneuvers should be seen in the context of the larger politics of developmentalism. The CNOP had become an indispensable component of urban political machines but also represented the most diverse and unruly of the party's "sectors." At the same time, the CNOP remained in competition with the CTM for influence within the party.[109] Uruchurtu and Peña Manterola's market policies, then, should be seen as attempts to unify the vendor movement within the CNOP and to thereby strengthen the CNOP within the PRI, along the way enhancing their own political standing against rival cliques.[110] This was how they sought to achieve the governability that was so necessary to enable economic growth.

The sticks came before the carrots. From Uruchurtu's very first week in office he launched a campaign to remove market stalls from the city center.[111] The repression of street vendors would continue throughout his long tenure. Despite this, available archival sources do not contain explicit attacks on the jefe del departamento. Uruchurtu's nickname, "Regente de Hierro," denoted strength as much as anything else. Rather, it is his jefe de mercados who is constantly criticized. In February 1953, "one hundred and thirty vendors who used to make an honest living on the streets of Eligio Ancona" complained they had been "vilely abused by the head of the market department." They demanded justice, which they believed they deserved because "we were Ruiz Cortinistas and contributed actively to your campaign. Is this how we are paid for our humble services?"[112] The Frentes de Comerciantes en Pequeño and Femenil de Protección de Comerciantes, both self-declared "active members of the Frente Coordinador de Unificación Nacional pro-Adolfo Ruiz Cortines," also censured the jefe de mercados, who "with excessive force and disregard for the most elementary rights of citizens persecutes [vendors,] confiscating their merchandise, fining them, charging them excessive fees."[113] The Alianza de Comerciantes en Pequeño del Mercado de Jamaica wrote to Uruchurtu and to Ruiz Cortines to denounce him. In the letter to the president, they called Peña Manterola their "inquisitor and tormentor."[114]

Reports from the new intelligence services, the Dirección Federal de Seguridad (DFS), documented this discontent.[115] In October 1953, after Peña Manterola announced that hundreds of market stalls would be shut down, DFS agents followed a rally of eight hundred vendors to the offices of the Department of the Federal District. Uruchurtu offered new sites for the relocation of the stalls, the agents reported, which the vendors' leaders were willing to accept. But vendors still demanded guarantees against his head of markets, who "in the presence of the jefe del departamento is a white dove, and in his offices is a Nero who treats the public to infamies and insults."[116] In January 1954, La Lagunilla's Frente de Protección Mutua de Comerciantes en Pequeño requested the president order "an immediate and energetic investigation to corroborate the unspeakable abuses inflicted upon us by Peña Manterola."[117] Later that year, the DFS recorded, 150 members of this frente marched to the National Palace with placards reading, "Mr. President: Our children are hungry. We can no longer put up with Peña Manterola," and "Mr. President we expect you to hear us and do us justice." The secretary of the president had no option but to receive them and at least acknowledge their grievances.[118]

Attacks on vendor organizations prompted fury but did not represent a repression of the vendor movement as a whole. Instead, the attacks functioned to reduce the fragmentation that had undermined previous urban renewal projects and to strengthen Peña Manterola's political position and the power of the Department of the Federal District. Congressman Víctor Manuel Ávila, in his role as secretary general of the United Front of Locatarios and Small-Scale Vendors of the Federal District, wrote to President Ruiz Cortines to inform him that Peña Manterola had created a rival federation "to which he is giving all the help and support imaginable." He asserted that Peña Manterola was trying to dissolve the United Front by slandering its leaders in the press, forcefully removing the stalls of its rank and file, imposing illegal fines, and encouraging violent confrontations among vendors. "These scandalous practices," Congressman Ávila claimed, "had already caused them the loss of several organizations."[119]

These accusations are repeated and expanded in a document dated February 2, 1954. Its provenance is unclear, but it is part of a file in the presidential archives devoted to complaints against Peña Manterola. The first section of this document reproduced Ávila's accusations, using almost his exact words. It then broadened the scope, confirming that Peña Manterola sought to dissolve all vendor federations in order to favor his own, the Federación de Comerciantes en Pequeño de los Mercados del Distrito Federal, and that to do this he played the others against one another, even accusing their leaders of being enemies of the government. Peña Manterola and his clique, the document related, had "managed to impress Mr. Francisco Galindo Ochoa, regional executive president of the PRI, who receives them and gives them preferential treatment." Following their request, Galindo Ochoa had assembled the representatives of all vendor federations to ask them to merge into one. This unification, the document claimed, would allow Peña Manterola to eliminate uncooperative leaders.[120] Consistent with these complaints, in June 1955, DFS agents recorded La Merced vendor leaders calling the jefe de mercados "Maquiavelo Manterola."[121]

As Peña Manterola was solidifying the department's control of the vendor movement, vendors used the opportunities opened by the growing institutional capacity of the PRI to express their demands. As María Cristina Sánchez Mejorada indicates, congressional representatives for the Federal District became important mediators between their local constituents and the federal authorities.[122] In February 1953, Juan José Osorio Palacios, congressman for the second electoral district, wrote to Uruchurtu to "bring to your attention some of the most urgent problems confronting the aforementioned district... and which diverse social sectors have put in my hands, with the desire to see them resolved in the shortest possible time." Almost all of the problems he described related to markets and reflected the demands that vendors had repeatedly made through their organizations—hardly surprising, given that his constituency was home to the markets and zonas de mercados of Abelardo Rodríguez, Tepito, La Lagunilla, 2 de Abril, Santa Ana, and Martínez de la Torre. The list begins with a demand for "indispensable" childcare facilities in the district's markets, identifying two locations which, vendors had suggested, could be suitable for the children of Tepito and La Lagunilla. All markets also needed their streets repaved and their drainages fixed. The congressman noted that vendors had been promised all of these improvements since the administration of Javier Rojo Gómez in the early 1940s, but that this area remained an embarrassment to the city and its government. Better markets, Osorio Palacios insisted, would be able to house more of the growing number of street vendors. He ended by acknowledging the numerous constraints facing Uruchurtu, but "on behalf of my constituents I cannot but make you aware of the needs of the district's residents."[123]

Vendors found an unexpected additional channel of communication with the government through the intelligence services. Spreading rumors and passing information to known DFS agents became an instrument for political maneuvering. On March 1, 1955, Agent 88 interviewed a vendor of pencils and fountain pens named Antonio López Hernández, who denounced politically motivated harassment by Federal District employees. This vendor explained that he usually set up his stall next to 55 Corregidora Street, using a loudspeaker to announce his merchandise. Following the instructions of the secretary general of the Sindicato Independiente de Comerciantes en Pequeño del Mercado de la Merced, Francisco Islas, he had recently begun to take time off every half an hour to use his microphone to urge passersby to register to vote in the upcoming midterm elections. But on Saturday, February 26, the driver of truck number 949 showed up accompanied by policeman number 3039. La Merced vendors knew that this truck was used to remove street stalls, but on this occasion López Hernández was the only one picked up out of more than two hundred vendors in Corregidora Street. Given that he was also the only one carrying out "democratic labors," he objected that he was being unfairly targeted. Angry at being questioned, the driver and the policeman unplugged the vendor's equipment and by blows got him and his merchandise on board the truck. After beating him, the driver told the vendor that if he wanted an explanation he should speak with Peña Manterola, because it was he who had given the orders.

Agent 88 noted, moreover, that he had interviewed López Hernández on the recommendation of the same Francisco Islas who had instructed him to carry out his "democratic labors." Islas clearly wanted this matter communicated to the DFS. Islas also told the agent that the altercation was purely a political matter. "Far from executing the postulates of this administration," claimed Islas, "many high-up government employees, among them Peña Manterola and the head of the Transit Department, are committing many injustices to discredit it and turn public opinion against it."[124] Islas declared himself, in contrast, one of the president's trustworthy collaborators in the city and, as proof, he promised to unify small-scale commerce on the PRI's behalf. He saw Peña Manterola as his direct competitor in this endeavor. Moreover, as Agent 88 would soon learn, Islas had political goals of his own.

While the PRI dominated Congress, there were intense political negotiations over which sector of the party, or which groups within a sector, would capture a particular electoral district. In Mexico City, vendor organizations like Sindicato Independiente de Comerciantes en Pequeño de la Merced competed among themselves and with other "popular sector" groups as well as with the CTM, for nominations. On March 23, 1955, Agent 88 visited the offices of the sindicato, where he had a conversation with Francisco Navarro. Navarro was *diputado suplente*, or alternate deputy, for the fifth electoral district. This position did not carry any specific powers, but it implied a degree of official access and political legitimation. Navarro informed Agent 88 that two days earlier, eighteen representatives of La Merced vendors' and merchants' organizations had gathered in the union's offices to express the support of the district's "popular sector" for a ticket led by him as diputado, with Islas as his diputado suplente, for the upcoming congressional elections. This would be a rise in position for both men. Navarro, who knew his comments to the agent would make their way up official channels, said that "if the PRI wants to win the elections in this district they should not impose outsiders, because that would give the PAN, which has supporters in this district, the opportunity to beat the official party." He insisted he had been working for the district for years and was able to gather more than five thousand resident voters in under five hours.[125] Elections gave vendor leaders a chance to demonstrate their strength.

Agent 88 returned to La Merced daily during the election season, and on March 29 he witnessed an assembly held at the offices of the Sindicato Independiente, now converted into the "office of political affairs" for the fifth electoral district. Under the banner of the PRI and the CNOP, he reported, all the organizations of comerciantes of La Merced showed discipline and "revolutionary unity," vowing to fight opposition parties.[126] But two days later, the mood changed drastically: newspapers had announced the candidacy of Alfonso Sánchez Madariaga from the CTM for the district, instead of Navarro, causing widespread discontent in La Merced. Odilón Posadas, from a wholesalers' organization, announced that the PRI was not going to trick them this time, and that if they wanted to impose a workers' candidate then they would simply vote for any opposition ticket available. Francisco Robles Rodríguez, secretary general of the separate Unión de Comerciantes Detallistas de La Merced and an ally of Navarro and Islas, commented that it looked like the government was scared of the CTM. Otherwise, he could not understand why they would nominate a workers' candidate when the district was so clearly "popular." On election day, he warned, they would "show their worth, driving the PAN candidate to victory."[127] Despite capitalist merchants' and proprietary vendors' threats, the CTM candidate carried the district—although, as a compromise, the position of diputado suplente was taken for the CNOP by Francisco Robles Rodríguez. The PRI leadership was right not to disregard vendors' threats completely. In the 1955 congressional election the PAN obtained three of the nineteen seats for the Federal District, which was very high for the period.[128]

While Peña Manterola battled to unify and control the vendor movement, and vendor leaders maneuvered through available channels to secure a place within the new political order, Uruchurtu's campaign of market building, for

FIGURE 13. La Merced Market, 1957. Source: Mediateca INAH, Colección Archivo Casasola.

which vendors had been lobbying for years, was reaching its peak. Between 1955 and 1958, Uruchurtu tore down what was left of the city's Porfirian markets and replaced them with sixty-nine halls with room for more than 29,000 vendors.[129] Twenty thousand stalls were built in 1957 alone, a year in which the Departamento del Distrito spent one-quarter of its budget on the construction of thirty-eight market halls.[130] This was the most intensive rate of market building that Mexico City had ever seen. In the new markets, vendors were provided with refrigerators and scales, while maintenance, security, electricity, and water were paid for by the city, all for a nominal rent. There were day care facilities. Vendors were also offered medical checkups and literacy programs in the markets' premises.[131] In other words, for the tens of thousands of organized vendors who found a place in the new markets, they represented dramatic material progress, providing access to conveniences and social services that had seemed unattainable ten years earlier.

La Merced's inauguration in September 1957 was the most celebrated of all market openings. The departamento had contracted one of the most renowned Mexican architects of the twentieth century, Enrique del Moral, to design it. The market was composed of seven different and separate halls: the

FIGURE 14. Main hall in La Merced Market, 1957. Source: AGN, Fondo Hermanos Mayo, Sección Concentrados, Sobre 1661, 1957.

enormous Nave Mayor, with capacity for 3,205 vendors of fruits and vegetables; the Nave Menor, with 496 stalls dedicated to meat, fish, and dry goods; an adjacent annex devoted to hardware and leather goods; and three smaller sections located in front of the Nave Mayor, one selling toys and clothes, another occupied by 106 stalls selling plants and flowers, and a third for traditional Mexican sweets; finally, there was a separate unit for vendors of prepared foods and drinks. In total, 5,825 comerciantes found a home in La Merced. The complex included a loading and unloading platform that could receive 150 trucks simultaneously as well as parking for 400 vehicles. It had refrigeration chambers, an area for washing fruit and vegetables, public toilets, first aid stations, a police station, and daycare units for the vendors' children.[132] La Merced embodied the promises of a Mexican capitalist modernity, shaped for proprietary vendors.

The public was thrilled. Under headlines such as "Monumental Markets," and "The Biggest Market in the World," the press reported that "more than fifty thousand people of all social classes" had gathered to attend the opening ceremony, presided over by Ruiz Cortines and Uruchurtu. The municipal band played for the crowds. Víctor Manuel Ávila was the first to speak on behalf of the vendors, to express gratitude for the transformation of the area, which until recently, he said, had resembled an unaesthetic "oriental souk," where transit had come to a halt. Addressing the president, he declared that "your ability to coordinate and equilibrate the interests of all sectors guarantees harmony and progress." The president and his jefe del departamento, accompanied by several secretaries of state, then toured the seven buildings of the La Merced complex, receiving "demonstrations of sympathy and affection" at every step of the way.[133]

Excélsior called La Merced "enormous and beautiful." It described the crowds that attended the inauguration as "one of the most spontaneous demonstrations of popular gratitude the city remembered." Cheers of "Long live President Ruiz Cortines, the most conscientious president of Latin America" and "Long live the best regente the city's ever had" resonated in the Nave Mayor.[134] *El Universal* celebrated "the disappearance of the old La Merced and Jamaica Markets," stating that even if with them the city lost "two points of reference for our traditions and history," this was "the natural tribute we must pay to the imperative of modernization." With the inauguration of new markets, Mexico City "has taken a giant step to put itself among the greatest metropolises of the world."[135] *El Nacional* proclaimed that La Merced "dignified small-scale vendors, providing for the health and well-being of their children," and bringing them "comfort and hygiene." The new halls were "works that represent progress and social justice."[136]

Vendor organizations were just as effusive in their praise of the new markets. President Ruiz Cortines received congratulatory telegrams from scores of vendor leaders. Jesús Jiménez Torres for the Alianza de Comerciantes del DF affirmed that "with works like this, Mr. President, you justify the revolution. . . . You have benefited not only small-scale vendors but also the city's consumers, who will now buy their goods at fair prices."[137] Congressman Javier Salgado, in the name of the locatarios of La Merced, sent congratulations for the new market he had given them and reported that the new locatarios pledged to respect official prices and help beat the high cost of living. He assured the president of their most loyal collaboration.[138]

The combination of Uruchurtu's leadership in building new market facilities and Peña Manterola's politicking, including his favoritism in the allocation of market stalls, selective use of violence, and other abuses of office, was a success. As the 1958 election approached, vendors showed their gratitude to the government. In February, combining support for both the government's registration campaign and its efforts to reduce the cost of living,

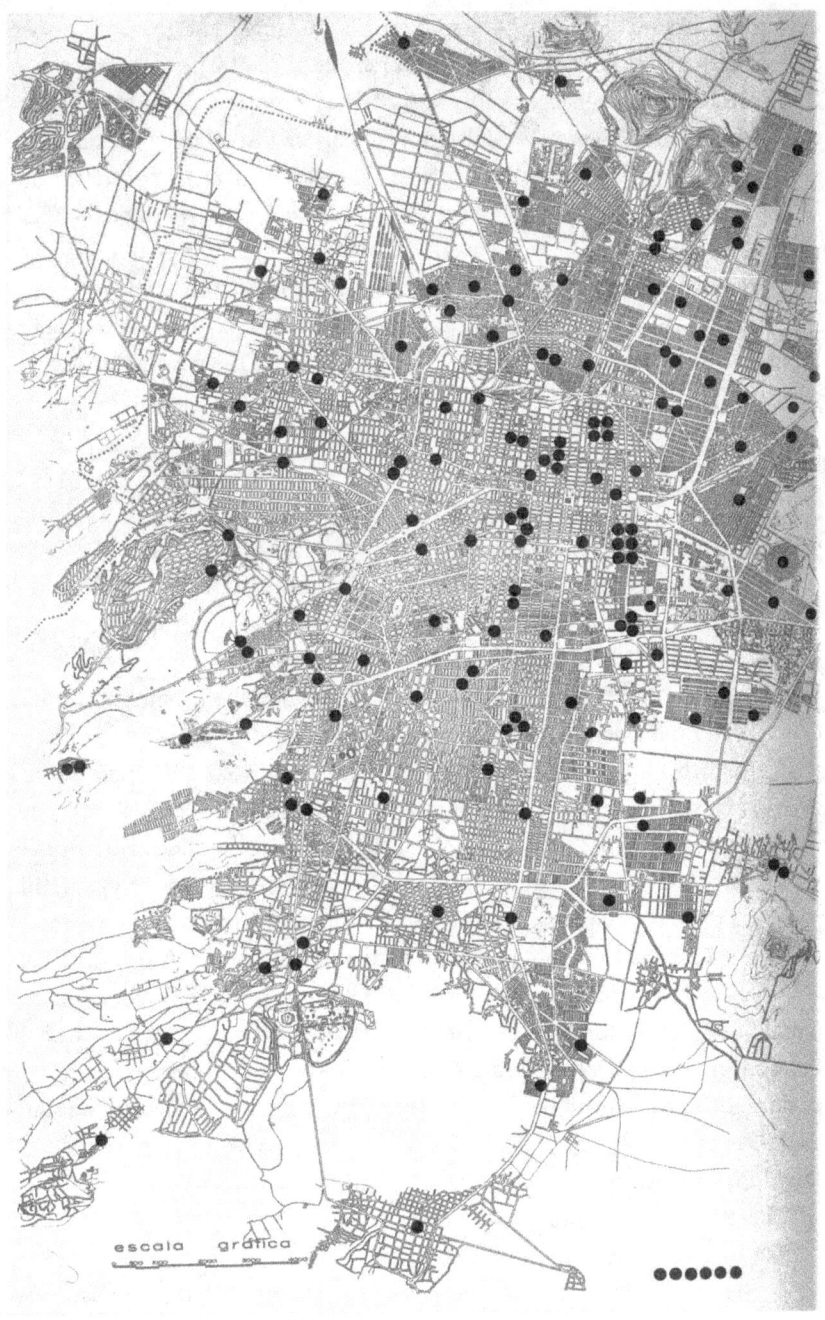

FIGURE 15. Market halls built under Ernesto P. Uruchurtu by 1964. Source: AHCDM. La Ciudad de México, Departamento del Distrito Federal, 1952–1964.

representatives of five organizations, claiming to represent 70,000 vendors, announced they would be offering a 10 percent discount to customers who showed them their registered voter card.[139] That same day, 40,000 vendors attended a rally for the presidential candidacy of the PRI's López Mateos; they explicitly connected their backing with his commitment to continue with Uruchurtu's policies.[140] The July 1958 presidential election was to be the PRI's all-time best in the Federal District.[141] Uruchurtu and Peña Manterola were reappointed by the next two administrations. In their unprecedented fourteen years running the Departamento del Distrito Federal, the city built a total of 174 markets with space for over 52,000 stalls.[142] The payoffs for participating in the politics of developmentalism had never been higher.

Exclusive Inclusion

On May 25, 1961, three hundred vendor representatives gathered in the Folies Bergere Theater to celebrate the Second Congress of CNOP-affiliated locatarios' organizations. The president of the congress, Adolfo Enríquez Guzmán, remarked that "until 1945 the locatarios constituted an anonymous sector in the concert of Mexican progress, a sector that now, with the new public markets built by the federal government . . . takes its rightful place, to contribute with its efforts to collective advancement."[143] Leonardo Salas Valencia, for the Federación de Comerciantes en Pequeño de los Mercados del Distrito Federal, proclaimed the new stalls an invaluable patrimony for locatarios. But, he insisted, their job was not done. It was their duty to protect and augment this patrimony. Salas Valencia vowed to fight for a better functioning of the Banco del Pequeño Comercio; to mobilize to secure direct purchases from producers; and to seek official support for the creation of a colonia where vendors could build houses for their families, as well as for scholarships so that their children could continue their studies. He exhorted the assembly to continue to fight for vendors' unity and for further improvements in their living standards. Buttressed by state support, organized vendors, who had pushed for so long to be included in the drive for modernity, found themselves closer to a middle-class way of life than ever before.

Yet further tens of thousands of vendors remained on the streets, which were even less welcoming than before. While the new markets represented significant material progress for vendors who obtained a stall, those who were left out faced the repressive end of the government's policies. At the time of

La Merced's inauguration, the department bulldozed 3,000 fixed and movable stalls in the area as part of an informal agreement between locatarios and the city government.[144] The authorities would keep the streets surrounding the new markets clear in order to protect those inside the halls from competition. According to the intelligence services, by November 1961 the leaders of the six largest umbrella vendor organizations were meeting every Monday morning to coordinate and organize their petitions to Uruchurtu and to allocate the patronage offered by Peña Manterola's office among their members. They also discussed and negotiated the removal of street vendors, including among their affiliates. The previous month, the department had banned street sales of sweets, *tacos de cabeza*, sandwiches, flavored ices, and thirteen other such products, leaving 15,000 ambulantes without a livelihood. To enforced the prohibition, the police and market inspectors acted brutally against these vendors, beating them and stealing their merchandise. At least 400 vendors had ended up in jail.[145] In the city's public markets, the dark underbelly of developmentalism was as evident as its achievements.

Epilogue

FOR ALMOST A HUNDRED YEARS, Mexico's tumultuous history played out in its public markets. Between 1867 and 1966 proprietary vendors remained at the heart of the political economy of the capital city, both as providers of a key public service and as protagonists in the multiple overlapping conflicts generated by economic development. While the way they made their living showed a high degree of continuity, the country's economy and the social and political structures in which vendors were embedded underwent dramatic transformations. With resilience and creativity, market vendors learned to navigate the changes. They also learned to resist exploitation by suppliers and creditors, and to manage bitter competition within their class. As the city industrialized and the working class grew, vendors' role of supplying urban populations with everyday essentials increasingly meant supplying wage goods. This generated further tensions, particularly in times of high inflation. Throughout it all, vendors demanded a state that promoted, or at least protected, their interests. The negotiations required to sustain the smooth functioning of the city's markets underlay the creation of institutions that supported economic growth. Vendors' collective actions shaped the evolution of the local public sphere, the ebbs and flows of the city council, the corporatist experiments of the 1930s, and eventually the formation of the PRI. For these reasons, vendors' experiences and trajectories provide an apt vantage point from which to study the history of the expansion of capitalism as it unfolded in Mexico.

The market halls that organized vendors obtained in the late 1950s and early 1960s represented the culmination of the trends analyzed in this book.

But the economic and political settlements that had made them possible would not last. Under regente del Departamento del Distrito Federal Ernesto P. Uruchurtu, capitalist development had gone hand in hand with support for selected groups of proprietary producers and traders. Their downfall was the result of a combination of pressures from above and below. Increasingly, big domestic capital in alliance with foreign capital pushed the policy agenda away from the promotion of small- and medium-sized national firms.[1] At the same time, the city's population exploded, despite the efforts of the authorities to control urban growth. A bustling urban economy in the midst of rural poverty generated constant migration to the city and its environs. With a capitalist sector too small and weak to incorporate the young and the newcomers, modernity remained exclusive, at its best broadening participation in economic progress, but leaving vast numbers behind. As the population of poor and self-employed grew, so did the ranks of street vendors. Eventually, their organizations tipped the balance against the smaller constituency of market vendors. In the calculus of the PRI's electoral strategies the streets now counted for more. An already-weakened Uruchurtu was finally ousted in September 1966 in response to outcry at his repression of squatter settlements, home to street vendors and others determined to expose the limits of Mexico's capitalist progress.[2]

After Uruchurtu left office, the construction of new market halls slowed to a trickle. Repairs became rare and sporadic, while the population of ambulantes and other forms of street commerce continued to boom.[3] The fate of public markets foreshadowed a radical shift in the country's (and the region's) political economy. The debt crisis of 1982 catalyzed a wholesale repudiation of state-led development. The growth model that had ushered in the Mexican miracle and given coherence to the state for the previous five decades took the blame for the unsustainability of government debt, more than the spike in international interest rates created by the US Federal Reserve in 1980. The neoliberal turn that followed embraced austerity, liberalization of trade and capital flows, privatizations, and deregulation as the panacea for the country's troubles. Public investment collapsed in the 1980s and 1990s.[4] Per capita GDP did not regain its 1981 peak until 1997; in 2020 real wages had still not regained the levels they reached in the mid-1970s.[5]

A wave of foreign investment after the passage of NAFTA brought the country's maquiladoras to the front pages of the international business press and finally swept in the expansion of supermarkets and convenience stores. Led by Walmart, by 2001 supermarkets accounted for 45 percent of food retailing in the largest cities, perhaps as much as 70 percent in Mexico City.[6] When in 2011 the city's legislature tried to protect public markets by forbidding the construction of new supermarkets and convenience stores within 500 meters of existing halls, the Supreme Court overturned it, citing the constitutional prohibition on monopolies.[7] This was the very same principle that market vendors had deployed during the Mexican Revolution to defend their right to make a living in the city. In 2012 Walmart de México was the largest private employer in the country, with 221,000 employees working across 2,275 supermarkets, stores, and restaurants.[8] Despite supermarkets' dominance, however, the proprietary sector has not been superseded. In Mexico City, according to the local authorities there were still 265,000 vendors across 329 public markets, 1,303 outdoor markets or *tianguis*, 52 mobile markets or *mercados sobre ruedas*, and 215 concentrations of street vendors.[9] Nationally, more than half of the working population remains engaged in the informal economy, most in small operations in production and trade.[10]

Vendors' role in the city's political economy continues to be a subject of tense, at times violent, disputes. In the early hours of February 27, 2013, a fire consumed 7,000 square meters and 1,200 stalls in La Merced Market complex, the largest and most emblematic retail outlet in Mexico. In the days and months that followed, some vendors managed to relocate to other markets, or to improvise tents on nearby streets. Many decided to stay put and continued to ply their trade among the debris. The city government, in partnership with urban planners and real estate developers, saw the conflagration as an opportunity to propose an overhaul of the area. The winning project for the "integral recovery of La Merced" envisioned the creation of a large open square, the development of pedestrian walkways, the restoration of the main market halls, and the replacement of buildings considered of little architectural value. It also proposed the construction of a national culinary center and the modernization of vendors' business models by introducing credit card terminals and shopping carts as well as the suppression of most street sales and other measures to improve traffic flows.

To its critics, this is a project for gentrification, aimed at valorizing downtown real estate and attracting tourists, and bound to exclude the existing vendors and residents.[11] In the 2016 documentary *Permanecer en La Merced*,[12] vendors echo their forbears, expressing their openness to the "revitalization" of their market, as long as they receive specific guarantees that they will be allowed to return to stalls of similar dimensions and in similar locations to those they currently occupy. Their greatest fear, however, is that the government is attempting to privatize public markets, abdicating its historic responsibility to maintain and manage them. To this perceived threat to their patrimony and identity they once again responded by organizing and building solidarity. In the face of their resistance the negotiations with the city government came to a halt and the project stalled. As fortune would have it, on Christmas Eve 2019, La Merced caught fire yet again. The last standing of the locatarios of the main hall have now agreed to vacate the premises, and works are progressing apace. We cannot know what the future will bring, but as the vendors chant, *la lucha sigue*.

Notes

Introduction

1. Neruda, "México florido y espinudo."
2. While historians of Mexico have explored state formation in depth, the process of economic development has not been a focus of historical narratives in recent decades. For the seminal work on state formation, see Joseph and Nugent, *Everyday Forms of State Formation*. What is more, with the exception of Susan Gauss, historians have rarely interrogated the relationship between the two processes. Gauss, *Made in Mexico*.
3. This paragraph and the next synthesize my interpretation of John Womack Jr.'s lecture series at Harvard University on Latin America since 1914 and provide the conceptual underpinnings of this book. Historians of Latin America have a long tradition of analyzing the different modes of production that developed and operated in different times and places, in particular in relationship to the region's participation in the global economy. The emphasis, however, was on the colonial period and the nineteenth century. For an overview, see Stern, "Feudalism, Capitalism, and the World-System in the Perspective of Latin America and the Caribbean." After the 1980s the historiography moved away from these topics as economic history migrated to economics departments and historians embraced the cultural turn. For the case of Mexico, John Tutino's attempt to bridge the global *longue durée* and local social and cultural histories of the Bajío marks the return of capitalism to the tool kit of historians of the region. Tutino, *Making a New World*.
4. Structuralist economic sociologists have analyzed these practices from the perspective of the links between formal and informal economic sectors. Manuel Castells and Alejandro Portes, "World Underneath: The Origins, Dynamics, and Effects of the Informal Economy," in Portes, Castells, and Benton, *Informal Economy*;

Portes and Schauffler, "Competing Perspectives on the Latin American Informal Sector." More recently, historians of global labor have also explored the multiple ways in which value is created, distributed, and appropriated in the world economy, both in the past and in the present. Van der Linden, *Workers of the World*; Komlosy, *Work: The Last 1,000 Years*.

5. Adelman and Levy, "Fall and Rise of Economic History."

6. Sociologist Diane Davis bases her analysis of the political economy of the city between 1929 and 1943 on the *Actas y Versiones del Consejo Consultivo*. She consulted them in what she calls a "semiprivate archive in the Departamento del Distrito Federal." Davis, *Urban Leviathan*, appendix, 325–26. After a long search I found bound volumes containing these sources tucked away on a top floor of the library of the old ayuntamiento building. They were moved to the library of the Archivo Histórico de la Ciudad de México, where I studied them in 2006.

7. The federal government declassified a large body of intelligence reports in 2002, and historians immediately saw their potential. See Aviña, *Specters of Revolution*; McCormick, *Logic of Compromise in Mexico*; Mendiola García, *Street Democracy*. For the methodological and historiographical innovations allowed by the availability of intelligence files, see Padilla and Walker, "In the Archives."

8. There is a dearth of archival materials pertaining to Ernesto P. Uruchurtu's tenure as *regente* of the Federal District between 1952 and 1966 in both the Archivo General de La Nación and Archivo Histórico de la Ciudad de México. Rachel Kram Villarreal reports that according to his relatives, he had kept the files at his personal residence but decided to burn them shortly before his death. By the time they gave her access Uruchurtu's private office, all she found was twenty-five empty filing cabinets. Kram Villarreal, "Gladiolas for the Children of Sánchez, 21–22. His nephew, Alejandro Gárate Uruchurtu, gave me the same account in 2006. It is plausible that the study of Mexico City's midcentury urban redevelopment projects has suffered from the resulting lack of substantive materials. With regard to the CNOP, as Louise Walker writes, to date there is no available archive of this branch of the PRI, which might help explain why we know so little about the middle classes and about how their confederation worked. Walker, *Waking from the Dream*, 16n84 and 17.

9. Thompson's notion of the moral economy refers to the emotions and confrontations over the marketing of foodstuffs in times of severe scarcity in a very specific historical context. E. P. Thompson. "Moral Economy of the English Crowd in the Eighteenth Century"; and "Moral Economy Reviewed," chap. 5. James C. Scott extended the use to peasant studies more broadly in *Moral Economy of the Peasant*, and *Domination and the Arts of Resistance*. For a discussion of the development of the concept of moral economy in European religious and philosophical circles starting in the mid-eighteenth century, see Götz, "Moral Economy." For its application to contemporary Latin America, see Aguirre Rojas, "Edward Palmer Thompson en América Latina."

10. As I discuss in chapter 1, markets produced on average 10 percent of the city council's yearly income between 1869 and 1880. Calculation based on Rodríguez Kuri, *La experiencia olvidada, el Ayuntamiento de México*, 120; *Memoria que*

el Ayuntamiento Constitucional de 1879 presenta a sus comitentes, 220; and *Discurso pronunciado por el Dr. Manuel Domínguez, Regidor 1º del Ayuntamiento Constitucional de México en 1880 al separarse de su puesto el 1º de Enero de 1881, y contestación del C. Pablo de Lascurain, Regidor 2º del Ayuntamiento Constitucional de 1881*, 12. Market revenues were also the most stable source of month-to-month funds. Márquez Colín, "Entre dos mundos."

11. There is growing interest in the role of religion in public life and the construction of the social identities of the popular classes in Mexico. Buffington, *Sentimental Education for the Working Man*; Barajas Durán, *Posada, mito y mitote*; and Forment, *Democracy in Latin America, 1760–1900*.

12. Following Habermas, I understand the public sphere "as a forum in which the private people, come together to form a public, readied themselves to compel public authority to legitimate itself before public opinion." Habermas, *Structural Transformation of the Public Sphere*, 25. However, as many authors have demonstrated, some caveats apply. The construction of a public sphere involved the exclusion of multiple sectors of society, and the model needs rethinking for its application to Latin American realities. Guerra and Lempérière, Introducción; Palti, "Guerra y Habermas"; Piccato, "Public Sphere in Latin America."

13. Evidence of a capitalist expansion can be found in indicators such as the kilometers of railway track, the level of foreign trade and investment, the creation of banking institutions, and the growth of productivity implicit in the growth of GDP per capita. The literature on the economics of the Porfiriato is vast. For two examples, see Kuntz Ficker, *Empresa Extranjera y Mercado Interno*; Connolly, *El Contratista de Don Porfirio*.

14. Lear, "Mexico City, Space and Class"; Tenorio Trillo, "1910 Mexico City."

15. In this chapter I build on a rich body of literature that explores how vendors experienced and reacted to attempts at urban modernization during the Porfiriato. Historians Pablo Piccato, Christina Jiménez, and Mario Barbosa Cruz highlight vendors' creative responses to the elite's attempts to constrain their use of public space between the 1880s and the 1930s, in Mexico City and Morelia. Susie Porter and Judith Martí unearth the gender relations of this period, showing the ways female street and market vendors coped with, and to some extent challenged, upper-class discourses of morality, hygiene, and public order in the national capital and Guadalajara. See Piccato, "Urbanistas, Ambulantes, and Mendigos; Jiménez, "Performing Their Right to the City"; Barbosa Cruz, *El trabajo en las calles*; Porter, "And That It Is Custom Makes It Law"; Martí, "Nineteenth-Century Views of Women's Participation in Mexico's Markets."

16. On the criminalization of the city's popular classes, see Piccato, *City of Suspects*.

17. The implications of the political and administrative reorganization of the city, in terms of both changes and continuities, remain understudied. Two notable exceptions are Rodríguez Kuri, *La experiencia olvidada, el Ayuntamiento de México*; Barbosa Cruz, "La Política en la Ciudad de México."

18. González y González, "La Revolución Mexicana"; Rodríguez Kuri, *Historia del desasosiego*.
19. On workers' activism in these years, see Womack, "Luchas sindicales y liberalismos sociales, 1867–1993"; Lear, *Workers, Neighbors, and Citizens*.
20. "¿Quién disparó?" *El Demócrata*, August 4, 1924, 3.
21. "El pueblo ametrallado por intereses políticos," *El País*, August 3, 1924, 1.
22. Pablo Piccato demonstrates that starting in the 1920s the *nota roja* became an avenue for debates about "the places, characters, motives and outcomes of a public event." As journalists gathered and reproduced testimonies from victims and perpetrators, they fostered discussions about violence in social life among an increasingly engaged public. Piccato, "Murders of *Nota Roja*," 229.
23. Here I am drawing on Davis, *Urban Leviathan*, 65–72. On the government and management of the Federal District, see Sánchez Mejorada's *Rezago de la modernidad*.
24. On the conflicts that pitted the owners of the largest bakeries against small-scale, independent producers and traders of bread, see Weis, "Immigrant Entrepreneurs, Bread, and Class Negotiation in Postrevolutionary Mexico City." A similar trend is discernible in the milk industry. Ochoa, "Reappraising State Intervention and Social Policy in Mexico."
25. This was part of a broader urban reform program that politicians and businessmen pursued in Mexico City in the 1930s. Olsen, *Artifacts of Revolution*; Ageeth Sluis, *Deco Body, Deco City*, chaps. 5–7. For the changing patterns of economic development that underpinned urban reforms of these years, see Cárdenas, *La industrialización mexicana durante la Gran Depresión*; Gauss, *Made in Mexico*.
26. Art historian James Oles considers this market one of the most important urban renovation projects of the decade. Oles, "Noguchi in Mexico," 16.
27. As inflation mounted, price controls and food subsidies were offered as substitutes for nominal wage gains. This trend continued in the 1940s, when the state food agencies NADYRSA (1941–1949) and CEIMSA (1949–1961) became primary vehicles the government used to manage industrial relations. Ochoa, *Feeding Mexico*, chaps. 3–5.
28. The economics of the so-called Mexican miracle have not received significant attention from scholars in recent times. Raymond Vernon's *The Dilemma of Mexico's Development*, published in 1963, remains the most eloquent characterization of the period's political economy. See also Hansen, *Politics of Mexican Development*; Garza, *El proceso de industrialización en la ciudad de México*. For a critical view of the developmental potential of the midcentury economic model, see Carmona et al., *El Milagro Mexicano*. While I do not disagree with Carmona and coauthors that poverty and inequality remained high, my recent work with Amílcar Challú and Paul Segal finds that from the 1950s to the 1970s economic growth was more inclusive than in any other period since independence. Bleynat, Challú, and Segal, "Inequality, Living Standards, and Growth: Two Centuries of Economic Development in Mexico."
29. Ochoa, *Feeding Mexico*, 112–13, 127.

30. Bertaccini, *El régimen priísta frente a las clases medias*, 256–66; Garrido, *El partido de la revolución institucionalizada*, 331–40; Schers, *Popular Sector of the Partido Revolucionario Institucional in Mexico*, 1–20. Alternatively, those scholars who have focused on the groups that constituted the CNOP have seen its creation as the result of the growing power of middle-class professionals and state employees. Soledad Loaeza goes as far as claiming that after 1946 the middle classes held the state hostage. Loaeza, *Clases medias y política en México*, 230.

31. Kram Villareal, "Gladiolas," 17, 51–53. There are not many historical studies of the urban transformations of these years, probably because of the paucity of archival material, as discussed in note 8.

32. John C. Cross and Gary Gordon examine the political behavior of street vendors in Mexico City from 1952 to the 1990s, arguing that a combination of market construction and repression allowed the government to bring vendor organizations under tight control. While there is no doubt this is true, the process was more nuanced. These authors disregard organized vendors' decades-long attempts to engage the state to improve their material condition. They also assume the existence of a coherent state attempting to bend vendor organizations to its will. By tracking vendor activism in the previous decades, and by building on a more recent historiography on the strengths and limitations of the PRI's rule, I show the extent to which the incorporation of vendors to the corporatist structures of midcentury was the product of both negotiation and contestation. Cross, *Informal Politics*; Gordon, "Peddlers, Pesos, and Power."

33. Soledad Loaeza and Louise Walker highlight the importance of the middle classes and the realization of their material and cultural aspirations to the consolidation and legitimation of the PRI. See Loaeza, *Clases medias*; Walker, *Waking from the Dream*. My book finds that market vendors were a crucial part of this story. Walker's groundbreaking book analyzes how the "endless unraveling and remaking" (4) of these middle classes after 1968 illuminate the connections between the dismantling of the midcentury economic development model in the 1980s and the transition to procedural democracy in the 1990s.

34. Given growth in street vendor numbers, in contrast to the fixed number of market stalls after 1966, their political weight within the PRI would overpower that of market vendors in the coming decades. But with further population growth compounded by de-industrialization in the 1980s leading to ever more people taking to the streets to make a living, street vendors also began to organize outside of the PRI. Attempts at managing *ambulantes* and their use of public spaces in the 1990s featured prominently in the demise of the PRI in the capital. Cross, "Debilitando al clientelismo"; Silva Londoño, "Comercio ambulante en el Centro Histórico de la ciudad de México." On the struggles of street vendors in the neoliberal city, see Crossa Niell, *Luchando por un espacio en la ciudad de México*. In contrast to the case of Mexico City, Sandra Mendiola's pioneering work on the economic and political activism of radical street vendors in the city of Puebla shows that starting in the early 1970s their organizations fought hard to reject incorporation by the state, in stark defiance of the PRI. Mendiola, *Street Democracy*.

35. See Delgadillo, "La disputa por los mercados de La Merced," and Téllez Contreras, "Los mercados de San Juan."

36. In contrast, at the turn of the twenty-first century markets only traded around 22 percent of the city's food supply. Castillo Berthier, "Los mercados públicos de la Ciudad de México."

Chapter 1

1. On postindependence turmoil, see MacLachlan and Beezley, *Mexico's Crucial Century, 1810–1910*; on how Maximilian's short-lived reign must necessarily be understood within Mexico's own political developments, see Pani, *Para mexicanizar el segundo imperio*.

2. 7/10/1867, AHCDMX, ACM, RyM, vol. 3733, exp. 446.

3. Katz, "Liberal Republic and the Porfiriato," 49–124; Hamnett, *Juárez*; Knapp, *Life of Sebastián Lerdo de Tejada*; Knight, "El liberalismo mexicano," 59–92.

4. See papal encyclical *Quanta Cura* and its appendix, the *Syllabus Errorum*, both from December 8, 1864. On September 30, 1861, Pius IX had publicly condemned the 1857 Constitution. The Church hierarchy in Mexico had repeatedly threatened to excommunicate anybody who purchased confiscated Church property and, after 1857, public officials who swore allegiance to the Constitution. It had also supported the French intervention. See MacLachlan and Beezley, *Mexico's Crucial Century, 1810–1910*, 90–91; García Ugarte, *Poder político y religioso*.

5. On liberal infighting, see Hamnett, "Liberalism Divided," 659–89; Perry, *Juárez and Díaz*, 184–185; Hale, *Transformation of Liberalism in Late Nineteenth-Century Mexico*. For an analysis of Liberalism from the bottom up, see Thomson, "Popular Aspects of Liberalism in Mexico, 1848–1888," 265–92.

6. On liberalism as an economic project, see Gómez-Galvarriato Freer and Kourí, "La reforma económica"; Carmagnani, *Estado y Mercado*. On economic performance: Cárdenas, *Cuando se originó el atraso económico de México*, chap. 4; Riguzzi, "Los caminos del atraso," 31–97.

7. *Estadísticas históricas de México* (Aguascalientes: Instituto Nacional de Estadística, Geografía e Informática, 1990), 1:24.

8. López Cámara, *La estructura económica y social de México*, 227–28; González y González, Cosío Villegas, and Monroy, *La República Restaurada*, 100. In 1874, a traveler described "The leperos [sic] of the city of Mexico [as] that peculiar nondescript class which in Europe is only to be found in the lazzaroni of Naples. Clad in rags, with no fixed abode, they earn their livelihood in the most mysterious manner, and ever cheerful in temperament, they combine unusual shrewdness with a remarkable ability for repartee." Geiger, *A Peep at Mexico*, 294; on the popularization of the term in Mexico following Humboldt's use of it, see Silvia M. Arrom, *Containing the Poor*, 34–35.

9. Illades, "Composición de la fuerza de trabajo," 2:265–68; Calderón, *La República Restaurada*, 87–88; Castillo Méndez, *Historia del comercio en la Ciudad*

de México, 45–46. On bakeries, see Weis, *Bakers and Basques*. In contrast, larger factories tended to be in the city's outskirts; for example, glass was produced near el Paseo de la Viga, crockery at Salto del Agua on the road to San Ángel, and cloth and paper in San Ángel, la Magdalena, and Tlalpan. López Monjardin, "El espacio en la producción," 57. On textile production, see Keremitsis, *La industria textil mexicana en el siglo XIX*. A list of types of commercial and industrial establishments in Mexico in 1879 and a census of industrial establishments in the capital can be found in volume 1 of Busto, *Estadística de la República Mexicana*.

10. Geiger, *Peep at Mexico*, 250.

11. Arróniz, *Manual del viajero en Méjico; o, Compendio de la historia de la Ciudad de Méjico*, 41.

12. Pilcher, "Fajitas and the Failure of Refrigerated Meatpacking in Mexico," 417. Popular consumption of meat was not a new phenomenon: Quiroz, *Entre el lujo y la subsistencia*.

13. López Cámara, *Estructura económica y social*, 83–84.

14. Several examples can be found in Gortari Rabiela and Hernández Franyuti, *Memoria y encuentros*, 3:188–207.

15. Geiger, *Peep at Mexico*, 290–91. *Aguadores* are water carriers; *carboneros* are sellers of charcoal, their *huacalitos* being their baskets. *Dulces* is a generic word for sweets; *agua fresca* is flavored water, usually with fruits or flowers.

16. Porter, *Working Women in Mexico City*, 133–38; Arrom, *Women of Mexico City*, 158–59; Thompson, "Artisans, Marginals, and Proletarians," 1:308–12.

17. *Memoria que el Ayuntamiento Popular de 1869 presenta a sus comitentes*, 159–60. Hereafter *Memoria 1869*. The same applies to other *Memorias*.

18. Earlier in the century, customers had gone to public markets in search of both imported and Mexican products as well as to provide themselves with luxury and basic items. The richest retail merchants, those with shops in El Parián Market in the city center, had sold imported luxury goods, including textiles from Japan and the Philippines. Looted in 1828 in the midst of the Acordada revolt, El Parián went into a decline that lasted until 1843 when President Santa Anna ordered its demolition. As importers sought private accommodations, public markets became specialized in the sale of Mexican products for everyday consumption while retailers of more luxury goods relocated to private establishments. Prieto, *Memorias de mis tiempos*, 33–35; Arrom, "Popular Politics in Mexico City," 256; Yoma Medina and Martos López, *Dos mercados de en la historia de la Ciudad de México*, 58–59; for the revolt in the broader political context, see Warren, *Vagrants and Citizens*, chap. 4; Stevens, "Riot, Rebellion, and Instability in Nineteenth-Century Mexico," 1:344–54. For a thorough history of El Parián as well as of the foodstuffs and secondhand goods markets that occupied the Plaza Mayor from the sixteenth century to the 1790s, see Olvera Ramos, *Los mercados de la Plaza Mayor de México*; on el Baratillo in particular, see Konove, *Black Market Capital*.

19. *Memoria que el Ayuntamiento constitucional del año de 1868 presenta para el conocimiento de sus comitentes*, 149.

20. The plaza where vendors gathered was the result of the demolition of part of the ex-convent of the order La Merced. 3/1/1865, AHCDMX, ACM, RyM, vol. 3733, exp. 424; 2/28/1865, vol. 3733, exp. 427.

21. *Memoria 1868*, 155–56.

22. Fires were increasingly common in this period, not just in markets. Alexander, *City on Fire*.

23. Alexander, *City on Fire*, 154; *Memoria 1869*, 161.

24. "Sobre ordenanzas de los mercados," in Castillo Velasco, *Colección de leyes*, 319–23; *Reglamento para el nuevo mercado de San Juan de la Penitenciaria de la Ciudad de México*, 1850, arts. 3, 6, and 11. A complete version of this document can be found in Archivo Salubridad Pública: Fondo Salubridad Pública, sección Higiene Pública, serie Inspección de Alimentos y Bebidas, caja 1, exp. 3. It is also reproduced, though partially, under the title of "Reglamento para el mercado Iturbide," in Gortari Rabiela and Hernández Franyuti, *Memoria y encuentros*, 3:219–20. The references in this chapter are from the complete document, hereafter referred to as *Reglamento mercado San Juan*.

25. *Memoria 1868*, 154; "Informe presentado el 16 de Junio por la Comisión de Mercados," *Municipio Libre*, June 26, 1879, 1.

26. *Reglamento mercado San Juan*, arts. 7, 8, 10, 11, and 12.

27. This will eventually change, as later governments tried to free up space in order to increase the number of vendors located within halls.

28. 10/25/1877, AHCDMX, ACM, RyM, vol. 3735, exp. 789; "De la Comisión de Mercados," *Municipio Libre*, November 24, 1877, 1; 1/31/1878, AHCDMX, ACM, RyM, vol. 3736, exp. 813; "De la Comisión de Hacienda," *Municipio Libre*, February 9, 1878, 1.

29. *Reglamento mercado San Juan*, art. 43; "Informe presentado el 16 de Junio por la Comisión de Mercados," *Municipio Libre*, June 26, 1879, 1; "[De la] Comisión de Mercados," *Municipio Libre*, April 21, 1887, 1.

30. Pilcher, "Fajitas," 416.

31. *Reglamento mercado San Juan*, art. 35. In 1862 the ayuntamiento had decided that contracts should not exceed three years, though they could be renewed. 6/27/1862, AHCDMX, ACM, RyM, vol. 3732, exp. 359; 6/20/1862, AHCDMX, ACM, RyM, vol. 3732, exp. 361. Merchants, however, continued to request longer leases, especially after investing in improvements to the stalls, and often obtained them. 09/27/1866, AHCDMX, ACM, RyM, vol. 3733, exp. 431.

32. Castillo Méndez, *Historia del comercio*, 46. *Petates* were multipurpose mats used by those in the lower classes during their complete life cycle, starting as cradle, then as bed, tablecloth, and umbrella, and finally as shroud. González y González, Cosío Villegas, and Monroy, *La República Restaurada*, 255.

33. *Memoria que el Ayuntamiento Popular de 1869 presenta a sus comitentes*, 165. For the following decades, Diego G. López Rosado puts the total number of people selling in public markets every day at more than three thousand. López Rosado, *Los mercados de la Ciudad de México*, 189. He gives no indication of the source of this estimate, however.

34. Martí, "Subsistence and the State," 131; *Memoria 1868*, 157–59.
35. Pilcher, "Fajitas," 417; *Memoria 1868*, 153.
36. Silva Riquer, "El abasto al mercado urbano de la Ciudad de México, 1830–1860," 182.
37. Gibson, *Aztecs under Spanish Rule*, 321. The major chinampa region, which extended from Santa Ana, Ixtacalco, and San Juanico to Mexicalzingo and Xochimilco, survived into the twentieth century.
38. Bullock, *Six Months Residence and Travels in Mexico*, 188–89. In late January 1873, a Spanish journalist traveling to the city on the occasion of the inauguration of the first railway connecting Veracruz with the capital, visited the chinampas and wrote, eloquently if naively, "I think I have just contemplated Moctezuma's empire as Cortés found it, with its flower islands, its delicious *huertas*, its canoes, and its Indians." Vérgez, *Recuerdos de Méjico*, 197. This was not just a foreigner's view; for similar claims by a famous local chronicler, see García Cubas, "Las Estaciones en el Valle de México," in *Escritos Diversos de 1870 a 1874*, 107.
39. Pérez Hernández reports the number of canoe loads entering Mexico City as 78,934 and 81,217 in 1860 and 1861 respectively, in Pérez Hernández, *Estadística de la República Mejicana*, 171.
40. 05/22/1871, AHCDMX, ACM, RyM, vol. 3734, exp. 550.
41. *Reglamento mercado San Juan*, in particular, arts. 4–5, 18, 24–25, 27, and 60–65. A short description of the administrator's job can be found in 12/10/1869, AHCDMX, ACM, Empleados, Mercados, vol. 965, exp. 18.
42. "Ordenanzas formadas por la Junta Departamental en el año de 1840," in Castillo Velasco, *Colección de leyes*, 293–339.
43. Rodríguez Kuri, *La experiencia olvidada, el Ayuntamiento de México*, 26.
44. The ayuntamiento's control over public markets developed not only in competition with other authorities but also by removing certain lucrative assets and activities from private hands. Over the first two decades after independence, for instance, the council bought the plazas in which markets were held from their individual owners and began renting out its own tripod parasols, the *sombras*. Most significantly, in 1837 the ayuntamiento bought the property on which El Volador Market was located from the Marquesado del Valle de Oaxaca, the biggest nonecclesiastic urban real estate holder of the time. Morales, "Estructura urbana y distribución de la propiedad de la Ciudad de México en 1813," 385–86, 399–400. In the case of the sombras, the ayuntamiento had been calling attention to the need to secure their rents from at least as early as 1830, when it had reported that three individuals were renting out five hundred tripod parasols, producing 4,800 pesos per annum, in violation of the principle that markets were "for the benefit of the ayuntamiento." The markets commission recommended that the council either build or buy the parasols and hire employees, who, under the watch of the administrator, would set them up and put them away each day. *Memoria económica de la Municipalidad de México formada por orden del Exceléntisimo Ayuntamiento, por comisión de su seno en 1830* (Mexico City: Martín Rivere, 1830), quoted in Gortari Rabiela and Hernández Franyuti, *Memoria y*

encuentros, 3:168. By the late 1830s the council had purchased 797 sombras from four individuals. 03/15/1836, AHCDMX, ACM, RyM, vol. 3730, exp. 130. By the late 1870s this had become standard practice. See, for example, "De la [Comisión] de Mercados," *Municipio Libre*, July 11, 1878, 1.

45. Orozco y Berra, *Historia de la Ciudad de México, desde su fundación hasta 1854: Selección de artículos publicados en el Diccionario Universal de Historia y Geografía (1854) preparada por el Seminario de Historia Urbana del Departamento de Investigaciones Históricas del INAH* (Mexico City: Secretaría de Educación Pública, Septentas, 1973), 122–31.

46. On how this fiscal structure was inherited from colonial times, and on how it changed in the 1810s and then as a result of independence, see Moncada González, *La libertad comercial*, chap. 3; on the proportion of *propios* and *arbitrios* during the first half of the nineteenth century, see Gamboa Ramírez, "Las finanzas municipales de la Ciudad de México, 1800–1850"; on the importance of the derechos municipales: Rodríguez, Kuri, *La Experiencia olvidada, el Ayuntamiento de México*, chap. 4; on the *alcabalas*: Silva Riquer, "El abasto," 64–76; on the fiscal structure of another Mexican city: Téllez Guerrero and Brito Martínez, "La hacienda municipal de Puebla en el siglo XIX," 951–78; on the state of Mexico, including its relationship with the national government: Marichal, Miño Grijalva, and Riguzzi, *El primer siglo de la hacienda pública del Estado de México*; on the political tenets of Mexican liberal fiscal policy, see Carmagnani, "El liberalismo, los impuestos internos y el estado federal mexicano," 471–96.

47. Gamboa Ramírez, "Las finanzas," 50–55.

48. Constitution of 1857, art. 23. On desamortization of ecclesiastical properties: Bazant, *Alienation of Church Wealth in Mexico*; on the liberal reforms the desamortization laws were part of, see Sinkin, *Mexican Reform*.

49. Morales, "Espacio, propiedad y órganos de poder en la ciudad de México en el siglo XIX," 169.

50. Beyond markets, hospitals, abattoirs, and cemeteries made the bulk of the properties that would remain in the hands of the ayuntamiento.

51. "Ley para la dotación del fondo Municipal de México, decreto de la Regencia del Imperio del 25 de septiembre de 1863," reproduced in *Memoria de los principales ramos de la policía urbana y de los fondos de la Ciudad de México presentado a la Serenísima Regencia del Imperio en cumplimiento de sus órdenes y de las leyes por el Prefecto Municipal*, 198–209; "Ley de 28 de noviembre de 1867," in Islas y Bustamante, *Colección de leyes y disposiciones gubernativas*, 1:6–7.

52. *Memoria que el Ayuntamiento Constitucional de 1870 presenta a sus comitentes*, 159.

53. There are notes on the scarcity the ayuntamiento endured in literally every Memoria Municipal, especially in the section on public works; a straightforward editorial describing the scope of the responsibilities of the city council, and expressing frustration about the financial constraints it faced when attempting to act on them, as well as about the dependency on federal authorities, can be found in the council's periodical, "Administración Municipal," *Municipio Libre*, July 28, 1877, 1.

54. Market revenues were also the ayuntamiento's most stable source of funds. Márquez Colín, "Entre dos mundos."

55. *Memoria 1868*, 151.

56. *Memoria 1869*, 159–60.

57. *Memoria 1869*, 159–60.

58. 12/23/1873, AHCDMX, GD, OP, vol. 1755, exp. 124.

59. "Comisión de Mercados," *Municipio Libre*, January 10, 1884, 2.

60. According to the city authorities, it was the small number and poor state of public markets that led so many people to sell *al viento*. On how the lack of a market in the sixth borough meant that stalls were scattered around, see *Memoria 1869*, 172. On how the poor state of La Merced Market made many vendors prefer to sell on other locations: *Memoria 1870*, 190.

61. *Memoria del Ayuntamiento que comenzó a funcionar el 5 de Diciembre de 1876 y concluyó el 31 de Diciembre de 1877*, 90–91.

62. *Memoria 1877*, 89–90.

63. According to Gamboa, during the first half of the nineteenth century paternalistic attitudes were still more important than economic reasons when it came to the ayuntamiento's collection of rents over its rural and urban properties, including markets. Gamboa Ramírez, "Las finanzas," 35. Compassion extended beyond markets. Warren believes that ayuntamiento members were fully aware of the city's population's "real opportunities and obstacles," and that this is why, despite the criticism it attracted, no more than 10 percent of the people brought in front the Vagrancy Tribunal between 1828 and 1850 were convicted. Warren, *Vagrants and Citizens*, 14. Arrom argues that a customary tolerance of the poor throughout most of the nineteenth century meant that mendicancy was a socially acceptable way to earn a living. She also finds that *Reforma* Liberals' (including Juárez's) views of welfare had clear Christian connotations, and that Christian charity had not given way to secular beneficence in the early 1870s. Arrom, *Containing the Poor*, 220–22; 284; Blum shows that civic piety remained at the center of elite identity during the Porfiriato. Ann S. Blum, "Conspicuous Benevolence," 7–38; for a general treatise on nineteenth-century public morality, see Escalante Gonzalbo, *Ciudadanos imaginarios*.

64. Thompson, "Moral Economy of the English Crowd," 76–136; Fox-Genovese, "Many Faces of Moral Economy," 161–68; Thompson, "Moral Economy Reviewed," chap. 5. The more recent literature follows Scott's *Moral Economy of the Peasant*, and *Domination and the Arts of Resistance*.

65. 1 Corinthians 13:13; Thomas Aquinas, *Summa Theologica*, I-II, Question 114, "Merit," art. 4. More broadly, see *Summa*, II-II, Questions 23–122, "Charity," "Prudence," and "Justice."

66. *Summa*, II-II, Question 30, "Mercy," art. 1; more broadly, see *Summa*, II-II, Questions 23–122, on charity, prudence, and justice.

67. On how in the second half of the nineteenth century Catholic theologians turned to Aquinas to respond to the infiltration of post-Enlightenment philosophy into Catholicism, see McCool, *Catholic Theology in the Nineteenth Century*, chap. 1;

MacIntyre, *Three Rival Versions of Moral Enquiry*, chap. 3. On how a minority of senior Catholic clergy in Europe met in several conferences to debate the "social question," eventually shaping the Church's social doctrine, see Aubert, "Aux origines de la doctrine sociale catholique," 249–78. These debates and discussions would crystallize in Pope Leo XIII's encyclicals "Aeternis Patris" ("On the Restoration of Christian Philosophy"), 1879, and "Rerum Novarum" ("On Capital and Labor"), 1891.

68. "Un obsequio al Federalista," La Voz de México, June 3, 1871, 1; more generally, see Adame Goddard, *El pensamiento político y social de los Católicos Mexicanos*, 115–17.

69. *Instrucción pastoral que los Illmos. Sres. Arzobispos de México, Michoacán y Guadalajara dirigen a su venerable clero y a sus fieles con ocasión de la Ley Orgánica expedida por el Soberano Congreso Nacional en 10 de diciembre del año próximo pasado [1874] y sancionada por el Supremo Gobierno en 14 del mismo mes*, 25.

70. *Catálogo comentado del acervo del Museo Nacional de Arte. Pintura Siglo XIX*, vol. 1 (Mexico City: Museo Nacional de Arte, 2002), 323–28. The painting received much praise; it would be sent to the Paris Universal Exhibition of 1889 and to the Chicago World's Columbian Exposition of 1893 to represent the country's artistic achievements.

71. Buffington, *Sentimental Education for the Working Man*, 54. Some Liberal criticisms of the hypocrisy of the Conservatives and the Church were grounded in the teachings of the New Testament. Barajas Durán, *Posada, mito y mitote*, 91, quoted in Buffington, *Sentimental Education for the Working Man*, 55.

72. Buffington, *Sentimental Education for the Working Man*, 57.

73. Chenillo Alazraki, "Liberalismo a prueba: La expulsión de 'extranjeros perniciosos'," *Revista de Indias* 72, no. 255 (2012): 377–408, at 396.

74. Philosophers had pondered the relation between authority, prosperity, and subordination since Aristotle. Mexican Liberals might have encountered these ideas in Edmund Burke's writings. On Burke's political economy, including his view that "natural subordination" was necessary for industriousness and economic progress, see Macpherson, *Burke*, 51–70.

75. *Fiscal Law of 1867*, art. 116, quoted in "Oficio del 21 de octubre," *Municipio Libre*, November 7, 1878, 1–2.

76. In Arteaga's arguments we find evidence of the three elements or moments that theologians associate with compassion: having awareness and knowledge of another's distress (cognitive), being moved by or suffering because of this distress (affective), and taking actions to try to remedy it (volitional). Davies, *A Theology of Compassion*. See also Nussbaum, "Compassion: The Basic Social Emotion," 27–58.

77. The presentation of the case in the ayuntamiento meeting, the letter by Arteaga to the governor of the Federal District and secretario de gobernación, and the national executive's response and decree can be found in *Recopilación de leyes, decretos y providencias de los poderes legislativo y ejecutivo de la Unión*, 442–50.

78. Júarez's antagonistic decree might have been a response to the fact that several ayuntamiento members had supported Sebastián Lerdo de Tejada against the

president in his quest for reelection in the summer of 1871. Perry, *Júarez and Díaz*, 153–57.

79. *Memoria 1872*, 141.
80. *Memoria 1872*, 141.
81. *Memoria 1877*, 94.
82. *Memoria 1870*, 190.
83. 4/27/1870, AHCDMX, ACM, RyM, vol. 3733, exp. 536. The weather reference probably refers to the fact that all of the comerciantes there sold al viento.
84. La Merced was one of the lowest points of the city and therefore one of the most severely affected by the recurrent floods of the period.
85. *Memoria 1870*, 191.
86. Some of these documents were produced with the help of a scribe, or "evangelista." Though the scribes might have added their own opinions and biases to the correspondence, the fact that vendors repeatedly paid for their services indicates they were confident that their interests were well represented.
87. 4/29/1868, AHCDMX, ACM, RyM, vol. 3733, exp. 484.
88. *Memoria Corporación Municipal que funcionó de Agosto a Diciembre de 1867*, 30; *Memoria 1868*, 149.
89. This, of course, did not mean they would always succeed; 1/28/1874, AHCDMX, ACM, RyM, vol. 3735, exp. 643.
90. 9/11/1872, AHCDMX, ACM, RyM, vol. 3734, exp. 576.
91. 11/29/1875, AHCDMX, ACM, RyM, vol. 3735, exp. 689.
92. Under the provisions of art. 9 of the 1857 Constitution and the Civil Code of 1870, artisans and workers (including commercial employees) organized "voluntary associations." In their struggles against capitalists and bosses, these mutualist societies sometimes worked like trade unions, fighting privately, as did the hatters in Mexico City, which held a successful strike in 1875. Most often, though, they sought protection and privileges from the authorities by participating in political activities and campaigns. While those belonging to losing factions were repressed, those with successful patrons gained access to scarce public funds and some degree of political representation. Womack, "Luchas sindicales y liberalismos sociales, 1867–1993," 418–19; Walker, "Porfirian Labor Politics," 257–89; Illades, "Organizaciones laborales y discurso asociativo en el siglo XIX," 245–74.
93. "La Comisión de Hacienda," *Municipio Libre*, November 1, 1878, 1.
94. "Oficio del 21 de octubre," *Municipio Libre*, November 7, 1878, 1–2.
95. *Memoria de los ramos municipales correspondiente al semestre de Julio a Diciembre de 1866 presentada a S.M. el Emperador por el Alcalde Municipal de la Ciudad de México D. Ignacio Trigueros* (Mexico City: Imprenta Económica, 1867), 8.
96. *Memoria que el Ayuntamiento Popular de 1868 presenta a sus comitentes y corresponde al semestre corrido desde el 1 de Enero al 30 de Junio* (Mexico City: Imprenta de Ignacio Cumplido, 1868), 2–3. Following Jürgen Habermas's development of the concept, the public sphere is tentatively understood "as a forum in which the private people, come together to form a public, readied themselves to compel public authority

to legitimate itself before public opinion." Habermas, *Structural Transformation of the Public Sphere*, 25. Some caveats apply, however. The construction of a public sphere involved the exclusion of different sectors of society, as many authors have demonstrated. Moreover, there are limitations to the appropriation of the model of the public sphere for understanding Latin American realities. There, not only women, whether literate or not, were excluded from the public sphere, but possessing enough cultural capital to access printed material was a necessary, though not sufficient, condition for men. Also, unlike the European cases Habermas analyzed, in Latin America modern political forms did not emerge out of the needs of any particular social class but out of the political crisis generated by the collapse of the Spanish Empire. Besides, these societies still lacked a local bourgeoisie with the potential to become a dominant class. Guerra and Lempérière, Introducción to *Los espacios públicos*; Piccato, "Introducción: ¿Modelo para armar?"

97. "La Comisión de Hacienda," *Municipio Libre*, November 1, 1878, 1.

98. For example, in the late 1870s *La Patria* was directed by old-time liberal Ireneo Paz. Vicente García Torres, the owner of *El Monitor Republicano*, was a member of the ayuntamiento in 1872. Between 1878 and 1880 José María Vigil was also an active writer in *El Monitor*. Moisés González Navarro, *Porfiriato: Vida social*, vol. 4, *Historia moderna*, Cosío Villegas (1957), 675–82; Perry, *Juárez and Díaz*, 184–85; Hale, *Transformation of Liberalism*, 64–69, 92; Piccato, "Honor y opinión pública," 145–78, esp. 151–55.

99. Perry, *Júarez and Díaz*, 184nn15–16.

100. 04/9/1878, AHCDMX, ACM, RyM, vol. 3736, exp. 800. The outsourcing of the management and administration of markets had been common in colonial and early republican times. See Moncada González, "La gestión municipal," 39–62.

101. Quoted in "Una pregunta," *Monitor Republicano*, July 11, 1878, 3; "Más sobre el arrendamiento de los mercados," *La Colonia Española*, July 26, 1878, 3.

102. Quoted in "También La Patria," *Monitor Republicano*, July 19, 1878, 3.

103. "Es la ruina," *Monitor Republicano*, July 18, 1878, 3.

104. "Las rentas de los mercados públibos," *La Patria*, June 13, 1878, 2.

105. "Mercados," *Monitor Republicano*, August 3, 1878, 3.

106. "Mercados," *Monitor Republicano*, August 3, 1878, 3.

107. For a discussion of the idea of public opinion as a tribunal, see Palti, "La transformación del liberalismo mexicano en el siglo XIX," 67–95; on journalists as an honor group pronouncing on vital issues, Piccato, "Honor y opinión pública," 146.

108. Piccato, *Tyranny of Opinion*.

109. "La Comisión de Hacienda," *Municipio Libre*, November 1, 1878, 1.

110. "Falta de higiene," *Monitor Republicano*, January 17, 1875, 3.

Chapter 2

1. Arguments invoking rights "since time immemorial" had a long history in Mexico. For examples related to colonial disputes over land, see Gibson, *Aztecs under*

Spanish Rule, 577–99. Rural villagers and municipal authorities continued to use these rights in the nineteenth century: Craib, *Cartographic Mexico*; in urban contexts herbs vendors in public markets did as well: Campos, *Home Grown*, 149; finally, female street vendors tried to bring these claims into the early twentieth century: Porter, "And That It Is Custom Makes It Law," 135–37.

2. Riguzzi, "México, Estados Unidos y Gran Bretaña, 365–436; Hart, *Empire and Revolution*; Riguzzi, *¿La reciprocidad imposible?*; Pletcher, *Rails, Mines, and Progress*); Tischendorf, *Great Britain and Mexico in the Era of Porfirio Díaz*; Schell, *Integral Outsiders*.

3. On the social savings produced by railroads, see the classic Coatsworth, *Growth against Development*; on their contribution to the development of a national market, Kuntz Ficker, "Los ferrocarriles y la formación del espacio económico en México," 105–37; on the effects of railroads on the textile industry, Gómez-Galvarriato Freer, *Industry and Revolution: Social and Economic Change in the Orizaba Valley*. On industrial policy, Beatty, *Institutions and Investment: The Political Basis of Industrialization in Mexico before 1911*. On terms of trade and industrialization, Aurora Gómez-Galvarriato and Jeffrey Williamson, "Was It Prices, Productivity, or Policy? Latin American Industrialisation after 1870," *Journal of Latin American Studies* 41, no. 4 (November 2009): 663–94. On foreign trade and federal finances, Kuntz Ficker, "Las nuevas series del comercio exterior de México," 213–70; Carmagnani, *Estado y Mercado*. On land sales, Holden, *Mexico and the Survey of Public Lands*.

4. Because of the fluctuating and declining price of silver in international markets, which hurt Mexico's terms of trade and the value of the silver-based Mexican peso, the fulfilment of foreign obligations at times became burdensome. The situation was most critical between 1890 and 1894 when, with conditions aggravated by a global recession, the federal government came close to bankruptcy and default. On institutions and debt, Marichal, "Construction of Credibility," 93–119; Zabludovsky, "La deuda externa pública," 152–89. On the price of silver and terms of trade in general, Pletcher, "Fall of Silver in Mexico," 33–55; Beatty, "Impact of Foreign Trade on the Mexican Economy," 399–433.

5. Valadés, *El Porfirismo, historia de un regimen*; Katz, "Liberal Republic and the Porfiriato," 49–124.

6. Tenorio Trillo, *Artilugio de la nación moderna*, 56.

7. A summary of the economic trends in this period can be found in Cárdenas, *Cuando se originó el atraso económico de México*, chap. 5. A new price index can be found in Gómez-Galvarriato Freer and Musacchio, "Un Nuevo Índice de Precios para México, 1886–1929," 45–91.

8. Lear, "Mexico City: Space and Class in the Porfirian Capital," 454–92; Tenorio Trillo, "1910 Mexico City," 75–104. State capitals underwent similar transformations. For the case of Mérida, for example, see Wells and Joseph, *Summer of Discontent, Seasons of Upheaval*, chap. 5.

9. Rodríguez Kuri, *La experiencia olvidada, el Ayuntamiento de México*, 104–13; Barbosa Cruz, *El trabajo en las calles*, 31–47.

10. On the territorial expansion of the city, see Morales, "La expansion de la ciudad de México (1858–1910)," 64–68; Morales, "La expansion de la ciudad de México en el siglo XIX," 189–200. On population: *Estadísticas históricas de México*, 1:24; Davies, "Tendencias demográficas urbanas durante el siglo XIX en México," 481–524. On colonias and their developers, Jiménez Muñoz, *La traza del poder*, chaps. 1–5. On public works, Kuntz Ficker and Connolly, *Ferrocarriles y obras públicas*, part 2.

11. In these years, despite significant GDP per capita growth, real wages in Mexico City saw no upward trend. While they grew between 1881 and 1888, they then declined again so that in 1900 they were slightly lower than around 1880. Bleynat, Challú, and Segal, "Inequality, Living Standards and Growth."

12. Lear, *Workers, Neighbors, and Citizens*, 21, 27.

13. *Discurso 1884*, 5. Ann Blum finds that public symbols of charity and social control such as correctional schools and insane asylums were central to the construction and consolidation of the civic identity of the social and political classes loyal to Díaz. Blum, "Conspicuous Benevolence," 7–38. According to Manuel Perló Cohen, Porfirio Díaz's personal word, honor, and prestige were invested in the city's drainage project, an enterprise that embodied his quest for modernity and civilization. Perló Cohen, *El paradigma porfiriano*, 296–97. Mauricio Tenorio Trillo argues that the attempt to construct a modern and cosmopolitan image of Mexico at the world fairs gave the Porfirian elite a sense of identity and unity. Tenorio Trillo, *Artilugio de la nación moderna*, 38.

14. *Discursos Ayuntamiento 1880*, 10–11.

15. *Discurso pronunciado por el Dr. Manuel Domínguez*, 3–5, 9, 39–40; *Discurso pronunciado por el Sr. Pedro Rincón Gallardo*, 5.

16. *Discursos Ayuntamiento 1881*, 7. Antonio García Cubas, probably our best source for this period, puts the population of Mexico City at 225,000 in 1870 and at 300,000 in 1884. Davies, "Tendencias demográficas urbanas durante el siglo XIX en México," 501.

17. Rodríguez Kuri shows that in the 1880s nominal municipal revenue doubled, with nominal expenditure per capita growing by 96 percent between 1885 and 1890. Rodríguez Kuri, *La experiencia olvidada, el Ayuntamiento de México*, 118. Real figures are calculated by deflating nominal revenues with Aurora Gómez-Galvarriato and Aldo Musacchio's inflation estimates.

18. *Reseña leída por el Presidente Municipal en nombre de la corporación que funcionó en 1882, contestación del Segundo Regidor Lic. Guillermo Valle y discurso del C. Gobernador del Distrito Federal al instalar el Ayuntamiento de 1883*, 48.

19. *Discurso leído el 1º de Enero de 1884 por el C. Pedro Rincón Gallardo como Presidente del Ayuntamiento de 1883 dando cuenta de su administración, contestación del C. Lic. Guillermo Valle Presidente del Ayuntamiento de 1884 y discurso del C. Gobernador del Distrito Federal al instalar la nueva corporación*, 38. When I quote one of these publications more than once, I refer to it by the administrative year that ends at the time of the addresses, so for the present case, subsequent quotes will read *Discursos Ayuntamiento 1883*. The documents describe works that took place that year, as well as expectations for the following one.

20. Ródiguez Kuri, *La experiencia olvidada, el Ayuntamiento de México*, 59. More broadly, the author traces the municipal government's gradual political and institutional decline starting in 1880.

21. *Discursos Ayuntamiento 1883*, 29.

22. At one point in August 1893, there were twenty-nine journalists from nine different newspapers in prison. Piccato, "Honor y opinión pública," 160–69.

23. Connolly, *El contratista de don Porifirio*; Rodríguez Kuri, "Gobierno local y empresas de servicios," 165–90.

24. *Reseña Ayuntamiento 1882*, 46–48.

25. Davies, "Tendencias demográficas urbanas durante el siglo XIX en México," 501.

26. Lanny Thompson maintains that a common laborer needed between two and two and a half times his or her customary wage to support a family of four, while skilled artisans, factory mechanics, and other better paid workers needed up to one and a half times their wage. Thompson, "Artisans, Marginals, and Proletarians," 1:308. While the dearth of social statistics demands caution, scattered information on high mortality rates, incidence of disease, and overcrowded housing conditions support this view. Agostoni, *Monuments of Progress*, 26–27, 65–76.

27. The largest sources of municipal revenue were fees for markets and abattoirs, water rights, and taxes on alcohol sales. For the different categories contributing to the city's coffers, see Rodríguez Kuri, *La experiencia olvidada, el Ayuntamiento de México*, 279–83.

28. *Discursos Ayuntamiento 1883*, 27–28.

29. *Discursos Ayuntamiento 1883*, 18.

30. *Discurso leído el 1º de Enero de 1885 por el C. Guillermo Valle, como Presidente del Ayuntamiento de 1884 dando cuenta de su administración, contestación del Lic. Pedro Rincón Gallardo, Presidente del Ayuntamiento de 1885, y discurso del C. Gobernador del Distrito Federal al instalar la nueva Corporación*, 34–35; *Discurso leído el 1º de Enero de 1886 por el C. Pedro Rincón Gallardo como Presidente del Ayuntamiento de 1885, dando cuenta de su administración, contestación del C. Manuel González Cosío y Discurso del C. Gobernador del Distrito al instalar la nueva Corporación*, 32.

31. This was not a new debate, but in the context of the economic dynamism of the 1880s it took new relevance.

32. Rodríguez Kuri, "Gobierno local y empresas de servicios"; *Discursos Ayuntamiento 1884*, 34.

33. López Rosado, *Los servicios públicos de la Ciudad de México*; Connolly, *El contratista de don Porifirio*.

34. *Discursos Ayuntamiento 1881*, 5–6; Rodríguez Kuri, *Experiencia olvidada, el Ayuntamiento de México*, 134–37; *Reseña 1882*, 50–51; *Discursos Ayuntamiento 1883*, 5–10, 15.

35. *Discursos Ayuntamiento 1883*, 15.

36. *Discursos Ayuntamiento 1883*, 55.

37. That year Mexico City borrowed £1,500,000 in London.

38. Vassallo, "La construcción de los mercados públicos," 78–99.

39. Palti, "La transformación del liberalismo mexicano en el siglo XIX," 87.
40. *Discursos Ayuntamiento 1880*, 7–9, 11–13.
41. "Nuevo Mercado de La Merced," *Monitor Republicano*, September 2, 1880, 2.
42. *Discursos Ayuntamiento 1880*, 7.
43. *Discursos Ayuntamiento 1881*, 13–14, 20.
44. 3/17/1882, AHCDMX, ACM, RyM, vol. 3737, exp. 898; *Reseña Ayuntamiento 1882*, 72.
45. *Discursos Ayuntamiento 1885*, 26; 10/5/1886, AHCDMX, ACM, FM, vol. 1101, exp. 28.
46. 3/17/1882, AHCDMX, ACM, RyM, vol. 3737, exp. 898.
47. "El Mercado del Volador," *Monitor Republicano*, October 22, 1882, 3.
48. 5/9/1882, AHCDMX, ACM, RyM, vol. 3737, exp. 898.
49. 5/25/1886, AHCDMX, ACM, FM, vol. 1101, exp. 28.
50. 10/5/1886, AHCDMX, ACM, FM, vol. 1101, exp. 28.
51. 10/5/1886, AHCDMX, ACM, FM, vol. 1101, exp. 28; *Discurso leído el 4 de enero de 1887 por el C. Gral. Manuel G. Cosío como Presidente del Ayuntamiento de 1886 dando cuenta de su administración, contestación del ciudadano Francisco Mejía, segundo regidor del Ayuntamiento de 1887*, 31–32.
52. Yoma Medina and Martos López, *Dos mercados de en la historia de la Ciudad de México*, 163–67; 5/17/1888, AHCDMX, ACM, FM, vol. 1102, exp. 31. Blanco's letterhead read: Contractor, Developer and Importer. General Representative for the Mexican Republic of the Electric Lighting System "Without Dynamo."
53. 3/24/1890, AHCDMX, ACM, FM, vol. 1102, exp. 33.
54. Quoted in "Mercado de Loreto," *El Universal*, September 27, 1889, 2.
55. Juvenal was editorialist Enrique Chávarri's pseudonym. "Mal andamos," *Monitor Republicano*, August 1, 1890, 1. This newspaper maintained the same position for years: "El Bazar Porfirio Díaz," *Monitor Republicano*, May 7, 1885, 1; "El Mercado del Volador," *Monitor Republicano*, December 12, 1889, 3.
56. "Comisión de mercados," *Municipio Libre*, August 28, 1884, 1–2.
57. 3/17/1882, AHCDMX, ACM, RyM, vol. 3737, exp. 898; "El mercado de La Merced," *Monitor Republicano*, October 1, 1880, 2; "Comisión de mercados," *Municipio Libre*, August 28, 1884, 1–2; "Comisión de mercados," *Municipio Libre*, April 21, 1887, 1.
58. "Informe que rinde el intendente de mercados a la comisión del ramo," *Municipio Libre*, August 24, 1884, 2.
59. *Discurso leído el 1º de Enero de 1888 por el C. Gral. Manuel G. Cosío como Presidente del Ayuntamiento de 1887, dando cuenta de su administración, contestación del Ciudadano Manuel Gargollo Segundo Regidor del Ayuntamiento de 1887 y discurso del C. Gobernador del Distrito Federal al instalarse la nueva corporación*, 30.
60. *Discursos Ayuntamiento 1887*, 29–30, 46; "Comisión de Mercados," *Municipio Libre*, October 1, 1888, 1. This campaign had the added benefit of bringing basic provisions to parts of the city where the arm of the council had yet to reach. "Comisión de mercados," *Municipio Libre*, April 21, 1987, 1.
61. "Comisión de mercados," *Municipio Libre*, August 28, 1884, 1–2; 6/14/1884, AHCDMX, ACM, FM, vol. 1101, exp. 26. A new set of regulations from 1885 restated

the ayuntamiento's jurisdiction over markets, in particular its right to authorize the formation of new ones, whether they be in halls, plazas, or other public spaces. *Reglamento para el servicio y recaudación del ramo de mercados* (Mexico City: Imprenta de Francisco Díaz de León, 1885). Hereafter, *Reglamento mercados 1885*.

62. "El mercado del Volador," *Municipio Libre*, April 30, 1887, 1.

63. The separate series for viento and arrendamientos go up to 1884, while from 1885 onward the ayuntamiento only reports for "mercados." The figures for "mercados" in 1885 and subsequent years, however, are substantially below the sum of viento and arrendamientos up to 1884 and more consistent with the viento-only totals. It is therefore reasonable to assume that "mercados" refers to the old viento category, and that figures for arrendamientos stopped being reported by the markets commission.

64. 5/9/1882, AHCDMX, ACM, RyM, vol. 3737, exp. 898; *Discursos Ayuntamiento 1886*, 32.

65. *Discursos Ayuntamiento 1886*, 32.

66. *Reseña Ayuntamiento 1882*, 31; "Informe que rinde el Intendente de mercados a la Comisión del ramo," *Municipio Libre*, August 28, 1884, 2; *Discursos Ayuntamiento 1885*, 26; *Discurso leído el 1° de enero de 1889 por el Lic. Gral. Manuel González Cosío como Presidente del Ayuntamiento de 1888 dando cuenta de su administración y discurso del C. Gobernador del Distrito Federal al instalar la nueva corporación* (Mexico City: Imprenta de Francisco Díaz de León, 1889), 29; 67/1901, AHCDMX, ACM, RyM, vol. 3740, exp. 1203.

67. 5/25/1886, AHCDMX, ACM, FM, vol. 1101, exp. 28.

68. "Comisión de mercados," *Municipio Libre*, April 21, 1887, 1.

69. "Mercados," *Municipio Libre*, June 4, 1889, 1.

70. *Discurso leído al 1° de enero de 1890 por el C. Gral Manuel González Cosío como Presidente del Ayuntamiento de 1889, y discurso del C. Gobernador del Distrito Federal al instalar la nueva corporación* (Mexico City: Imprenta de Francisco Díaz de León, 1890). San Lucas was inaugurated on September 16, 1889; Loreto on September 18; San Juan on November 27; La Merced on February 5, 1890.

71. *Discurso del C. Ingeniero Sebastián Camacho, Presidente del Ayuntamiento de 1895, al instalarse el de 1896, contestación del C. Gobernador del Distrito Federal Gral. Pedro Rincón Gallardo y memoria documentada de los trabajos municipales de 1895*, 127–29.

72. "El Mercado Martínez de la Torre," *El Tiempo*, June 5, 1895.

73. 1/24/1890, AHCDMX, ACM, FM, vol. 1102, exp. 31; "Mercados," *Municipio Libre*, February 7, 1890, 1.

74. 4/7/1890, AHCDMX, ACM, FM, vol. 1102, exp. 33.

75. *Discurso leído el 1 de enero de 1891 por el C. Gral. Manuel González Cosío como Presidente del Ayuntamiento de 1890 dando cuenta de su administración y discurso del C. Gobernador del Distrito Federal al instalar la nueva corporación* (Mexico City: Imprenta de Francisco Díaz de León), 42.

76. "Comisión de mercados," *Municipio Libre*, January 17, 1891, 1. On another occasion, in 1897 the council hoped to concentrate those vendors who sold clothes

outside of other markets in El Volador. 7/27/1897, AHCDMX, ACM, RyM, vol. 3739, exp. 1136.

77. "De la comisión de mercados," *Municipio Libre*, July 26, 1890, 3.
78. "Comisión de mercados," *Municipio Libre*, January 17, 1891, 1.
79. "Obstruyen las aceras," *El Universal*, October 12, 1888, 7; "El mercado de La Merced," *Monitor Republicano*, December 17, 1896, 2.
80. "¿Para qué?" *El Universal*, March 18, 1890, 2. My emphasis. A village *tianguis* is a market, which in general gathers on specific days in specific locations. The expression had a negative connotation, village as opposed to city, *tianguis* as opposed to modern market.
81. "Los mercados," *El Nacional*, January 5, 1892, 2.
82. "Vendedores ambulantes," *El Universal*, October 22, 1892, 3.
83. *Discursos Ayuntamiento 1888*, 29; "Comisión de mercados," *Municipio Libre*, January 17, 1891, 1; "Nuestro colega," *Municipio Libre*, December 18, 1896, 2; *Discurso del C. Lic. Miguel S. Macedo, Presidente del Ayuntamiento, contestación del C. Gobernador del Distrito Federal C. Lic. Rafael Rebollar y memoria documentada de los trabajos municipales de 1898, formada por el Secretario Lic. Juan Bribiesca* (Mexico City: Tip. y Lit. "La Europea" de J. Aguilar Vera y Cía., 1899), 221.
84. "Comisión de mercados," *Municipio Libre*, November 13, 1892, 2.
85. These licensed peddlers were now officially categorized as vendedores ambulantes. *Discurso del S. Don Guillermo de Landa y Escandón, Presidente del Ayuntamiento de México en 1900, discurso del S. Don Ramón Corral, gobernador del Distrito Federal y memoria documentada de los trabajos municipales de 1900*, 369; 4/9/1901, AHCDMX, GD, M, vol. 1727, exp. 8; 11/29/1902, AHCDMX, GD, M, vol. 1727, exp. 64; *Discursos del Sr. D. Fernando Pimentel y Fagoaga, Presidente interino del Ayuntamiento en 1902, del Sr. D. Ramón Corral, gobernador del Distrito Federal, y del Sr. D. Guillermo de Landa y Escandón* (Mexico City: Tip. y Lit. "La Europea" de J. Aguilar Vera y Cía., 1903), 428.
86. Porter, "And That It Is Custom Makes It Law," 134.
87. "El Municipio y las necesidades de la capital," *El Universal*, March 12, 1900, 1.
88. 6/7/1901, AHCDMX, ACM, RyM, vol. 3740, exp. 1203.
89. "Los mercados," *Boletín Municipal*, July 11, 1902, 4. The provisional status of ambulantes's licences reflected both the ayuntamiento's rejection of these vendors' presence in the streets and the difficulty of collecting fees from them. *Discursos Ayuntamiento 1900*, 369. In 1902 there were 1,333 licensed ambulantes. *Discursos Ayuntamiento 1902*, 429.
90. *Discurso del C. Ingeniero Sebastián Camacho, presidente del Ayuntamiento de 1897 al instalarse el de 1898discurso del C. Lic. Miguel S. Macedo, presidente del Ayuntamiento de 1898, contestación del C. Gobernador del Distrito Federal C. Lic. Rafael Rebollar, y memoria documentada de los trabajos municipales de 1897, formada por el Secretario C. Lic. Juan Bribiesca* (Mexico City: La Europea de J. Aguilar Vera y Cía., 1898), 192.
91. Barbosa Cruz, *El Trabajo*, 16. He borrows the phrase from Luis Alberto Romero, *¿Qué hacer con los pobres? Elite y sectores populares en Santiago de Chile* (Buenos Aires: Sudamericana, 1997), 165–74.

92. Locatarios are those who rent a locale in a public market from the relevant authorities. A more approximate though archaic translation is stallenger.
93. 2/12/1881, AHCDMX, ACM, RyM, vol. 3736, exp. 873; "Nuevo mercado de La Merced," *Monitor Republicano*, September 26, 1880, 3.
94. 2/12/1881, AHCDMX, ACM, RyM, vol. 3736, exp. 873.
95. 4/19/1881, AHCDMX, ACM, RyM, vol. 3736, exp. 873.
96. Christina Jiménez has shown how during this period in Morelia, Michoacán, local residents from the popular classes co-opted certain elements of the government's modernizing agenda as well as its rhetoric about liberal rights and responsibilities to advance their own interests and demand that the authorities fulfill their self-imposed responsibilities over the urban built environment. Jiménez, "Popular Organizing for Public Services," 495–518. In another article, this author also demonstrates how in their correspondence to municipal authorities Morelia's vendors "performed" their commitment to the city's aesthetic and hygiene and their contribution to local commerce and taxation in a way that legitimized them as members of the community, that is, as *vecinos* and citizens. Jiménez, "Performing Their Right to the City," 435–56.
97. 9/15/1888, APD, CDP, leg. 13, caja 18, d. 008807–08.
98. *Discursos Ayuntamiento 1888*, 29.
99. 7/30/1890, AHCDMX, ACM, RyM, vol. 3739, exp. 1198.
100. 3/26/1901, AHCDMX, ACM, RyM, vol. 3740, exp. 1223.
101. 11/17/1902, AHCDMX, GD, M, vol. 1727, exp. 64.
102. 12/05/1896, AHCDMX, ACM, RyM, vol. 3739, exp. 1110.
103. 12/15/1896, AHCDMX, ACM, RyM, vol. 3739, exp. 1110.
104. 7/22/1897, AHCDMX, ACM, RyM, vol. 3739, exp. 1136; "Comisión de mercados," *Municipio Libre*, August 5, 1897, 1.
105. 1/24/1901, AHCDMX, ACM, RyM, vol. 3740, exp. 1249; 1/29/1901, AHCDMX, GD, M, vol. 1727, exp. 1.
106. 4/2/1901, AHCDMX, ACM, RyM, vol. 3740, exp. 1233.
107. Buffington, *Sentimental Education for the Working Man*, 25.
108. 4/14/1897, AHCDMX, ACM, RyM, vol. 3739, exp. 1128.
109. 4/24/1897, AHCDMX, ACM, RyM, vol. 3739, exp. 1128.
110. 5/9/1899, AHCDMX, ACM, RyM, vol. 3739, exp. 1166.
111. 5/9/1899, AHCDMX, ACM, RyM, vol. 3739, exp. 1166.
112. Rodríguez Kuri, *La experiencia olvidada, el Ayuntamiento de México*, 14, 29–31, 137–45.
113. Congress had authorized the national executive to reform the political organization of the Federal District in December 14, 1900; the *Ley de Organización Política y Municipal del Distrito Federal* was then passed in March 26, 1903, coming into effect on July 1 of that same year.
114. 9/30/1880, AHCDMX, ACM, RyM, vol. 3736, exp. 870.
115. 4/19/1881, AHCDMX, ACM, RyM, vol. 3736, exp. 873.
116. 5/25/1886: AHCDMX, ACM, FM, vol. 1101, exp. 28.
117. "Dice La Patria," *Monitor Republicano*, September 1, 1882, 2.
118. *Reglamento mercados 1885*, art. 4.

119. He had to content himself with relocating them to the old Volador Market. "Sección Oficial," *Municipio Libre*, January 17, 1891, 1.

120. "El Bazar Porfirio Díaz," *Monitor Republicano*, May 7, 1885, 1.

121. Porter, "And That It Is Custom Makes It Law."

122. Porter, "And That It Is Custom Makes It Law."

123. *Discurso del Sr. D. Fernando Pimentel y Fagoaga, Presidente del Ayuntamiento en 1903 y Memoria documentada de los trabajos municipales en el primer semestre de 1903* (Mexico City: La Europea, 1903), 5.

Chapter 3

1. "Corrió la sangre ayer frente al Palacio Municipal," *El Demócrata*, 2nd ed., August 2, 1924, 1; 9; 12; 14.

2. "Corrió la sangre ayer frente al Palacio Municipal," *El Demócrata*, 2nd ed., August 2, 1924, 1; 9; 12; 14.; "Sangriento conflicto por una manifestación," *Excélsior*, 2nd ed., August 2, 1924, 1.

3. "¿Quién disparó?" *El Demócrata*, August 4, 1924, 3.

4. "El pueblo ametrallado por intereses políticos," *El País*, August 3, 1924, 1.

5. *Discursos del Sr. D. Fernando Pimentel y Fagoaga, Presidente interino del Ayuntamiento en 1902, del Sr. D. Ramón Corral, gobernador del Distrito Federal, y del Sr. D. Guillermo de Landa y Escandón* (Mexico City: Tip. y Lit. "La Europea" de J. Aguilar Vera y Cía., 1903), 38.

6. According to Mario Barbosa, the ayuntamiento remained a useful platform for capitalist interests as it could still emit opinion on the planning and contracting out of public works. Between 1909 and 1913 it handled the changing nomenclature and numbering of streets and avenues and discussed projects for opening new thoroughfares. Barbosa Cruz, "La Política en la Ciudad de México en tiempos de cambio (1903–1929)," 264–71.

7. Tenorio Trillo, "1910 Mexico City," 75–77.

8. Lear, *Workers, Neighbors and Citizens*, chap. 1.

9. Piccato, "Urbanistas, Ambulantes, and Mendigos."

10. Piccato, *City of Suspects*, chaps. 1 and 2.

11. Congress had authorized the National Executive to reform the political organization of the Federal District in December 14, 1900; the Ley de Organización Política y Municipal del Distrito Federal was then passed in March 26, 1903, going into effect on July 1 of that same year. *Discurso del Sr. D. Fernando Pimentel y Fagoaga, Presidente del Ayuntamiento en 1903 y Memoria documentada de los trabajos municipales en el primer semestre de 1903* (Mexico City: La Europea, 1903), 5.

12. *Discurso del Sr. D. Fernando Pimentel y Fagoaga, Presidente del Ayuntamiento en 1903*, 48–55.

13. *Memoria del Consejo Superior de Gobierno del Distrito Federal correspondiente al período transcurrido del 1 de Julio de 1903 al 31 de Diciembre de 1904*, 2:9. The markets in question were La Merced, San Juan, Santa Catarina, Martínez de la Torre, San Cosme, Dos de Abril, Santa Ana, and San Lucas.

14. 8/29/1905, AHCDMX, GD, M, vol. 1728, exp. 162; 9/2/1905, AHCDMX, GD, M, vol. 1728, exp. 162.

15. 9/25/1903, AHCDMX, CSG, vol 608, exp. 5; 10/19/1903, AHCDMX, GD, M, vol. 1728, exp. 162, exp.1.

16. 11/14/1904, AHCDMX, GD, M, vol. 1728, exp. 117.

17. 9/25/1903, AHCDMX, CSG, vol. 608, exp. 5.

18. *Memoria del Consejo Superior de Gobierno del Distrito Federal correspondiente al período transcurrido del 1 de Julio de 1903 al 31 de Diciembre de 1904*, 2 vols. (Mexico City: Talleres de Pablo Rodríguez, 1906), 2:9.

19. 9/21/1906, AHSSA, Salubridad Pública, Higiene Pública, Inspección de Alimentos y Bebidas, caja 1, exp. 21.

20. "Notas Locales," *La Patria*, September 26, 1906, 2.

21. 2/21/1907, AHCDMX, GD, M, vol. 1729, exp. 190.

22. 1/16/1909, AHCDMX, GD, M, vol. 1733, exp. 594; 1/19/1909, AHCDMX, GD, M, vol. 1733, exp. 594.

23. 5/27/1905, AHDF, GD, M, vol. 1728, exp. 151.

24. 5/30/1905, AHDF, GD, M, vol. 1728, exp. 151.

25. 8/15/1908, AHDF, CSG, vol. 608, exp. 18.

26. 2/18/1905, AHCDMX, CSG, vol. 608, exp. 7.

27. 3/24/1905, AHCDMX, CSG, vol. 608, exp. 7.

28. *Memoria del Consejo Superior de Gobierno del Distrito Federal correspondiente al período transcurrido del 1 de enero al 31 de diciembre de 1905 presentada al Señor Secretario de Estado y del Despacho de Gobernación* (Mexico City: Talleres de Pablo Rodríguez, 1907), 200.

29. 3/24/1905, AHCDMX, CSG, vol. 608, exp. 7.

30. 10/1/1910, AHCDMX, GD, M, vol. 1737, exp. 896. In vendors' minds, earlier notions of compassion merged with this period's industrial labour relations. As class tensions mounted, and as both workers and capitalists sought governmental protection and support in their struggles, former ayuntamiento president, then governor of the Federal District Guillermo Landa y Escandón became the center of what Womack calls an informal institution of conciliation and arbitration. Landa y Escandón toured factories and workshops, giving speeches and listening to the concerns of industrialists, shop owners, and workers. When a strike or lockout could not be avoided, he personally intervened in its resolution. Subsidized newspapers and plays publicized his role as a negotiator of social harmony, which might explain vendors' phrasing in the first sentence of the quote. Womack, "Luchas sindicales y liberalismos sociales, 1867–1993," 426–28. On workers' grievances and labor conflicts in the Federal District in the late Porfiriato, see Anderson, *Outcasts in Their Own Land*, 194–201; 224–29; 334–38; on how the authorities responded to these conflicts following well-established precedents, see Walker, "Porfirian Labor Politics"; on the particular efforts made by Landa y Escandón, see Lear "Del mutualismo a la resistencia," 275–85.

31. 10/19/1910, AHCDMX, GD, M, vol. 1737, exp. 896.

32. The forceful determination to broaden US influence in the American hemisphere was demonstrated in the annexation of Puerto Rico in 1900, the incorporation

of the Platt Amendment into the Cuban constitution in 1902, the secession of Panama from Colombia in 1903 and the securing of the Canal Zone in 1904, the control assumed by US bankers over customs and national debt in the Dominican Republic in 1905, and the deployment of troops in Nicaragua from 1909 onward. For an introduction to the concept of "big stick" diplomacy, see John M. Dobson, *Belligerents, Brinkmanship, and the Big Stick : A Historical Encyclopedia of American Diplomatic Concepts* (Santa Barbara, CA: ABC-CLIO, 2009), 137–41; on how it developed in the greater Caribbean, see Veeser, *A World Safe for Capitalism*.

33. Katz, "Liberal Republic and the Porfiriato," 49–124; Cosío Villegas, *El Porfiriato*; Weiner, "Battle for Survival," 645–70; Katz, *Secret War in Mexico*, 21–27.

34. The subsequent paragraphs draw extensively on Womack, "Mexican Revolution," 125–200.

35. Katz, *Life and Times of Pancho Villa*.

36. Womack, *Zapata and the Mexican Revolution*.

37. Anderson, *Outcasts in Their Own Land*.

38. Gilly, *Mexican Revolution*. Zapatistas and Villistas remained in arms for the rest of the decade, but were by then reduced to mostly defensive guerilla operations.

39. Knight, *Mexican Revolution*, 2:469–76; Florescano, *El nuevo pasado mexicano*, 87.

40. Obregón was eventually recognized in 1923 as US oil companies lost ground to US bankers, who favored a functioning Mexican government with the capacity to collect taxes and thus with the revenue to repay its foreign debts. Financial sovereignty was another matter, the opening of the Banco de México in 1925 notwithstanding. Smith, *United States and Revolutionary Nationalism in Mexico*; Meyer, *Mexico y Estados Unidos en el conflicto petrolero*; Zebadúa, *Banqueros y revolucionarios*; Zebadúa, "El Banco de la Revolución," 67–98.

41. Meyer, *Cristero Rebellion*.

42. Rodea, *Historia del movimiento obrero ferrocarrilero en México*, 468–91. Rodríguez, "Beginnings of a Movement," chap. 3.

43. 7/27/1911, AHCDMX, CSG, vol. 608, exp. 24; 8/2/1911, AHCDMX, GD, M, vol. 1739, exp.1000; 8/9/1911, AHCDMX, CSG, vol. 608, exp. 24.

44. 6/29/1912, AHCDMX, CSG, vol. 608, exp. 25; 7/11/1912, AHCDMX, CSG, vol. 608, exp. 25.

45. 10/19/1911, AHCDMX, GD, M, vol. 1738, exp. 961.

46. 7/18/1911, AHCDMX, GD, M, vol. 1741, exp. 1030.

47. 7/10/1911, AHCDMX, GD, M, vol. 1740, exp. 1024.

48. 7/15/1911, AHCDMX, GD, M, vol. 1740, exp. 1024.

49. Rodríguez Kuri, *Historia del desasosiego*, 11–28. By emphasizing these changes, Rodríguez Kuri and Lear move beyond what historians of the revolution have termed the *revisionist position*, which tended to see the revolutionary agency of popular groups at best as short-lived. Bailey, "Revisionism and the Recent Historiography of the Mexican Revolution," 62–79; Knight, "Interpretaciones recientes de la Revolución Mexicana," 23–43; Knight, "Revisionism and Revolution," 159–99; Matute Aguirre, "Orígenes del revisionismo historiográfico," 29–48.

50. 8/28/1912, AHCDMX, GD, M, vol. 1743, exp. 1161.

51. In fact, the meat sales bylaw had been issued on April 14, 1904; August 14, 1904, was the date when it went into effect.

52. Rojas, Madrigal, and Rodríguez were not alone in denouncing the connection between the 1904 bylaw and El Popo's monopolistic practices. According to Jeffrey Pilcher, from 1908 El Popo came under attack from a cross-class alliance of livestock importers, slaughterhouse workers, and butchers. Pilcher, *Sausage Rebellion*, 143-70.

53. 1/23/1912, AHCDMX, GD, M, vol. 1739, exp. 999. The vendors in question simplified or misremembered the history of the city's meat supply. They conflated the Terrazas clan's Compañía Empacadora La Internacional, which had attempted to sieze control of the city's meat distribution system in the early 1900s, and John Wesley DeKay's Anglo-American Compañía Empacadora Nacional Mexicana, whose products bore the label "El Popo," and which bought El Peralvillo's slaughterhouse from La Internacional in 1908 after the operation went bankrupt. On how these companies had tried to gain market power in Mexico City in the late Porfiriato, see Pilcher, *Sausage Rebellion*, chaps. 3 and 4.

54. On workers' militancy and its consequences, see Leal and Villaseñor, *La clase obrera en las historia de México*; Lear, *Workers, Neighbors, and Citizens*, chaps. 5-7; Carr, *El movimiento obrero y la política en México*, 2 vols., 1: 55-120; Womack, "Luchas sindicales," 432-36. Womack emphasizes that with all the new authorities brought by the revolution, conciliation increasingly became a legal matter and government arbitration obligatory.

55. 2/14/1912, AHCDMX, GD, M, vol. 1739, exp. 999.

56. As Huerta tried to enlarge the army, for example, the National Preparatory School was turned into a military academy, and forced conscription, the infamous *leva*, made roaming the city dangerous for the lower classes, especially after dark. Meyer, "The Militarization of Mexico, 1913-1914," 299-300; Gonzales, *Mexican Revolution, 1910-1940*, 93, 101. Huerta also shut down the Casa del Obrero, which by then included teachers, carpenters, shoemakers, printers, textile workers, and streetcar workers.

57. 7/14/1913, AHCDMX, SG, RyM, vol. 1238, exp. 64.

58. Boletín Oficial del Consejo Superior de Gobierno del Distrito Federal, vol. 21, July-December 1913 (Mexico City: Talleres de la Tipografía Mexicana, 1913), 274.

59. 9/22/1913, AHCDMX, GD, M, vol. 1744, exp. 1208.

60. 8/26/1913, AHCDMX, SG, RyM, vol. 1283, exp. 63.

61. 1/27/1914, AHCDMX, SG, RyM, vol. 1283, exp. 63; 1/30/1914, AHCDMX, SG, RyM, vol. 1283, exp. 63.

62. Rodríguez Kuri, "Desabasto, hambre y respuesta politica, 1915." On the commercial practices of the city's flour mill and bakery owners during this period, Weis, *Bakers and Basques*, chap. 5.

63. Knight, *Mexican Revolution*, 2:413; Ochoa, *Feeding Mexico*, 28.

64. Molina de Villar, "El Tifo en la Ciudad de México."

65. Ramírez Plancarte, *La Ciudad de México durante la revolución constitucionalista*, 250, 252, 254, 299, 314-17, 324, 366, 397, 424-27, 509, 525-26, 533.

66. "30 tiendas y 5 mercados fueron saqueados ayer," *Mexican Herald*, June 26, 1915, 1, 4.

67. Lear, *Workers, Neighbors, and Citizens*, 301–15.

68. In September 1914, Carranza had repealed Porfirio Díaz's 1903 decree removing all executive powers from the city council, only to reintroduce it in August 1915. In November, Enriquez was succeeded by Coronel Ignacio Rodríguez, who continued efforts to guarantee the city's supply. Rodríguez Kuri finds that the militarization of the city's bureaucracies paralleled the growing social tensions. The need to normalize the provision of basic goods and keep labor militancy in check paved the way for the reinstatement of the ayuntamiento's full powers in 1917. Rodríguez Kuri, "Desabasto, hambre y respuesta política."

69. Rodríguez Kuri, "Desabasto, hambre y respuesta política," 155–59. Only the council's fishmongers were located in public markets. And in these cases, inspectors carefully monitored that employees did not sell to locatarios or private shops. 3/6/1916, AHCDMX, Reguladora de comercio, Comisión de inspectores, vol. 3857, exp. 10. Note that in a revised version of this essay, the author eliminated the only reference to public markets. Rodríguez Kuri, *Historia del desasosiego*, 169.

70. Womack, "Luchas sindicales," 433–34. Womack highlights that the electricians' importance derived from their strategic position, notably their capacity to turn off the electric supply to the country's central grid and thus bring all production to a halt. Unless otherwise stated, references to the labor movement in this period are based on this article.

71. Discussions about the desirability and viability of reinstating the Ayuntamiento de la Ciudad de México began as early as 1911. On the failure of municipal reform under Madero see Rodríguez Kuri, *La experiencia olvidada, el Ayuntamiento de México*, chaps. 7 and 8. On how the wars between Constitucionalistas, Zapatistas, and Villistas informed the reappearance of the ayuntamiento in the capital, see Rodríguez Kuri, "El año cero." The constitutional reintroduction of the ayuntamiento and the political conflicts that shaped its evolution between 1917 and 1928 are chronicled in Hoffmann Calo, *Crónica Política del Ayuntamiento de la Ciudad de México*; and in Miranda Pacheco, *Historia de la desaparición del Municipio*, 127–59.

72. Hart, *Anarchism and the Mexican Working Class*, 159–74.

73. Guadarrama, *Los sindicatos y la política en México*; Rivera Castro, *La clase obrera en la historia de México*, 17–34.

74. Whoever controlled the governorship of the Federal District held sway over the local Junta de Conciliación y Arbitraje as well as the local policía. Control of the ayuntamiento entailed influence over municipal jobs and contracts. On Ross, see 12/5/1929, AGN, DGIPS, c. 47, exp. 7; on Serrano's role in keeping the *laboristas* in check, see Hoffman Calo, *Cronica Política del Ayuntamiento*, 109–10. On how the CROM made use of public office, see Womack, "Luchas sindicales," 438; Davis, *Urban Leviathan*, 52–59.

75. Hoffman Calo, *Cronica Política del Ayuntamiento*, 61.

76. FAPECFT, PEC, serie Ramón Medina, exp. 30, legajo 2, fojas 6, inventario 3604.

77. 5/24/1922, AGN, O-C, caja 114, 242-M1-M-1. Other public services were equally affected by political rivalries. When in November 1922 the mismanagement of a technical malfunction led to the interruption of the city's water supply, President Alonzo Romero and PLC councilors came under attack again. The CROM organized a demonstration for November 30, which ended in a violent confrontation between the municipal guard and the protestors. The day after the riots, Cooperativista Jorge Prieto Laurens, who expected his party to win the following months' ayuntamiento elections, and aspired to its presidency, blamed the lack of water on the corruption in the PLC and the lack of maintenance of the pumps by the previous year's PLC-dominated council. Both the PLM and the Cooperativistas demanded the resignation of the Peleceanos. Rodríguez Kuri, "Desabasto de agua y violencia política," 167–201; Salazar and Escobedo, *Las pugnas de la Gleba*, 1: 210–12. Hoffman Calo, *Cronica Política del Ayuntamiento*, 72–74. Alonzo Romero left his testimony of the political pressures he endured as president of the ayuntamiento in Alonzo Romero, *Un año de sitio a la presidencia municipal*.

78. *Estadísticas históricas*.

79. López Rosado, *Los servicios públicos de la Ciudad de México*, 213, 264–65; *Boletín Municipal*, June 30, 1925, 30; *Boletín Municipal*, October 31, 1926, 20; *Obras Públicas* 1, no. 4 (April 1930), 238.

80. For the expansive use of the city's streets as markets and, more generally, as spaces where vast numbers of people made a living, see Barbosa Cruz, *El trabajo en las calles*, 143, 151–55. This trend would only be exacerbated over the next two decades.

81. *Boletín Municipal*, March 21, 1919, 297.

82. *Boletín Municipal*, June 3, 1924, 377. The following year, in 1925, the council built the markets of La Dalia and Hidalgo; a new flower market was inaugurated in 1927. López Rosado, *Los servicios públicos*, 143, 151–55.

83. In this period there was no clear definition of which groups could legally form unions and have them registered with the authorities. Even prisoners in Galley 3 of the Belem prison formed a union in 1922. Piccato, *City of Suspects*, 206–7. On how before the passing of the Federal Labor Law in 1931 the Supreme Court had to decide what was legally cognizable under Article 123 of the 1917 Constitution, informing the development of labor legislation and the system of industrial relations, see Suarez-Potts, *Making of Law*.

84. 6/30/1923, AGN, O-C, c. 167, 425-J-2.

85. 5/24/1922, AGN, O-C, c. 114, 242-M1-M-1.

86. 6/28/1922, AGN, O-C, c. 246, 802-5-11.

87. In the 1920s locatarios with stalls within market halls, in theory, paid both federal taxes and municipal market fees, called "derecho de piso." 7/12/1922, AGN, O-C, caja 114, 242-M1. Between 1922 and 1926 the federal government attempted several fiscal innovations, without much success. Aboites Aguilar, *Excepciones y privilegios*, 101–29.

88. Hoffman Calo, *Cronica Política del Ayuntamiento*, 94.

89. The account of the demonstration that follows has been reconstructed on the basis of: "Corrió la sangre ayer frente al Palacio Municipal," *El Demócrata*, 2nd ed. August 2, 1924, 1, 9, 12, 14; "Small Riot in the Zocalo," *Excélsior*, English section, August 2, 1924, 1; "Sangriento conflicto por una manifestación," *Excélsior*, 2nd ed., August 2, 1924, 1, 5; "El alcalde, Sr. Raya, habla de los sucesos de ayer tarde," *El Universal*, August 2, 1924, 1; "Un muerto y once heridos en la Plaza de Armas," *El Universal*, 2nd ed., August 2, 1924, 1. For a discussion of the meaning of the *nota roja* and its richness as a historical source, see Piccato, "Murders of *Nota Roja*," 195–231.

90. "Corrió la sangre ayer frente al Palacio Municipal," *El Demócrata*, 2nd ed., August 2, 1924, 14. In 1893 Justo Sierra had used the biblical phrase "hambre y sed de justicia," quoting the Sermon on the Mount (Matthew 5:6), in arguing for an independent judiciary. In English it is usually translated as "Blessed are those who hunger and thirst for righteousness," but the Spanish, like the Latin, says "justicia." Vendors now appropriated the phrase, and the moral force it carried, to bring to the realm of the political their unfulfilled material needs. As they brought to the public sphere their social relations of production, they began to interpret justice as social justice.

91. See n. 75 in this chapter.

92. "Sangriento conflicto por una manifestación," *Excélsior*, 2nd ed., August 2, 1924, 5.

93. "Hubo políticos entre los mercaderes que organizaron la protesta del día primero," *El Demócrata*, 2nd ed., August 6, 1924, 11; "No se hará luz en la tragedia del viernes," *Excélsior*, 2nd ed., August 6, 1924, 6.

94. "El alcalde, Sr. Raya, habla de los sucesos de ayer tarde," *El Universal*, August 2, 1924, 1.

95. "Se investiga el asesinato de locatarios," *Excélsior*, August 5, 1924, 5.

96. "¿Quién disparó?" *El Demócrata*, August 4, 1924, 3.

97. "El pueblo ametrallado por intereses políticos," *El País*, August 3, 1924, 1.

98. "El pueblo ametrallado por intereses políticos," *El País*, August 3, 1924, 1.

99. "Trágicos sucesos del viernes causados por la baja política," *Excélsior*, August 3, 1924, 1.

100. "Se investiga el asesinato de locatarios," *Excélsior*, August 5, 1924, 3.

101. "Las últimas investigaciones en los sangrientos sucesos del viernes último," *El Demócrata*, 2nd ed., August 4, 1924, 1; "Las siluetas de los verdaderos promotores del motín en el Ayuntamiento comienzan a condensarse," *El Demócrata*, August 3, 1924, 1, 14.

102. "No se hará luz en la tragedia del viernes," *Excélsior*, 2nd ed., August 6, 1924, 1, 6. According to the *Boletín Municipal*, the "Unión de Comerciantes del Exterior de los Mercados de esta Capital" was formally constituted on October 3, 1912, with Pascual Paz as its secretary general. *Boletín Municipal*, December 30, 1921, 836–37.

103. 8/6/1924, "Hubo políticos entre los mercaderes que organizaron la protesta del día primero," *El Demócrata*, 2nd ed., 11.

104. 8/4/1924, "Las últimas investigaciones en los sangrientos sucesos del viernes último," *El Demócrata*, 2nd ed., 1.

105. The FSC's affiliation with the CGT was through its membership of the Federación Local de Trabajadores del Distrito, while the UC's affiliation with the CROM was through the Federación de Sindicatos Obreros del Distrito Federal. Salazar, *Historia de las luchas proletarias de México*, 1:65; Guadarrama, *Los sindicatos*, 63.

106. "Fue anulado en nuevo impuesto de piso para los venderores del exterior de los mercados," *El Demócrata*, August 30, 1924, 4.

107. 11/11/1924, FAPECFT, PEC, Serie Dámaso F. Díaz, exp. 68, legajo 1, fojas 3, inventario 1533. After almost a decade and a half of population growth and lack of investment, by the mid-1920s public markets had expanded by attaching fee-paying stalls to the outside of existing halls; the vendors operating these stalls refered to themselves as external to, though still very much part of, public markets.

108. 8/4/1925, AGN, O-C, c. 114, exp. 242-M1-E-1.

109. Vendors were not the only ones who joined the CROM in this period. Between 1925 and 1928, when the PLM controlled the council, more than fifty-five groups joined the CROM. Davis, *Urban Leviathan*, chap. 3, n. 5.

110. 5/11/1926, AGN, SGG, 2-380.1 (5-1)-13.

111. 30/11/1927, AGN, SGG, 2-380.1 (5-1)-13; 12/9/1927, AGN, SGG, 2-380.1 (5-1)-13.

112. 11/13/1923, AGN, O-C, c. 241, exp. 802-D-9.

113. 4/8/1924, AGN, O-C, c. 241, exp. 802-D-9.

114. 7/29/1924, AGN, O-C, c. 241, exp. 802-D-9.

115. 3/4/1927, AGN, DT, c. 987, exp. 2. I am grateful to Miles Vincent Rodríguez for this reference.

116. 2/25/1828, AGN, DT, c. 1588, exp. 1.

117. *Estadísticas históricas*, table 4.1.2. Note that between 1920 and 1930, when the population grew by around 67 percent, a third of the increase was due to the expansion of the city's territory.

118. *Boletín Municipal*, June 30, 1925, 30; *Boletín Municipal*, October 31, 1926, 20; *Obras Públicas* 1, no. 4 (April 1930): 238.

119. Francisco Bulman, "La situación actual de la ciudad en lo relativo a mercados," *Obras Públicas* 2, no. 8–9 (August–September 1930): 83.

120. *Boletín Municipal*, February 16, 1918, 167.

121. *Boletín Municipal*, March 21, 1919, 296–97.

122. *Boletín Municipal*, March 31, 1925, 36–37, 12.

123. *Boletín Municipal*, April 11, 1919, 356.

124. *Boletín Municipal*, February 24, 1922, 123–24.

125. González y González, "La Revolución Mexicana desde el punto de vista de los revolucionados," 5–13; Rodríguez Kuri, *Historia del desasosiego*, 16–20.

Chapter 4

1. Cárdenas, *La hacienda pública y la política económica*, 23–27; Smith, *United States and Revolutionary Nationalism in Mexico*, 264.

2. Hernández Chávez, *Mexico: A Brief History*, 245–50.

3. Weis, "Revolution on Trial."
4. Garrido, *El partido de la revolución institucionalizada*, chap. 1; Knight, "Mexico's Elite Settlement."
5. Lieuwen, *Mexican Militarism*, 103.
6. Skirius, *José Vasconcelos y la cruzada de 1929*; Blanco, *Se llamaba Vasconcelos*.
7. Cárdenas, *La industrialización mexicana durante la Gran Depresión*.
8. Hamilton, *Limits of State Autonomy*, 81–83, 106–7, 119–24, 184–87; Reynolds, *Mexican Economy*, 284–85; Hernández, *Mexico*, 268.
9. This was not the first attempt to remove the city council. Miranda Pacheco, *Historia de la desaparición del Municipio en el Distrito Federal*; for a different interpretation, see Rodíguez Kuri, "Ciudad oficial," 417–23.
10. *Ley Orgánica del Distrito Federal y de los Territorios Federales*. Miranda Pacheco, *La creación del Departamento del Distrito Federal*.
11. For an analysis of the trial against the actual perpetrator, the public debates that it generated, and the challenges and opportunities it offered the Callista political leadership, see Weis, "Revolution on Trial."
12. The figure did not reflect fee-paying members, which numbered 20,000 nationwide. Vázquez Ramírez, *Organización y resistencia popular*, 35–40; Guadarrama, *Los sindicatos y la política en México*, 199–202.
13. Davis, *Urban Leviathan*, 65–72. For a thorough study of the government and management of the Federal District, see Sánchez Mejorada's *Rezago de la modernidad*. Her focus, however, is on the 1940s and early 1950s.
14. *Ley Orgánica del Distrito Federal*, arts. 92–96.
15. Davis argues that the overrepresentation of workers (three councilors) responded to the power of organized labor within the official coalition and incipient party, remarking that as recognition of particularly strong Cromista unions, the labor slots were consistently allocated to the Federación de Sindicatos Obreros del Distrito Federal, the Sindicato de Redactores de Prensa, and the Alianza de Camioneros.
16. The inclusion of mothers' associations in the Consejo Consultivo, more than two decades before women got the vote, is notable. Women also sometimes obtained the representation of public employees. On how the expansion of female office work in the public sector shaped class identities in Mexico City, and prompted feminist organizing, see Porter, *From Angel to Office Worker*.
17. 1/29/1929, AVCC, FR 328.38 M4c 1929. In November 1928, for example, as successor to the CROM's leader Luis N. Morones as secretary of industry, Puig Casauranc had convoked and then chaired a Worker-Employer Convention to debate Portes Gil's project for a Federal Labor Law. Rodríguez, "Beginnings of a Movement," 187–89, 194.
18. Dirección General de Estadística, *Primer censo industrial*.
19. Dirección General de Estadística, *Quinto censo de población 15 de mayo de 1930*, 53.
20. A report by a commission in charge of studying the feasibility of establishing a bank to extend loans to small-scale vendors claimed that in the summer of 1932

there were at least 20,000 active stalls licensed by the Oficina de Mercados of the Federal District. 07/12/1932, AGN, ALR, c. 148, exp. 531.1/37.
21. Suarez-Potts, *Making of Law*.
22. 3/20/1929, AVCC, FR 328.38 M4c 1929.
23. Weis, "Immigrant Entrepreneurs, Bread, and Class Negotiation in Postrevolutionary Mexico City," 71–100. A similar trend is discernible in the milk industry. Ochoa, "Reappraising State Intervention and Social Policy in Mexico," 78–82.
24. Weis, "Immigrant Entrepreneurs," 88.
25. 9/11/1930, AVCC, 004-ACT-04-1930.
26. Francisco Bulman, "La situación actual de la ciudad en lo relativo a mercados," *Obras Públicas* 2, no. 8–9, August–September 1930, 84.
27. By 1940, there were 35,000 cars (4,500 of which were taxis), and 10,000 trucks in Mexico City. Olsen, *Artifacts of Revolution*, 109, 128–29, 239.
28. Bulman, "La situación," 83.
29. 3/6/1929, AVCC.
30. 4/24/1929, AVCC.
31. 4/24/1929, AVCC.
32. 5/8/1930, AVCC.
33. 5/8/1930, AVCC.
34. 8/29/1930, AVCC.
35. 10/15/1930, AVCC.
36. 10/15/1930, AVCC.
37. 2/21/1931, AGN, DGIPS, c. 2, exp. 21.
38. 11/26/1930, AVCC.
39. 12/24/1930, AHCDMX, DDF, Oficina Consultiva, box 3. Similar letters were addressed to the president. See, for example, 2/21/1931, AGN, POR, c. 68, exp. 7/2986. On racism against the Chinese in Mexico, especially in the north, see Treviño Rangel, "Los 'hijos del cielo' en el infierno"; Bloch and Ortoll "Anti-Chinese and Anti-Japanese Movements in Cananea, Sonora, and Salt Lake River, Arizona"; on the history of Syrian and Lebanese immigration to Mexico, their commercial practices, and the discrimination they suffered, see Alfaro-Velcamp, *So Far from Allah, So Close to Mexico*; on anti-Semitism in Mexico, see Gojman de Backal, *Camisas, escudos y desfiles militares*.
40. 1/28/1931 and 2/4/1931, AVCC. For an account of the passing of the reglamento from a street vending perspective, see Gordon, "Peddlers, Pesos, and Power," 50–59.
41. According to available estimates, 100 pesos represented the minimum middle-class income in 1932. Iturriaga, *La estructura social y cultural de México*, 79.
42. 2/25/1931, AVCC.
43. Vázquez Ramírez, *Organización y resistencia popular*, 106. During the first quarter of 1931, two of the most widely read newspapers of the period, *El Nacional* and *Excélsior*, reproduced merchants' and vendors' antiforeign views. See Vázquez Ramírez, *Organización y resistencia popular*, nn. 17–29. That year, Jewish merchants were expelled from their shops outside of La Lagunilla Market. Gojman de Backal,

Camisas, escudos y desfiles militares, 165–66, 185–87. While vendors continued to decry foreigners' participation in markets for the rest of the decade, I did not find evidence of official support for their xenophobic complaints after these events.

44. 12/16/1931, AVCC.
45. 12/16/1931, AVCC.
46. 2/3/1932, AVCC; Vázquez Ramírez, *Organización y resistencia popular*, 117–18.
47. 9/3/1932, AVCC.
48. Vázquez Ramírez, *Organización y resistencia popular*, 111.
49. 7/12/1932, AGN, ALR, c. 148, exp. 531.1/37.
50. 12/2/1932, AGN, ALR, c. 148, exp. 531.1/37, exp. 531.1/21.
51. 2/10/1933, AGN, ALR, c. 148, exp. 531.1/37 exp. 531.1/37.
52. 1/5/1933, AVCC.
53. "Ley de planificación y zonificación del Distrito Federal y Territorios de la Baja California," *Diario Oficial*, January 17, 1933; "Reglamento de la ley de planificación y zonificación," *Diario Oficial*, February 22, 1933.
54. Davis, *Urban Leviathan*, 79–80.
55. Salmerón Sanginés, *Aarón Sáenz Garza, militar, diplomático, empresario*; James C. Hefley, *Aarón Sáenz, Mexico's Revolutionary Capitalist*.
56. Under President Pascual Ortíz Rubio, in comparison, the city had witnessed the appointment and removal of six different heads of the Federal District. Departamento del Distrito Federal, *Resumen de Actividades, 1949*, 10.
57. Olsen, *Artifacts*, chap. 3.
58. Nacional Financiera was created in 1933 to assist banks with liquidity problems and to support development projects in both rural and urban areas. "Decreto que autoriza a la Secretaría de Hacienda y Crédito Público para la fundación de una Sociedad Financiera con carácter de Institución Nacional," *Diario Oficial*, August 31, 1933; "Decreto que modifica al que autorizó a la Secretaría de Hacienda y Crédito Público para la fundación de una Sociedad Financiera, S.A., con carácter de Institución Nacional de Crédito," *Diario Oficial*, April 30, 1934. Cardero, "Estructura monetaria y financiera de México: 1932–1940," 752.
59. The National Bank for Urban Mortgages and Public Works was created in February 1933, and it lent 11.5 million pesos to the departamento during that year. *Informe presidencial y memoria del Departamento del Distrito Federal que rinde el C. Jeje del mismo por el período administrativo comprendido entre el 1 de julio del 1933 y el 30 de junio de 1934* (Mexico City: Talleres Gráficos de la Nación, 1934), 9.
60. Olsen, *Artifacts*, 76.
61. Sluis, *Deco Body, Deco City*, 251. The censure was so widespread that in the departamento's published report of activities for the year 1933 Sáenz found it necessary to defend his administration from accusations of "unspeakable squandering, and of having performed useless or non-urgent public works, for which they claim we have paid unjustifiable prices, within a system of favoritism and cronyism." *Gobernar la ciudad es servirlaInforme que rinde el C. Jefe del Departamento del Distrito Federal, Lic. Aarón Sáenz, a la ciudad de México* (Mexico City: [s.n.], 1934), 2–3.

62. Antonio Muñoz García, "Edificación llevada a cabo por el Departamento del Distrito Federal en el período 1932–1934," *Revista Mexicana de Ingeniería y Arquitectura* 13 (April 1935): 186. Muñoz García had been responsible for the city council's Architecture Office from the time it was created in 1924. From 1930 he was head of conservation services. Antonio Muñoz García, "Los mercados de la capital," *Obras Públicas* 2, no. 12 (December 1930).

63. 11/24/1934, AVCC.

64. 11/24/1934, AVCC.

65. 3/12/1930, AVCC.

66. 11/2/1933, AVCC. The departamento deemed both the Mixcalco and Jamaica Markets to be in a poor state. According to a survey by *Obras Públicas*, Mixcalco remained "to date, only a group of barracas, without a proper building," while Jamaica was "nothing but a cluster of more or less homogeneous stalls." In "Origen de los nombres de los mercados de la ciudad y fechas de construcción," *Obras Públicas* 1, no. 4 (April 1930): 288–89.

67. 2/13/1929, AVCC.

68. 2/12/1932, AVCC.

69. This was not altogether trivial, with market dues constituting the third largest source of revenue for the local government after property and business taxes. Sluis, *Deco Body, Deco City*, 251.

70. Muñoz García, "Los mercados de la capital," 270, 273.

71. Muñoz García, "Los mercados de la capital," 274.

72. Muñoz García, "Los mercados de la capital," 275–76.

73. *Gobernar la ciudad es servirla. Informe que rinde el C. Jefe del Departamento del Distrito Federal, Lic. Aarón Sáenz, a la ciudad de México* (Mexico City: [s.n.], 1934), 49.

74. *Gobernar la ciudad es servirla*, 49.

75. 3/16/1933, AVCC.

76. 4/27/1933, AVCC. This was part of a wider trend. In these years the federal government established an array of social assistance programs for mothers and children, especially in Mexico City. See Sanders, *Gender and Welfare in Mexico: The Consolidation of a Postrevolutionary State*.

77. 1/12/1934, AGN, ALR, c. 224, exp. 616/17-1.

78. 2/12/1934, AGN, ALR, c. 224, exp. 616/17-1.

79. 2/12/1934, AGN, ALR, c. 224, exp. 616/17-1.

80. *Informe que rinde el C. Jefe del Departamento del Distrito Federal de la obra realizada durante el año de 1934 a los habitantes de la ciudad* (Mexico City: [s.n.], 1935), 137–53.

81. Sluis, *Deco Body, Deco City*, chap. 6.

82. Whitney Museum of American Art, "The Abelardo L. Rodriguez Market / Vida Americana: Mexican Muralists Remake American Art, 1925–1945," https://whitney.org/media/46658 (video last accessed on July 27, 2020).

83. According to art historian Esther Acevedo, the Abelardo Rodíguez Market murals reflect the tension between the artists' stylistic and contractual commitment

to Rivera and their affinity to Siqueiros's more radical ideology. Acevedo, "Young Muralists at the Abelardo Rodríguez Market."

84. Oles, "Noguchi in Mexico," 16.
85. Sluis, *Deco Body, Deco City*, 300.
86. 8/30/1933, AGN, ALR, c. 224, exp. 616/17.
87. Neither Sáenz nor Herrera Salcedo, the Jefe de Mercados, was receptive to their plight. 12/15/1934, AGN, LC, c. 361, exp. 418.5/1; 12/18/1934, AGN, LC, c. 361, exp. 418.5/1.
88. 2/8/1935, AGN, LC, c. 361, exp. 418.5/1.
89. 2/26/1935, AGN, LC, c. 361, exp. 418.5/1.
90. 3/4/1935, AGN, LC, c. 361, exp. 418.5/1.
91. 4/11/1935, AGN, LC, c. 638, exp. 521/27.
92. 6/8/1935, AGN, LC, c. 361, exp. 418.5/2.
93. Hernández Chávez, *La Mecánica Cardenista*, 44–46, 96–104.
94. Hernández Chávez, *La Mecánica Cardenista*, 62–64.
95. Knight, "Rise and Fall of Cardenismo," 256–64; Carr, "Mexican Communist Party and Agrarian Mobilization in the Laguna?" 371–404; Fowler-Salamini, *Agrarian Radicalism in Veracruz*, 49–69.
96. Hernández Chávez, *Mexico: A Brief History*, 258.
97. Hamilton, *Limits of State Autonomy*, 125.
98. Spenser, *Unidad a toda costa*; Carr, *Marxism and Communism*, chap. 2.
99. Womack, "Luchas sindicales," 441–42; Middlebrook, *Paradox of Revolution*, 83–92.
100. Hernández Chávez, *La Mecánica Cardenista*, 64–69; Snodgrass, *Deference and Defiance in Monterrey*, chap. 8.
101. I have not been able to locate meaningful references to Alberto Cárdenas in the literature on the period. In 1938, a foreign correspondent described him as the president's "little-seen brother." In "Mexico: Troubles and Taxes," *Time Magazine*, July 11, 1938. Later on, he is mentioned as a supporter of opposition candidate Miguel Henríquez Guzmán during the presidential race of 1952. Oikión Solano, "La oposición Henriqusita en Michoacán," 98.
102. 8/9/1935, AGN, LC, c. 361, exp. 418.5/1.
103. 8/20/1935, AGN, LC, c. 361, exp. 418.5/1.
104. 8/27/1935, AGN, LC, c. 361, exp. 418.5/1.
105. 8/30/1935, AGN, LC, c. 361, exp. 418.5/1.
106. 9/24/1935, AGN, LC, c. 638, exp. 521/48; 10/16/1935, AGN, LC, c. 638, exp. 521/48.
107. 4/19/1934, AVCC.
108. 8/15/1935, AVCC.
109. Sluis, *Deco Body, Deco City*, 232–35.
110. Departamento del Distrito Federal, *Memoria presentada al H. Congreso de la Unión por el período comprendido de septiembre de 1935 a agosto de 1936* (Mexico City: [s.n.], 1936), 30. Markets' higher visibility did not translate into higher levels of tax collection. While markets continued to represent a significant source of income

for the departamento, the total nominal revenue they generated increased very little during the 1930s. Given the fact that inflation rates were positive, this implies a decline in real terms. Moreover, the share of total revenue due to markets consistently fell during this decade. For total revenues, see: Up to 1937, *Memoria del Departamento del Distrito Federal: Del 1 de septiembre de 1937 al 30 de agosto de 1938*, 334; 1938–1939, *Memoria del Departamento del Distrito Federal: Del 1 de septiembre de 1939 al 31 de agosto de 1940*, 9. For market revenues see: Up to 1937, *Memoria del Departamento del Distrito Federal: Del 1 de septiembre de 1937 al 30 de agosto de 1938*, 346; 1938 and 1939, *Memoria del Departamento del Distrito Federal: Del 1 de septiembre de 1940 al 31 de agosto de 1941*, figure 114.

111. Departamento del Distrito Federal, *Memoria presentada al H. Congreso de la Unión por el período comprendido de septiembre de 1935 a agosto de 1936*, 31.

112. Departamento del Distrito Federal, *Memoria del Departamento del Distrito Federal presentada por el C. Jefe del mismo, al H H. Congreso de la Unión por el período comprendido del 1 de septiembre de 1936 al 31 de agosto de 1937*, 62. The daily average was calculated assuming 260 working days per year.

113. 8/28/1935, AGN, LC, c. 361, exp. 418.5/15.

114. 6/23/1936, AGN, LC, c. 361, exp. 418.5/15.

115. 9/30/1936, AGN, LC, c. 361, exp. 418.5/10.

116. Cárdenas, *La hacienda pública y la política económica*, 75. In Mexico City, the general cost of living rose by 6 percent in 1936, 21 percent in 1937, and then by an additional 11 percent in 1938. Ochoa, *Feeding Mexico*, 46, table 3-1.

117. 03/04/1936, AGN, LC, c. 638 , exp. 521/35.

118. 12/31/1936, AGN, LC, c. 638 , exp. 521/35.

119. Ochoa, *Feeding Mexico*, 46–49.

120. 6/12/1937, AGN, LC, c. 638 , exp. 521/35.

121. 1/21/1938, AGN, LC, c. 361, exp. 418.5/15.

122. 4/2/1938, AGN, LC, c. 361, exp. 418.5/15.

123. Hamilton, *Limits of State Autonomy*, 241–58.

124. Azpeitia Gómez, *Compañía Exportadora e Importadora Mexicana*, 28–29.

125. Ochoa, *Feeding Mexico*, 59.

126. 10/20/1938, AGN, LC, c. 638 , exp. 521/35. The title of the report was "Shortcomings of the Working of the Comité Regulador del Mercado de las Subsistencias and How to Correct Them."

127. 1/16/1939, AGN, LC, c. 638 , exp. 521/35. It is hard to discern derogatory bureaucratic jargon from reality. On the one hand, Albert Michaels suggests government officials tended to label all opposition forces as fascist. Michaels, "Las Elecciones," 123. On the other hand, according to historian Alicia Gojman de Backal, sentiments akin to those behind fascism were not uncommon among public market vendors. For example, in November 1937 locatarios from La Merced formed an organization called the Legión Mexicana Nacionalista "to fight tenaciously to reclaim our economy from the hands of undesirable foreigners, and defend the history, tradition, and customs of our homeland." Gojman de Backal, *Camisas, escudos y desfiles militares*, 164. Shortly before that, the president of the Cámara Israelita de Industria y Comercio de México

had written an "urgent telegram" to Lázaro Cárdenas requesting an audience to discuss the actions of the Bloque de Acción Revolucionaria Pro-Pequeño Comercio e Industria, which was campaigning "to restrict the civil rights of Jewish people, and the cancelation of legally granted licenses." 10/4/1937, AGN, LC, c. 637, exp. 521/4. Tiziana Bertaccini also points at small-scale vendors' flirtation with right-wing groups such as the openly xenophobic Comité Pro-Raza and the Confederación de la Clase Media. Bertaccini, *El régimen priísta*, 227–32. In any case, what matters here is that this period, as Alan Knight reminds us, saw high levels of popular mobilization on the right. Knight, "Cardenismo: Juggernaut or Jalopy?" 92.

128. 8/14/1939, AVCC.

129. 7/10/1939, AVCC; 31/7/1939. Tensions between the concessioner, the local authorities, and market vendors had been ongoing for almost four years. "Nuevo mercado en populosa colonia de esta capital," *Excélsior*, December 22, 1935. The original contract had been approved in December 1935. AVCC, 12/5/1935.

130. Ochoa, *Feeding Mexico*, 60.

131. Davis, *Urban Leviathan*, 91–98.

132. Davis, *Urban Leviathan*, 91–98.

133. Navarro, *Political Intelligence*, 21–22, 63–64.

134. 8/14/1939, AVCC.

135. Davis quotes estimates putting the size of the crowds between 200,000 and 250,000. *Urban Leviathan*, 97.

136. Gill, *El Sinarquismo: Su origen, su esencia, su misión*; Meyer, *El Sinarquismo: ¿Un fascismo Mexicano? 1937–1947*; Katz, "Algunos rasgos esenciales," 42–48.

137. For a history of the PAN, see Loaeza, *El Partido Acción Nacional*.

138. Michaels, *Mexican Election of 1940*; Contreras, *México 1940*; Navarro, *Political Intelligence*, chap. 1.

139. Davis, *Urban Leviathan*, 97–98. Marte R. Gómez, secretary of agriculture under Ávila Camacho, later admitted that while the official candidate had won throughout the country, he had lost in the Federal District. Wilkie, *Mexican Revolution*, 180.

140. Niblo, *War, Diplomacy, and Development*.

141. Meyer, "El conflicto petrolero entre México y los Estados Unidos," 149–50.

142. Roxborough, "Mexico," 194–202.

143. Jones, *The War Has Brought Peace to Mexico*.

144. Middlebrook, *Paradox of Revolution*, 111–12.

145. Hernández Chávez, *Mexico: A Brief History*, 288.

146. Bortz, *Los salarios industriales en México*, 266.

147. Middlebrook, *Paradox of Revolution*, 164, table 5.1.

148. Ochoa, *Feeding Mexico*, 80 and n. 36.

149. For example, in early 1942, intelligence agents reported that in response to a renewed surge in inflation, the Partido Autonomista Mexicano was launching a campaign against the high cost of living that included a "plan to cause a scandal" at a Comité de las Subsistencias depot, an attack on several La Merced wholesalers,

and PAM-organized meetings in several markets. 1/9/1942, AGN, DGIPS, c. 70, exp. 1; 1/10/1942, AGN, DGIPS, c. 70, exp. 1; 1/8/1942, AGN, MAC, c. 581, exp. 521.8/1; 1/20/1942, AGN, MAC, c. 581, exp. 521.8/1; 4/16/1942, AGN, DGIPS, c. 70, exp. 1; 4/20/1942, AGN, DGIPS, c. 70, exp. 1. Locatarios representatives from La Lagunilla, La Merced, and Martínez de la Torre attended a "secret" PAM assembly where they pledged to fight both "speculators" and the politicians "who monopolize access to basic goods, selling them at whatever price they want." 4/23/1942, AGN, DGIPS, c. 70, exp. 1. On surveillance of former Almazanista groups more generally, see Navarro, *Political Intelligence*, 171–74. By 1943, concerns about right-wing agitators combined with unease about the activities of communist organizers in markets. According to agent 184, a communist fee collector from the Tacubaya Market was forcing vendors to attend a party gathering at the Cine Regis under threat of increasing the cost of their stalls. 6/30/1943, AGN, DGIPS, c. 93, exp. 10. Agent 97, in turn, recounted a talk the Communist Party gave in the Ampudia Market to discuss trends in prices and the international situation as World War II was coming to an end. 2/14/1944, AGN, DGIPS, c. 95, exp. 9.

150. 12/26/1941, AGN, MAC, c. 769, exp. 542.21/52.

151. 8/10/1943, AGN, MAC, c. 769, exp. 542.21/52.

152. Gobierno del Distrito Federal, *Memoria del Gobierno del Distrito Federal, del 1 de Septiembre de 1944 al 31 de Agosto de 1945* (Mexico City: [s.n.], 1945), 91.

153. Davis, *Urban Leviathan*, 99–101.

154. Osorio Marbán, *El sector popular del PRI*, 41–43.

155. Schers, *Popular Sector*, 1–20; Bertaccini, *El régimen priísta*, 256–66; Garrido, *El partido de la revolución institucionalizada*, 331–40.

156. *Historia Documental CNOP*, 89.

157. Bertaccini, *El régimen priísta*, 256–66; Garrido, *El partido de la revolución institucionalizada*, 331–40; Schers, *Popular Sector of the Partido Revolucionario Institucional in Mexico*, 1–20.

158. 3/6/1944, AGN, MAC, c. 924, exp. 564.1/1014.

Chapter 5

1. Cárdenas, *La hacienda pública y la política económica*, 91–99.

2. Turrent Díaz, *México en Bretton Woods*.

3. *Estadísticas históricas*, tables 16.2 and 16.4; Smith, *Talons of the Eagle*, 118–19; Roxborough, "Mexico," 194–95.

4. US officials presented the Clayton Plan, so-called after US assistant secretary of state for economic affairs William L. Clayton, at the Inter-American Conference on the Problems of War and Peace in Mexico City, February 21 to March 8, 1945. José Galindo, "La Conferencia de Chapultepec (1945): El nacionalismo económico latinoamericano frente a la política librecambista de Estados Unidos," *Revista América Latina en la historia económica* 24, no. 2 (May–August 2017) 43–51; Leandro Morgenfeld, "Argentina y la vuelta al sistema interamericano: El largo camino a Chapultepec,"

Relaciones Internacionales 19, no. 39 (2010): 202–10; Kofas, *Foreign Debt and Underdevelopment*, 22–27.

5. Katz, "La guerra fría en América Latina," 18.

6. Niblo, *War, Diplomacy, and Development*, 143–46.

7. Puga, "La controversia sobre el proteccionismo en México," 195–239. Led by Lombardo Toledano, this was also the line of the Confederation of Latin American Workers. Alexander, *International Labor Organizations and Organized Labor in Latin America and the Caribbean*, 71–72.

8. Gauss, *Made in Mexico*, 169–71; Mosk, *Industrial Revolution in Mexico*, 33–35.

9. Cárdenas, *La hacienda*, 115–23, 130–33; Hansen, *Politics of Mexican Development*; Wionczek, *Nacionalismo mexicano*.

10. Loaeza, "Modernización autoritaria a la sombra de la superpotencia," 668.

11. Niblo, *War, Diplomacy, and Development*, 221–32; Shadlen, *Democratization without Representation*, 34–36. Raymond Vernon's *The Dilemma of Mexico's Development*, published in 1963, is an eloquent characterization of the period's political economy.

12. Ceceña, *México en la órbita imperial*, chap. 4; Shadlen, *Democratization without Representation*, 33–35; Niblo, *War, Diplomacy, and Development*, 225–26. For an analysis of the cultural maneuvers of large US corporations in their attempts to attract Mexican customers, see Moreno, *Yankee Don't Go Home!*

13. Niblo, *Mexico in the 1940s*, 187–88; Niblo, *War, Diplomacy, and Development*, 228, 266; Aboites Aguilar, *El norte entre algodones*, chap. 3.

14. Bertaccini, *El régimen priísta frente a las clases medias*, 256–66; Garrido, *El partido de la revolución institucionalizada*, 331–40; Schers, *Popular Sector of the Partido Revolucionario Institucional in Mexico*, 1–20. In the context of the hemispheric "democratic spring" that followed World War II, another key political change was the marginalization of the military sector of the party, which would no longer be able to compete for the presidency. Loaeza, "Modernización autoritaria," 656–57.

15. Selee, *Decentralization, Democratization, and Informal Power in Mexico*. See also Sabet, *Police Reform in Mexico*. An earlier sociological literature on urban informality argues that patronage networks fostered co-optation and dependency, the price the poor in Mexico City paid to be able to stake claims to land, shelter, and services. Eckstein, *Poverty of Revolution*; Gilbert and Ward, *Housing, the State, and the Poor*.

16. Medina Peña, *Civilismo y modernización del autoritarismo*, 112–94; Katz, "La guerra fría," 25; Carr, *Marxism and Communism in Twentieth-Century Mexico*, chap. 5.

17. The history of the government's handling of labor conflicts and the *charrismo* in the country's most powerful industrial unions is relatively well known. We now also have compelling accounts of the violence exerted on peasant communities and organizations. Padilla, *Rural Resistance in the Land of Zapata*; McCormick, *Logic of Compromise in Mexico*. However, just as important for the political stability of the

period were divisions within the labor and agrarian movements and electoral competition between these groups and the popular sectors now incorporated under the CNOP. Together, they allowed the government to avoid challenges to capital's dominance over policy. Womack, "Luchas sindicales y liberalismos sociales," 444–48; Middlebrook, *Paradox of Revolution*, chap. 4; Jorge Basurto, *Del avilacamachismo al alemanismo*; Reyna and Trejo Delarbre, *De Adolfo Ruiz Cortines a Adolfo López Mateos (1952–1964)*.

18. There is a rich and growing historiography that emphasizes the importance of political violence in this period. Smith, *Pistoleros and Popular Movements*; Rath, *Myths of Demilitarization*; Pensado, *Rebel Mexico*.

19. Niblo, *Mexico in the 1940s*, 150–59, 230–35.

20. Rubin, *Decentering the Regime*; Gillingham, "Maximino's Bulls"; Gillingham and Smith, *Dictablanda*.

21. Banco de México, *Indicadores económicos*, cuadro 7.1.

22. Garza, *El proceso de industrialización en la ciudad de México*, 141–43; Reynolds, *Mexican Economy*, 36–43, 58–64, 185–96. On real wages, see Bleynat, Challú, and Segal, "Inequality, Living Standards and Growth." See also Bortz, *Los salarios industriales en México*, 266–70.

23. Wilkie, *Mexican Revolution*, 158–69. Per capita social expenditures and education outlays grew during the Alemán and Ruiz Cortines administrations. According to this author, public health expenditures did not.

24. The Sinarquista movement, the most serious political threat of the late 1930s and early 1940s, now proclaimed President Alemán "the best sinarquista in Mexico" owing to his construction and public works projects. "Best Sinarquista in Mexico," *Novedades*, April 20, 1951. Quoted in Navarro, *Political Intelligence and the Creation of Modern Mexico*, 226, n. 123.

25. Knight, "Weight of the State in Modern Mexico." As Paul Gillingham puts it, the Mexican state of the 1940s and 1950s resembled a puffer fish, desperately inflating itself to look bigger than it really was. Gillingham, "Maximino's Bulls," 181.

26. Figures in constant 1950 pesos. Garza, *El proceso de industrialización*, 142–43.

27. In terms of production value. Gauss, *Made in Mexico*, 198.

28. Garza, *El proceso de industrialización*, 142–43.

29. Luis Unikel, *La dinámica del crecimiento de la Ciudad de México*, 9; Pick and Butler, *Mexico Megacity*, 54.

30. Ochoa, *Feeding Mexico*, 112–13, 127. In July 1949, the State Food Agency was revamped and taken over by the CEIMSA, a branch of the national export-import bank. Under Ruiz Cortines, the State Food Agency would receive more than twice the funds allocated to the Secretaría de Recursos Hidráulicos, and several times the money the federal government invested in agricultural credit. Ochoa, *Feeding Mexico*, 132.

31. While intelligence agents' reports provide a fascinating window into the period's popular politics, the agents' incentives to exaggerate threats and thus raise

their profiles should not be overlooked. Moreover, because they were under the purview of the secretary of gobernación, their content, especially any criticism of other high-level party and government officials, must be read in the light of the secretary's political agenda. After all, beginning with Alemán, four of the next five presidents would be former secretaries of gobernación. In 1948, Ruiz Cortines might have hoped to discredit Casas Alemán, who would later be his rival for the PRI's presidential nomination.

32. 7/22/1948, AGN, DGIPS, c. 111, exp. 1, 15–16.
33. 7/23/1948, AGN, DGIPS, c. 111, exp. 1, 25–26; 7/26/1948, AGN, DGIPS, c. 111, exp. 1, 54.
34. 7/30/1948, AGN, DGIPS, c. 111, exp. 1, 91.
35. 8/4/1948, AGN, DGIPS, c. 111, exp. 1, 175.
36. 8/10/1948, AGN, DGIPS, c. 111, exp. 1 254.
37. *El Universal*, August 14, 1948, in AGN, DGIPS, c. 111, exp. 3, 2.
38. "Enérgico plan para control de precios," *La Prensa*, August 14, 1948, in AGN, DGIPS, c. 111, exp. 3. 9; "Para frenar el alza," *El Universal*, August 11, 1948, in AGN, DGIPS, c. 111, exp. 1, 311. The mercados agrícolas were also referred to as "mercados de emergencia" or "mercados populares." For the sake of clarity and consistency, I always call them *agrícolas*.
39. Ochoa, *Feeding Mexico*, 111–12.
40. For example, see AGN, MAV, C.671, exp. 562.32/18–4.
41. 08/11/1948, AGN, DGIPS, c. 111, exp. 1, 316.
42. 8/14/1948, AGN, DGIPS, c. 111, exp. 3, 13.
43. Just as intelligence reports need to be read with an eye on the agents' personal interests and their bosses' political projects, journalists in this period had strong incentives to present the federal government in a positive light. See Niblo, *Mexico in the 1940s*, 346–50.
44. "Esta semana bajarán los precios de la carne," *Excélsior*, August 16, 1948, in AGN, DGIPS, c. 111, exp. 3, 15.
45. "La campaña de abaratamiento," *El Universal*, sección editorial, August 16, 1948, in AGN, DGIPS, c. 111, exp. 3, 22.
46. "Se instalarán todos los mercados de emergencia que sean necesarios," *El Nacional*, August 17, 1948, in AGN, DGIPS, c. 111, exp. 3, 59.
47. 08/18/1948, AGN, GDIPS, c. 111, exp. 3, 86.
48. "Limpia de políticos y acaparadores en los nuevos mercados," *Excélsior*, August 19, 1948, 17, 27, in BLT, AE.
49. "Esta semana bajarán los precios de la carne," *Excélsior*, August 16, 1948, in AGN, DGIPS, c. 111, exp. 3, 15.
50. Castillo Berthier, *Estructura de poder de los comerciantes mayoristas*, 17–71.
51. "Enérgico plan para control de precios," *La Prensa*, August 14, 1948, in AGN, DGIPS, c. 111, exp. 3, 9.
52. "Limpia de políticos y acaparadores en los nuevos mercados," *Excélsior*, August 19, 1948, 17, 27, in BLT, AE.

53. "Los coyotes de La Merced intervienen en los nuevos mercados de emergencia," *El Popular*, August 19, 1948, in AGN, DGIPS, c. 111, exp. 3, 100.

54. "Limpia de políticos y acaparadores en los nuevos mercados," *Excélsior*, August 19, 1948, 17, 27, in BLT, AE.

55. "Limpia de políticos y acaparadores en los nuevos mercados," *Excélsior*, August 19, 1948, 17, 27, in BLT, AE.

56. "Tendrá verdaderas proporciones populares la manifestación de hoy contra la carestía," *El Popular*, August 21, 1948, in AGN, DGIPS, c. 111, exp. 3, 163.

57. Open letter, *Excélsior*, August 21, 1948, in AGN, DGIPS, c. 111, exp. 3, 166. In the same issue, the newspaper published an interview with the secretary general of the progovernment CTM, who said the demonstration was a communist "training session . . . to test the efficacy of the slogans and tactics elaborated by international conspirators, experts in mutinies and coups d'état." No wonder the organizers of the demonstration were trying to explain themselves. "Dice la CTM que el mitín de hoy es de comunistas," *Excélsior*, August 21, 1948, in AGN, DGIPS, c. 111, exp. 3, 167. Though more circumspect in their statements, business leaders shared the CTM's opinion. "Clasificación divergente del desfile contra la carestía," *El Universal*, August 21, 1948, in AGN, DGIPS, c. 111, exp. 3, 169.

58. "Condenan a agitadores," *La Prensa*, August 21, 1948, in AGN, DGIPS, c. 111, exp. 3, 176.

59. 8/21/1948, AGN, DGIPS, c. 111, exp. 3, 191–94.

60. 8/21/1948, AGN, DGIPS, c. 111, exp. 3, 195–96.

61. "Cincuenta mil compradores," *Novedades*, August 23, 1948, in AGN, DGIPS, c. 111, exp. 3, 229.

62. "Apertura del segundo mercado de emergencia," *La Prensa*, August 21, 1948, in AGN, DGIPS, c. 111, exp. 3, 158–59.

63. 23/8/1948, AGN, MAV, c. 617, exp. 565.32/18-4.

64. "Derrumbe general de precios en los 60 mercados del distrito," *Excélsior*, August 21, 1948, in AGN, DGIPS, c. 111, exp. 3, 160.

65. "Los mercados de emergencia," *El Nacional*, August 23, 1948, in AGN, DGIPS, c. 111, exp. 3, 228.

66. 9/6/1948, AGN, MAV, c. 671, exp. 565.32/18-4. Apparently the president did not respond promptly enough. On September 20, 1948, the Federación de Comerciantes wrote to Alemán again to inform him of an assembly of representatives of sixty-three vendor organizations, where they decided that their markets should be turned into mercados agrícolas; they now asked for his backing to enjoy all the official exemptions that this would imply. The federación also requested assistance in buying their merchandise at production centers and to be able to transport them to the capital without paying taxes, bribes, or any other expenses that, they claimed, were partly responsible for making subsistence goods so expensive. 9/20/1948, AGN, MAV, c. 671, exp. 565.32/18-4.

67. 8/24/1948, AGN, DGIPS, c. 111, exp. 3, 240.

68. 9/18/1948, AGN, MAV, c. 671, exp. 565.32/18-4.

69. 9/17/1948, AGN, MAV, c. 671, exp. 565.32/18-4.

70. 3/5/1949, AGN, MAV, c. 804, exp. 703.4/476. Other small-scale producers reported Rojas telling them that "the mercados agrícolas have finished because the emergency has passed." 3/8/1949, AGN, MAV, c. 671, exp. 565.32/18-4.

71. 3/7/1949, AGN, MAV, c. 671, exp. 565.32/18-4.

72. 1/30/1950, AGN, MAV, c. 671, exp. 565.32/18-4.

73. 11/17/1949, AGN, DGIPS, c. 111, exp. 2, 64; 12/1/1949, AGN, DGIPS, c. 111, exp. 2, 97.

74. "Los mercados populares," *Excélsior*, December 9, 1949, in BLT, AE.

75. "La vuelta de los mercados populares," *Novedades*, December 18, 1949, in BLT, AE.

76. The State Food Agency, CEIMSA, announced that it would increase both the number of stores that sold directly to the public and those that supplied the city's market vendors. Ochoa, *Feeding Mexico*, 116.

77. 11/29/1945, AGN, MAC, c. 755, exp. 545.2/18.

78. "El problema del comercio en pequeño es de higiene," *Novedades*, May 25, 1945, in BLT, AE. In these years, the US department store Sears Roebuck also opened its first store, becoming an instant hit among the city's upper-middle-class eager to consume the latest fashions. Moreno, *Yankee Don't Go Home*, chap. 6.

79. Isbister, "Urban Employment and Wages in a Developing Economy," 30.

80. "El problema del comercio en pequeño es de higiene," *Novedades*, May 25, 1945, in BLT, AE. While CANACO claimed that this was the result of "a study" of the city's commerce, it would suit them to err on the side of exaggerating the number.

81. "El pequeño comercio en mala situación," *Excélsior*, April 11, 1945, in BLT, AE. Vendor organizations had reasons of their own to inflate the numbers.

82. According to Wayne Cornelius, almost half of urban population growth during the 1940 to 1960 period resulted from rural migration. Cornelius, *Politics and the Migrant Poor in Mexico City*, 16.

83. Eileen Ford draws attention to the fact that between 1940 and 1960, children, defined as people aged fourteen and under, went from 34.5 to 41 percent of the population of the Federal District, which she aptly calls a "city of children." Ford, *Childhood and Modernity in Cold War Mexico City*, 28. For a discussion of children's experiences of the working in the city, including vending, see chap. 1.

84. 1/28/1947, AVCC.

85. For all practical purposes, the zonas de mercado functioned as markets. Market administrators treated zonas de mercado as extensions of (or substitutes for) market halls, awarding licenses and charging fees for stalls in these areas.

86. The difficulty stemmed from the level of informality in fee collection as well as from vendors' reluctance to be surveyed. Bleynat, "Business of Governing."

87. 4/23/1947, AVCC.

88. "A vuelo de pluma trata importantes problemas el compañero Jesús Baustista, viejo comerciante," *La Gaceta de México, Quincenal de Información y Variedades*, September 1949, p. 4, in Fondo Presidente Miguel Alemán Valdés, Archivo General de la Nación (hereafter AGN, MAV), c. 318, exp. 433/152-A.

89. "Carece la capital de buenos mercados," *Excélsior*, September 12, 1945, in BLT, AE.
90. 6/2/1949, AGN, MAV, c. 286, exp. 418.5/2.
91. 10/7/1948, AGN, MAV, c. 286, exp. 418.5/2.
92. 6/2/1949, AGN, MAV, c. 286, exp. 418.5/2.
93. 5/2/1950, AGN, MAV, c. 579, exp. 545.22/466.
94. "Proyecto de ley para Bco. del Pq Comercio del DF, S.A. de C.V.," in 12/15/1948, AGN, MAV, c. 579, exp. 545.22/470.
95. 5/2/1950, AGN, MAV, c. 579, exp. 545.22/466.
96. 5/2/1950, AGN, MAV, c. 579, exp. 545.22/466.
97. 3/30/1950, AGN, MAV, c. 579, exp. 545.22/466.
98. 4/4/1950, AGN, MAV, c. 318, exp. 433.152.
99. 4/4/1950, AGN, MAV, c. 318, exp. 433.152.
100. 2/6/1951, AGN, MAV, c. 318, exp. 433.152.
101. 2/23/1951, AGN, MAV, c. 318, exp. 433.152.
102. Bojórquez proposed the bank should offer vendors twenty-four-hour-long loans at 0.5 percent interest. He defended this rate by comparing it with the *usureros'* practice of charging 5 percent, or even 10 percent for the same loans. It is no wonder that so many vendors preferred state control to remaining in the hands of their usual creditors.
103. 2/12/1951, AGN, MAV, c. 318, exp. 433/152; 3/8/1951, AGN, MAV, c. 318, exp. 433/152. Guillermo Martínez Domínguez was a man moving up the political ladder. After leaving the bank in 1955, he became oficial mayor of the Federal Electricity Commission, later becoming its director general. In 1970 he was appointed director general of the public financing agency Nacional Financiera, a post he held until 1974. His brother, Alfonso, rose even higher. After two stints as federal deputy for the Federal District (1946–49 and 1952–55), he became head of the PRI's Federal District regional committee in 1955, then secretary general of the CNOP between 1960 and 1965, and head of the Federal District in 1970–71.
104. 4/4/1952, AGN, MAV, c. 1265, exp. 243.2/34416.
105. "Promete Uruchurtu mejorar servicios públicos y frenar la carestía en el D.F.," *Excélsior*, December 6, 1952, in BLT, AE.
106. Davis, *Urban Leviathan*, 131; Oldman et al., *Financing Urban Development in Mexico City*, 29. These authors provide figures that are in nominal terms, reporting a 300 percent increase. When I deflate them using the index for the cost of living for workers in Mexico City (*Estadísticas Históricas Mexicanas*, table 17.20), it implies inflation of 54 percent over 1953–59.
107. Kram Villarreal, "Gladiolas for the Children of Sánchez," 17, 51–53.
108. Cross, *Informal Politics*, 160–72; see also Gordon, "Peddlers, Pesos, and Power," 98–100.
109. Sánchez Mejorada, *Rezago de la modernidad*, 67–75; Davis, *Urban Leviathan*, 102–5, 126, 132–36.
110. They both aimed high. According to gobernación agents, in 1955 Uruchurtu was considered a potential presidential contender, the candidate of the "organized

casasalemanismo," 3/26/55, DFS, exp. 10-26-55. Peña Manterola, for his part, sought Uruchurtu's post. In July 1957 he campaigned in the press and in the city's markets with a leaflet reading: "Whoever becomes president, Peña Manterola will be regent. Long live the protector of the poor! Long live the protector of the Mexican society and family!" 11/22/1957, DFS, 30-25-57. Instead, he was elected deputy for the Federal District for the 44th Legislature (1958–61) alongside his renewed position as head of the markets department. Camp, *Mexican Political Biographies*, 1100. The two appear to have abandoned public life after 1966.

111. Gordon, "Peddlers, Pesos, and Power," 83.
112. 2/18/1953, AGN, ARC, c. 677, exp. 521/1.
113. 10/9/1953, AGN, ARC, c. 677, exp. 521/1.
114. 8/7/1953, AGN, ARC, c. 411, exp. 418.5/3. The Alianza was a member of the Federación de Obreros del D.F. and was affiliated with the CTM. 5/17/1957, AGN, ARC, c. 677, exp. 521/1.
115. In August 1953, the DFS took over the surveillance of markets from the DGIPS. 8/18/1953, AGN, DFS, 52-8 L-1. There are some continuities between DFS and the DGIPS markets reports: agents continued to monitor prices and consumers' moods and opinions on the government. They both informed on vendors' and merchants' reactions to state intervention in the city's supply chains, in particular on their views on the functioning of the state food agency, CEIMSA. They also included commentary on the relationship between vendors and public officials. For example, see: 8/21/1953, AGN, DFS, 52-8 L-1; 8/29/1953, AGN, DFS, 52-8 L-1. Increasingly, though, the focus shifted toward the political behavior of vendor organizations. The presence of DFS agents in the city's markets underscores the growing importance of vendors in local and national CNOP politics. More broadly, it illustrates the politization of intelligence services and the DFS's centrality to the PRI's electoral dominance in this period. Navarro, *Political Intelligence*, 186. For a discussion of the methodological and historiographical innovations allowed by the use of intelligence files, see Padilla and Walker, "In the Archives: History and Politics," 1–10.
116. 10/26/1953, AGN, DFS, 30–21 53 L-1, H-2; 10/29/1953, AGN, DFS, 30–21 53 L-1, H-5.
117. 1/10/1954, AGN, ARC, c. 1240, exp. 703.2/209.
118. 11/17/1954, AGN, DFS 31-21 54.
119. 6/17/1953, AGN, ARC, c. 677, exp. 521/1. The list of organizations that Ávila claimed had left the Frente Único included: Obrero Mundial, Colima, Ambulantes, Churubusco, San Juan de Letrán, Arenal, Lagunilla, Circumvalación, Jesús María, and Venustiano Carranza.
120. 2/2/1954, AGN, ARC, c. 1240, exp. 703.2/209.
121. 6/11/1955, AGN, DFS, 30-21-55 H-79 L-1.
122. Sánchez Mejorada, *Rezago de la modernidad*, 88. Note that only in 1953 did Mexican women obtain the right to vote and to serve as congressional representatives. Hernández, "Women in Mexican Politics since 1953."
123. 2/9/1953, AHCDMX, DDF, OP, box 605.

124. 3/1/1955, AGN, DFS, 30-21-55 H-74 L-1.
125. 3/23/1955, AGN, DFS, 30-21-55 H-75 L-1.
126. 3/29/1955, AGN, DFS, 30-21-55 H-76 L-1.
127. 3/31/1955, AGN, DFS, 30-21-55 H-77/78 L-1.
128. Peschard, "Las elecciones en el Distrito Federal (1946–1970)," 238.
129. Only one Porfirian market remains, the 1903 iteration of the Mercado Dos de Abril. Vassallo, "La construcción de los mercados públicos," 92.
130. Gordon, "Peddlers, Pesos, and Power," 87.
131. A description of the markets built between 1955 and 1966 can be found in Pyle, "Public Markets of Mexico City," chap. 1.
132. López Rosado, *El abasto de productos alimenticios en la Ciudad de Mexico*, 450–51; "Dignificación del comerciante en pequeño, salud y bienestar para sus hijos, metas del D.F.," *El Nacional*, September 24, 1957, in BLT, AE.
133. "Monumentales centros de abastecimiento de La Merced y Jamaica, inaugurados ayer," *El Nacional*, September 24, 1957, in BLT, AE.
134. "Obras por 129 millones puso en servicio el Señor Presidente," *Excélsior*, September 24, 1957, in BLT, AE.
135. "Unidad técnica y social," *El Universal*, September 24, 1957, sección editorial, in BLT, AE.
136. "Dignificación del comerciante en pequeño, salud y bienestar para sus hijos, metas del D.F.," *El Nacional*, September 24, 1957, in BLT, AE.
137. 9/17/1957, AGN, ARC, c. 980, exp. 564.1/18.
138. 9/23/1957, AGN, ARC, c. 980, exp. 564.1/18.
139. "Descuento a quienes se empadronen," *Excélsior*, February 12, 1958.
140. Cross, *Informal Politics*, 170–71.
141. Peschard, "Las elecciones en el Distrito Federal," 233. It had still not gotten better when this study was published in 1988.
142. Cross, *Informal Politics*, 164. For an overview of Uruchuru's long tenure, see Garrido, "Ernesto P. Uruchurtu."
143. "Reconocen la gran obra del gobierno federal los locatarios de mercados," *El Universal*, May 25, 1961, in BLT, AE.
144. 9/30/1957, AGN, DFS, 30-21/224.
145. 11/16/1961, AGN, DFS, 30-21/4.

Epilogue

1. The conflicts surrounding the building of the subway system that Diane Davis studied exemplify this trend. As the city prepared for the 1968 Olympics, the country's most powerful engineering company, real estate developers, and finance capitalists pushed for this massive infrastructure project, to the detriment of Mexican bus operators and small factory owners who, like market vendors, had enjoyed Uruchurtu's protection. Davis, *Urban Leviathan*, 152–70.
2. Rodríguez Kuri, "Ciudad oficial, 1930–1979," 454–55.

3. Cross, *Informal Politics*, 163–82.

4. Real per capita investment calculated from public investment data in *Estadísticas Históricas de México*, table 15.23 and INEGI, using population and GDP deflator data from *World Bank Databank*.

5. Bleynat, Challú, and Segal, "Inequality, Living Standards, and Growth."

6. Chavez, "Transformation of Mexican Retailing with NAFTA," 503–13; Schwentesius and Gómez, "Supermarkets in Mexico," 487–502; Tilly, "Wal-Mart in Mexico," 189–209.

7. Delgadillo, "La disputa por los mercados de La Merced," 60–61.

8. David Barstow and Alejandra Xanic von Bertrab, "The Bribery Aisle: How Wal-Mart Got Its Way in Mexico," *New York Times*, December 17, 2012.

9. Delgadillo, "La disputa," 59.

10. "Statistical update on employment in the informal economy," *International Labour Organisation*, Department of Statistics, June 2012.

11. Delgadillo, "La disputa por los mercados de La Merced."

12. Left Hand Rotation Collective, in conjunction with Contested Cities and vendors and residents of La Merced, *Permanecer en La Merced*, Vimeo video, https://vimeo.com/156152727, 2016.

Bibliography

Archives and Collections

Archivo General de la Nación (AGN)
    Departamento de Trabajo (DT)
    Dirección Federal de Seguridad (DFS)
    Dirección General de Investigaciones Políticas y Sociales (DGIPS)
    Fototeca
Presidentes
    Obregón-Calles (O-C)
    Pascual Ortíz Rubio (POR)
    Abelardo L. Rodríguez (ALR)
    Lázaro Cárdenas (LC)
    Manuel Ávila Camacho (MAC)
    Miguel Alemán Valdés (MAV)
    Adolfo Ruiz Cortines (ARC)
    Secretaría General de Gobernación (SGG)
Archivo Histórico de la Secretaría de Salubridad y Asistencia (AHSSA)
Archivo Histórico de la Ciudad de México (AHCDMX)
    Actas y Versiones del Consejo Consultivo (AVCC)
    Ayuntamiento de la Ciudad de México, Fincas de Mercados (ACM, FM)
    Ayuntamiento de la Ciudad de México, Rastros y Mercados (ACM, RyM)
    Consejo Superior de Gobierno (CSG)
    Departamento del Distrito Federal, Oficina Consultiva (DDF, OC)
    Departamento del Distrito Federal, Obras Públicas (DDF, OP)
    Gobierno del Distrito, Mercados (GD, M)
    Reguladora de comercio, Comisión de inspectors (RC, CI)
    Secretaría de Gobernación, Rastros y Mercados (SG, RyM)

Archivo Porfirio Díaz (APD)
Biblioteca Lerdo de Tejada (BLT)
   Archivos Económicos (AE)
   Hemeroteca
Fideicomiso Archivos Plutarco Elías Calles y Fernando Torreblanca (FAPECFT)
   Plutarco Elías Calles (PEC)
Hemeroteca Nacional
Mediateca Instituto Nacional de Antropología e Historia

Newspapers and Periodicals

Boletín Oficial del Consejo Superior de Gobierno del Distrito Federal
Diario Oficial de la Federación
El Boletín Municipal
El Demócrata
Mexican Herald
El Monitor Republicano
El Municipio Libre
El Nacional
El País
El Popular
El Tiempo
El Universal
Excélsior
La Colonia Española
La Patria
La Prensa
Novedades
Obras Públicas
Revista Mexicana de Ingeniería y Arquitectura
Times Magazine

Published Primary Sources

Alonzo Romero, Miguel. *Un año de sitio a la presidencia municipal: Crónica y comentarios de una labor accidentada*. Mexico City: Hispano-Mexicana, 1923.
Arróniz, Marcos. *Manual del viajero en Méjico, ó Compendio de la historia de la Ciudad de Méjico*. Mexico City: Librería de Rosa y Bouret, 1858.
Bullock, William. *Six Months' Residence and Travels in Mexico*. Port Washington, NY: Kennikat Press, 1971. First printed in 1824.
Busto, Emiliano. *Estadística de la República Mexicana: Estado que guardan la agricultura, indutria, mineria y comercio; Resumen y análisis de los informes rendidos a la Secretaría de Hacienda por los agricultores, mineros, industriales y comerciantes*

de la República y los agentes de México en el exterior, en respuesta a las circulares de l de agosto de 1877. Mexico City: Imprenta de Ignacio Cumplido, 1880.

Castillo Velasco, José M. del, ed. *Colección de leyes, supremas órdenes, bandos, disposiciones de policía y reglamentos municipales de administración del Distrito Federal.* Mexico City: Castillo Velasco e Hijos, 1874.

Departamento del Distrito Federal. *Memoria del Departamento del Distrito Federal: Del 1 de septiembre de 1939 al 31 de agosto de 1940.* Mexico City: Talleres Gráficos de la Penitenciaría, 1940.

———. *Memoria del Departamento del Distrito Federal: Del 1 de septiembre de 1940 al 31 de agosto de 1941.* Mexico City: Talleres Gráficos de la Penitenciaría, 1941.

———. *Memoria del Departamento del Distrito Federal: Del 1 de septiembre de 1937 al 30 de agosto de 1938.* Mexico City: DAPP, 1938.

———. *Memoria del Departamento del Distrito Federal presentada por el C. Jefe del mismo, al H. Congreso de la Unión por el período comprendido del 1 de septiembre de 1936 al 31 de agosto de 1937.* Mexico City: (s.n.), 1937.

———. *Memoria presentada al H. Congreso de la Unión por el período comprendido de septiembre de 1935 a agosto de 1936.* Mexico City: (s.n.), 1936.

———. *Resumen de Actividades, 1949.* Mexico City: (s.n.), 1950.

Dirección General de Estadística. *Primer censo industrial: Resúmenes Generales.* Mexico City: Talleres Gráficos de la Nación, 1933.

———. *Quinto censo de población 15 de mayo de 1930: Distrito Federal.* Mexico City: Talleres Gráficos de la Nación, 1933.

Discurso del C. Ingeniero Sebastián Camacho, Presidente del Ayuntamiento de 1897, al instalarse el de 1898, discurso del C. Lic. Miguel S. Macedo, presidente del Ayuntamiento de 1898, contestación del C. Gobernador del Distrito Federal C. Lic. Rafael Rebollar, y memoria documentada de los trabajos municipales de 1897, formada por el Secretario C. Lic. Juan Bribiesca. Mexico City: La Europea de J. Aguilar Vera, 1898.

Discurso del C. Ingeniero Sebastián Camacho, Presidente del Ayuntamiento de 1895, al instalarse el de 1896, contestación del C. Gobernador del Distrito Federal Gral: Pedro Rincón Gallardo y memoria documentada de los trabajos municipales de 1895. Mexico City: Imp. y Lit. "La Europea" de Fernando Camacho, 1896.

Discurso del C. Lic. Miguel S. Macedo, Presidente del Ayuntamiento, contestación del C. Gobernador del Distrito Federal C. Lic. Rafael Rebollar y memoria documentada de los trabajos municipales de 1898, formada por el Secretario Lic. Juan Bribiesca. Mexico City: Tip. y Lit. "La Europea" de J. Aguilar Vera, 1899.

Discurso del S. Don Guillermo de Landa y Escandón, Presidente del Ayuntamiento de México en 1900, discurso del S. Don Ramón Corral, gobernador del Distrito Federal y memoria documentada de los trabajos municipales de 1900. Mexico City: Tip. y Lit. "La Europea" de J. Aguilar Vera, 1901.

Discurso del Sr. D. Fernando Pimentel y Fagoaga, Presidente del Ayuntamiento en 1903 y Memoria documentada de los trabajos municipales en el primer semestre de 1903. Mexico City: La Europea, 1903.

Discurso leído al 1º de enero de 1890 por el C. Gral Manuel González Cosío como Presidente del Ayuntamiento de 1889, y discurso del C. Gobernador del Distrito Federal al instalar la nueva corporación. Mexico City: Imprenta de Francisco Díaz de León, 1890.

Discurso leído el 1 de enero de 1891 por el C. Gral. Manuel González Cosío como Presidente del Ayuntamiento de 1890 dando cuenta de su administración y discurso del C. Gobernador del Distrito Federal al instalar la nueva corporación. Mexico City: Imprenta de Francisco Díaz de León.

Discurso leído el 1º de enero de 1889 por el Lic. Gral. Manuel González Cosío como Presidente del Ayuntamiento de 1888 dando cuenta de su administración y discurso del C. Gobernador del Distrito Federal al instalar la nueva corporación. Mexico City: Imprenta de Francisco Díaz de León, 1889.

Discurso leído el 1º de enero de 1884 por el C. Pedro Rincón Gallardo como Presidente del Ayuntamiento de 1883 dando cuenta de su administración, contestación del C. Lic. Guillermo Valle Presidente del Ayuntamiento de 1884 y discurso del C. Gobernador del Distrito Federal al instalar la nueva corporación. Mexico City: Imprenta de Francisco Díaz de León 1884.

Discurso leído el 1º de enero de 1885 por el C. Guillermo Valle, como Presidente del Ayuntamiento de 1884 dando cuenta de su administración, contestación del Lic. Pedro Rincón Gallardo, Presidente del Ayuntamiento de 1885, y discurso del C. Gobernador del Distrito Federal al instalar la nueva Corporación. Mexico City: Imprenta de Francisco Díaz de León, 1885.

Discurso leído el 1º de enero de 1886 por el C. Pedro Rincón Gallardo como Presidente del Ayuntamiento de 1885, dando cuenta de su administración, contestación del C. Manuel González Cosío y Discurso del C. Gobernador del Distrito al instalar la nueva Corporación. Mexico City: Imprenta de Francisco Díaz de León, 1886.

Discurso leído el 1º de enero de 1888 por el C. Gral. Manuel G. Cosío como Presidente del Ayuntamiento de 1887, dando cuenta de su administración, contestación del Ciudadano Manuel Gargollo Segundo Regidor del Ayuntamiento de 1887 y discurso del C. Gobernador del Distrito Federal al instalarse la nueva corporación. Mexico City: Imprenta de Francisco Díaz de León, 1888.

Discurso leído el 4 de enero de 1887 por el C. Gral. Manuel G. Cosío como Presidente del Ayuntamiento de 1886 dando cuenta de su administración, contestación del ciudadano Francisco Mejía, segundo regidor del Ayuntamiento de 1887. Mexico City: Imprenta de Francisco Díaz de León, 1887.

Discurso pronunciado por el Dr. Manuel Domínguez, Regidor 1º del Ayuntamiento Constitucional de México en 1880 al separarse de su puesto el 1º de enero de 1881, y contestación del C. Pablo de Lascurain, Regidor 2º del Ayuntamiento Constitucional de 1881. Mexico City: Imprenta de Francisco Díaz de León, 1881.

Discurso pronunciado por el Sr. Pedro Rincón Gallardo, Regidor primero del Ayuntamiento Constitucional de México en 1881 al alejarse del puesto conforme a la ley, el 1º de enero de 1882. Mexico City: Imprenta del Comercio de Dublán, 1882.

Discursos del Sr. D. Fernando Pimentel y Fagoaga, Presidente interino del Ayuntamiento en 1902, del Sr. D. Ramón Corral, gobernador del Distrito Federal, y del

Sr. D. Guillermo de Landa y Escandón. Mexico City: Tip. y Lit. "La Europea" de J. Aguilar Vera, 1903.

Esposición del Exmo. Sr. Ministro de Hacienda al Congreso dando cuenta del decreto de 6 de octubre último sobre dotación del fondo municipal de la Capital leída en la Cámara de Diputados el día 19 de enero de 1849. Mexico City: Imprenta de Vicente García Torres, 1849.

Estadísticas históricas de México. Aguascalientes: Instituto Nacional de Estadística, Geografía e Informática, 1990.

García Cubas, Antonio. *Escritos Diversos de 1870 a 1874.* Mexico City: Imprenta de Ignacio Escalante, 1874.

Geiger, John Lewis. *A Peep at Mexico: Narrative of a Journey across the Republic from the Pacific to the Gulf in December 1873 and January 1874.* London: Trübner, 1874.

Gobernar la ciudad es servirla: Informe que rinde el C. Jefe del Departamento del Distrito Federal, Lic. Aarón Sáenz, a la ciudad de México. Mexico City: (s.n.), 1934.

Gobierno del Distrito Federal. *Memoria del Gobierno del Distrito Federal, del 1 de Septiembre de 1944 al 31 de Agosto de 1945.* Mexico City: (s.n.), 1945.

Historia Documental CNOP. Mexico City: Instituto de Capacitación Política—PRI, 1984.

Informe presidencial y memoria del Departamento del Distrito Federal que rinde el C. Jeje del mismo por el período administrativo comprendido entre el 1 de julio del 1933 y el 30 de junio de 1934. Mexico City: Talleres Gráficos de la Nación, 1934.

Informe que rinde el C. Jefe del Departamento del Distrito Federal de la obra realizada durante el año de 1934 a los habitantes de la ciudad. Mexico City: (s.n.), 1935.

Instrucción pastoral que los Illmos: Sres. Arzobispos de México, Michoacán y Guadalajara dirigen a su venerable clero y a sus fieles con ocasión de la Ley Orgánica expedida por el Soberano Congreso Nacional en 10 de diciembre del año próximo pasado [1874] y sancionada por el Supremo Gobierno en 14 del mismo mes. Mexico City: Imprenta de José Mariano Lara, 1875.

Islas y Bustamante, Nicolás, ed. *Colección de leyes y disposiciones gubernativas, municipales y de policía vigentes en el Distrito Federal, formada por acuerdo del C. Gobernador Lic. Carlos Rivas.* 2 vols. Mexico City: Imprenta y litografía de Ireneo Paz, 1884.

Ley Orgánica del Distrito Federal y de los Territorios Federales. Mexico City: Talleres Gráficos de la Nación, 1929.

Los derechos del pueblo mexicano, México a través de sus constituciones. 15 vols. Mexico City: Cámara de Diputados del H. Congreso de la Unión / Porrúa Grupo Editorial, 2000.

Memoria con que da cuenta el C. Presidente del Ayuntamiento de 1875 al Ayuntamiento de 1876. Mexico City: Imprenta del Comercio de Dublán, 1876.

Memoria Corporación Municipal que funcionó de Agosto a Diciembre de 1867. Mexico City: Imprenta de J. Fuentes, 1868.

Memoria de los principales ramos de la policía urbana y de los fondos de la Ciudad de México presentado a la Serenísima Regencia del Imperio en cumplimiento de sus órdenes y de las leyes por el Prefecto Municipal. Mexico City: Imprenta de J. M. Andrade, 1864.

Memoria de los ramos municipales correspondiente al semestre de Julio a Diciembre de 1866 presentada a S. M. el Emperador por el Alcalde Municipal de la Ciudad de México D. Ignacio Trigueros. Mexico City: Imprenta Económica, 1867.

Memoria del Ayuntamiento que comenzó a funcionar el 5 de Diciembre de 1876 y concluyó el 31 de Diciembre de 1877. Mexico City: Imprenta de Ignacio Escalante, 1878.

Memoria del Consejo Superior de Gobierno del Distrito Federal correspondiente al período transcurrido del 1 de julio de 1903 al 31 de diciembre de 1904. 2 vols. Mexico City: Talleres de Pablo Rodríguez, 1906.

Memoria del Consejo Superior de Gobierno del Distrito Federal correspondiente al período transcurrido del 1 de enero al 31 de diciembre de 1905 presentada al Señor Secretario de Estado y del Despacho de Gobernación. Mexico City: Talleres de Pablo Rodríguez, 1907.

Memoria que el Ayuntamiento Constitucional de 1870 presenta a sus comitentes. Mexico City: Imprenta del Comercio de N. Chavez, 1871.

Memoria que el Ayuntamiento Constitucional de 1872 presenta a sus comitentes. Mexico City: Imprenta de I. Cumplido, 1873.

Memoria que el Ayuntamiento Constitucional de 1879 presenta a sus comitentes. Mexico City: Imprenta de Francisco Díaz de León, 1880.

Memoria que el Ayuntamiento Constitucional del año de 1868 presenta para el conocimiento de sus comitentes. Mexico City: Imprenta de Ignacio Cumplido, 1869.

Memoria que el Ayuntamiento Popular de 1868 presenta a sus comitentes y corresponde al semestre corrido desde el 1 de Enero al 30 de Junio. Mexico City: Imprenta de Ignacio Cumplido, 1868.

Memoria que el Ayuntamiento Popular de 1869 presenta a sus comitentes. Mexico City: Tipografía del Comercio de N. Chavez, 1870.

Orozco y Berra, Manuel. *Historia de la Ciudad de México, desde su fundación hasta 1854. Selección de artículos publicados en el Diccionario Universal de Historia y Geografía (1854) preparada por el Seminario de Historia Urbana del Departamento de Investigaciones Históricas del INAH.* Mexico City: Secretaría de Educación Pública, Septentas, 1973.

Osorio Marbán, Miguel. *El sector popular del PRI.* Mexico City: Coordinación Nacional de Estudios Históricos, Políticos y Sociales—PRI, 1994.

Pérez Hernández, José María. *Estadística de la República Mejicana.* Guadalajara: Tipográfica del Gobierno, 1862.

Prieto, Guillermo. *Memorias de mis tiempos, 1828 a 1840.* Mexico City: Librería de la Vda. de C. Bouret, 1906.

Recopilación de leyes, decretos y providencias de los poderes legislativo y ejecutivo de la Unión desde que se estableció en la Ciudad de México el Supremo Gobierno en 15 de julio de 1867, formada por la redacción del "Diario oficial." Vol. 12 (January–April 1872). Mexico City: Imprenta del Gobierno, 1873.

Reglamento para el servicio y recaudación del ramo de mercados. Mexico City: Imprenta de Francisco Díaz de León, 1885.
Reseña leída por el Presidente Municipal en nombre de la corporación que funcionó en 1882, contestación del Segundo Regidor Lic. Guillermo Valle y discurso del C. Gobernador del Distrito Federal al instalar el Ayuntamiento de 1883. Mexico City: Imprenta de Francisco Díaz de León, 1883.
Vérgez, José F. *Recuerdos de Méjico.* Barcelona: Imprenta de Henrich, 1902.

Secondary Sources

Aboites Aguilar, Luis. *Excepciones y privilegios: Modernización tributaria y centralización en México, 1922–1972.* Mexico City: El Colegio de México, 2003.
Acevedo, Esther. "Young Muralists at the Abelardo Rodríguez Market." In *Mexican Muralism: A Critical History*, edited by Alejandro Anreus, Leonard Folgarait, and Robin Adele Greeley. Berkeley: University of California Press, 2012.
Adame Goddard, Jorge. *El pensamiento político y social de los Católicos Mexicanos.* Mexico City: Universidad Nacional Autónoma de México, Instituto de Investigaciones Históricas, 1981.
Adelman, Jeremy, and Jonathan Levy. "The Fall and Rise of Economic History." *Chronicle of Higher Education*, December 1, 2014.
Agostoni, Claudia. *Monuments of Progress: Modernization and Public Health in Mexico City, 1876–1910.* Calgary, AB: University of Calgary Press, 2003.
Aguirre Rojas, Carlos Antonio. "Edward Palmer Thompson en América Latina: Sobre la economía moral de las multitudes latinoamericanas." *Autoctonía: Revista de Ciencias Sociales e Historia* 3, no. 1 (January–June 2019).
Alexander, Anna Rose. *City on Fire: Technology, Social Change, and the Hazards of Progress in Mexico City, 1860–1910.* Pittsburgh: University of Pittsburgh Press, 2016.
Alexander, Robert J. *International Labor Organizations and Organized Labor in Latin America and the Caribbean: A History.* Santa Barbara, CA: Praeger / ABC-CLIO, 2009, 71–72.
Alfaro-Velcamp, Theresa. *So Far from Allah, So Close to Mexico: Middle Eastern Immigrants in Modern Mexico.* Austin: University of Texas Press, 2007.
Anderson, Rodney D. *Outcasts in Their Own Land.* DeKalb: Northern Illinois University Press, 1976.
Arrom, Silvia M. *Containing the Poor: The Mexico City Poor House, 1774–1871.* Durham, NC: Duke University Press, 2000.
———. "Popular Politics in Mexico City: The Parian Riot, 1828." *Hispanic American Historical Review* 68, no. 2 (May 1988): 245–68.
———. *The Women of Mexico City, 1790–1857.* Stanford, CA: Stanford University Press, 1985.
Aubert, Roger. "Aux origines de la doctrine sociale catholique." *Dossiers de l'action sociale catholique* 43 (May 1966): 249–78.

Aviña, Alex. *Specters of Revolution: Peasant Guerrillas in the Cold War Mexican Countryside*. Oxford: Oxford University Press, 2014.
Azpeitia Gómez, Hugo. *Compañía Exportadora e Importadora Mexicana, S.A., 1949–1958: Conflicto y abasto alimentario*. Mexico City: CIESAS, 1994.
Bailey, David C. "Revisionism and the Recent Historiography of the Mexican Revolution." *Hispanic American Historical Review* 58, no. 1 (February 1978): 62–79.
Barajas Durán, Rafael. *Posada, mito y mitote: La caricatura política de José Guadalupe Posada y Manuel Alfonso Manilla*. Mexico City: Fondo de Cultura Económica, 2009.
Barbosa Cruz, Mario. "La Política en la Ciudad de México en tiempos de cambio (1903–1929). In *Historia Política de la Ciudad de México (Desde su fundación hasta el año 2000)*, edited by Ariel Rodríguez Kuri, 367–415. Mexico City: El Colegio de México, 2012.
———. *El trabajo en las calles: Subsistencia y negociación política en la Ciudad de México a comienzos del siglo XX*. Mexico City: El Colegio de México / Universidad Autónoma Metropolitana-Cuajimalpa, 2008.
Basurto, Jorge. *Del avilacamachismo al alemanismo (1940–1952)*. Vol. 11 of *La clase obrera en la historia de México*, edited by Pablo González Casanova. Mexico City: Siglo XXI Editores, 1984.
Bazant, Jan. *Alienation of Church Wealth in Mexico: Social and Economic Aspects of the Liberal Revolution, 1856–1875*. Cambridge: Cambridge University Press, 1970.
Beatty, Edward. "The Impact of Foreign Trade on the Mexican Economy: Terms of Trade and the Rise of Industry, 1880–1923." *Journal of Latin American Studies* 32, no. 2 (May 2000): 399–433.
———. *Institutions and Investment: The Political Basis of Industrialization in Mexico before 1911*. Stanford, CA: Stanford University Press, 2002.
Beezley, William H. *Judas at the Jockey Club and Other Episodes of Porfirian Mexico*. Lincoln: University of Nebraska Press, 1987.
Bertaccini, Tiziana. *El régimen priísta frente a las clases medias, 1943–1964*. Mexico City: Consejo Nacional para la Cultura y las Artes, 2009.
Blanco, José J. *Se llamaba Vasconcelos: Una evocación crítica*. Mexico City: Fondo de Cultura Económica, 1977.
Bleynat, Ingrid. "The Business of Governing: Corruption and Informal Politics in Mexico City's Markets, 1946–1958." *Journal of Latin American Studies* 50, no. 2 (2018): 355–81.
Bleynat, Ingrid, Amílcar Challú, and Paul Segal. "Inequality, Living Standards, and Growth: Two Centuries of Economic Development in Mexico." *Economic History Review* (forthcoming).
Bloch, Avital, and Servando Ortoll. "The Anti-Chinese and Anti-Japanese Movements in Cananea, Sonora, and Salt Lake River, Arizona, during the 1920 and 1930s." *Americana, E-Journal of American Studies in Hungary* 6, no. 1 (Spring 2010).
Blum, Ann S. "Conspicuous Benevolence: Liberalism, Public Welfare, and Private Charity in Porfirian Mexico City, 1877–1910." *The Americas* 58, no. 1 (July 2001): 7–38.

Bortz, Jeffrey L. *Los salarios industriales en México, 1939–1975*. Mexico City: Fondo de Cultura Económica, 1988.
Buffington, Robert M. *A Sentimental Education for the Working Man: The Mexico City Penny Press, 1900–1910*. Durham, NC: Duke University Press, 2015.
Calderón, Francisco R. *La República Restaurada: Vida Económica*. Vol. 2 of *Historia Moderna de México*, edited by Daniel Cosío Villegas. Mexico City: Hermes, 1955.
Camp, Roderic A. *Mexican Political Biographies, 1935–1993*. Austin: University of Texas Press, 2011.
Campos, Isaac. *Home Grown: Marijuana and the Origins of Mexico's War on Drugs*. Chapel Hill: University of North Carolina Press, 2012.
Cárdenas, Enrique. *Cuando se originó el atraso económico de México: La economía mexicana en el largo siglo XIX, 1720–1920*. Madrid: Biblioteca Nueva Fundación Ortega y Gasset, 2003.
———. *La hacienda pública y la política económica, 1929–1958*. Mexico City: El Colegio de México / Fondo de Cultura Económica, 1994.
———. *La industrialización mexicana durante la Gran Depresión*. Mexico City: El Colegio de México, 1987.
Cardero, María Elena. "Estructura monetaria y financiera de México: 1932–1940." *Revista Mexicana de Sociología* 41, no. 3 (July–September 1979): 729–68.
Carmagnani, Marcello. *Estado y Mercado: La economía pública del liberalismo mexicano, 1850–1911*. Mexico City: Fondo de Cultura Económica / Colegio de México, 1994.
———. "Finanzas y estado en México, 1820–1880." *Ibero Amerikanisches Archiv* 9, no. 3–4 (1983): 277–317.
———. "El liberalismo, los impuestos internos y el estado federal mexicano, 1857–1911." *Historia Mexicana* 38, no. 3 (January–March 1989): 471–96.
Carmona Fernando, Guillermo Montaño, Jorge Carrión, and Alonso Aguilar M. *El Milagro Mexicano*. Mexico City: Editorial Nuestro Tiempo, 1970.
Carr, Barry. *Marxism and Communism in Twentieth-Century Mexico*. Lincoln: University of Nebraska Press, 1992.
———. "The Mexican Communist Party and Agrarian Mobilization in the Laguna, 1920–1940: A Worker-Peasant Alliance?" *Hispanic American Historical Review* 67, no. 3 (August 1987): 371–404.
———. *El movimiento obrero y la política en México, 1910–1929*. 2 vols. Mexico City: Secretaría de Educación Pública, Dirección General de Divulgación, 1976.
Castillo Berthier, Héctor. *Estructura de poder de los comerciantes mayoristas de abarrotes de la Ciudad de México*. Mexico Instituto de Investigaciones Sociales, Universidad Nacional Autónoma de México, 1994.
———. "Los Mercados Públicos de la Ciudad de México: Características, Problemas y ¿Soluciones?" In *Políticas de Abasto Alimentario: Alternativas para el Distrito Federal y su Zona Metropolitana*, edited by Gerardo Torres Salcido, 187–94. Mexico City: Casa Juan Pablos / UNAM, Facultad de Ciencias Políticas, 2003.
Castillo Méndez, Laura Elena. *Historia del comercio en la Ciudad de México*. Mexico City: Departamento del Distrito Federal, Secretaría de Obras y Servicios, Colección Popular, 1973.

Ceceña, José Luis. *México en la órbita imperial*. Mexico City: Ediciones El Caballito, 1970.
Chavez, Manuel. "The Transformation of Mexican Retailing with NAFTA." *Development Policy Review* 20, no. 4 (2002): 503–13.
Chenillo Alazraki, Paola. "Liberalismo a prueba: La expulsión de 'extranjeros perniciosos' en México durante la República Restaurada (1867–1876)." *Revista de Indias* 72, no. 255 (2012): 377– 408.
Coatsworth, John H. *Growth against Development: The Economic Impact of Railroads in Porfirian Mexico*. DeKalb: Northern Illinois University Press, 1981.
Connolly, Priscilla. *El contratista de don Porifirio: Obras públicas, deuda y desarrollo desigual*. Mexico City: Fondo de Cultura Económica, 1997.
Contreras, Ariel J. *México 1940: Industrialización y crisis política*. Mexico City: Siglo XXI, 1977.
Cornelius, Wayne A. *Politics and the Migrant Poor in Mexico City*. Stanford, CA: Stanford University Press, 1975.
Cosío Villegas, Daniel. *El Porfiriato: Vida politica, politica exterior, parte segunda*. Vols. 5 and 6 of *Historia moderna de Mexico*, edited by Daniel Cosío Villegas. Mexico City: Hermes, 1960–63.
Cosío Villegas, Daniel, ed. *Historia moderna de México*. 9 vols. Mexico City: Hermes, 1955–72.
Craib, Raymond B. *Cartographic Mexico: A History of State Fixations and Fugitive Landscapes*. Durham, NC: Duke University Press, 2004.
Cross, John C. "Debilitando al clientelismo: La formalización del ambulantaje en la ciudad de México." *Revista Mexicana de Sociología* 59, no. 4 (October–December 1997): 93–115.
———. *Informal Politics: Street Vendors and the State in Mexico City*. Stanford, CA: Stanford University Press, 1998.
Crossa Niell, Verónica. *Luchando por un espacio en la ciudad de México: Comerciantes ambulantes y el espacio público urbano*. Mexico City: El Colegio de México, 2018.
Davies, Keith. "Tendencias demográficas urbanas durante el siglo XIX en México." *Historia Mexicana* 21 (July 1971–June 1972): 481–524.
Davies, Oliver. *A Theology of Compassion: Metaphysics of Difference and the Renewal of Tradition*. London: SCM Press, 2001.
Davis, Diane. *Urban Leviathan: Mexico City in the Twentieth Century*. Philadelphia: Temple University Press, 1994.
Delgadillo, Víctor. "La disputa por los mercados de La Merced." *Alteridades* 26, no. 51 (January–June 2016): 57–66.
Eckstein, Susan. *The Poverty of Revolution: The State and the Urban Poor in Mexico*. Princeton, NJ: Princeton University Press, 1977.
Escalante Gonzalbo, Fernando. *Ciudadanos imaginarios*. Mexico City: El Colegio de México, 1993.
Florescano, Enrique. *El nuevo pasado mexicano*. Mexico City: Cal y Arena, 1999.
Ford, Eileen Mary. *Childhood and Modernity in Cold War Mexico City*. New York: Bloomsbury, 2018.

Forment, Carlos A. *Democracy in Latin America, 1760–1900: Civic Selfhood and Public Life in Mexico and Peru*. Chicago: University of Chicago Press, 2003.

Fowler-Salamini, Heather. *Agrarian Radicalism in Veracruz, 1920–1938*. Lincoln: University of Nebraska Press, 1978.

Fox-Genovese, Elizabeth. "The Many Faces of Moral Economy: A Contribution to a Debate." *Past and Present*, no. 58 (February 1973): 161–68.

Gamboa Ramírez, Ricardo. "Las finanzas municipales de la Ciudad de México, 1800–1850." In *La Ciudad de México en la primera mitad del siglo XIX*, edited by Regina Hernández Franyuti, 1:11–63. Mexico City: Instituto de Investigaciones Dr. José Luis Mora, 1994.

García Ugarte, Marta Eugenia. *Poder politico y religioso: México siglo XIX*. Mexico City: UNAM / Porrúa, 2010.

Garrido, José. "Ernesto P. Uruchurtu (Distrito Federal, PRI, 1952–1966). Entre el equilibro autoritario nacional y el control del poder local." In *Los Gobernadores: Caciques del pasado y del presente*, edited by Andrew Paxman, 381–412. Mexico City: Grijalbo / Penguin Random House, 2018.

Garrido, Luis Javier. *El partido de la revolución institucionalizada: La formación del nuevo estado en México (1928–1945)*. Mexico City: Siglo XXI, 1982.

Garza, Gustavo. *El proceso de industrialización en la ciudad de México, 1821–1970*. Mexico City: El Colegio de México, 1985.

Gauss, Susan M. *Made in Mexico: Regions, Nation, and the State in the Rise of Mexican Industrialism, 1920s–1940s*. University Park: Pennsylvania State University Press, 2010.

Gibson, Charles. *Aztecs under Spanish Rule: A History of the Indians of the Valley of Mexico, 1519–1810*. Stanford, CA: Stanford University Press, 1964.

Gilbert, Alan, and Peter M. Ward. *Housing, the State, and the Poor*. Cambridge: Cambridge University Press, 1985.

Gill, Mario. *El Sinarquismo: Su origen, su esencia, su misión*. Mexico City: Olín, 1962.

Gillingham, Paul. "Maximino's Bulls: Popular Protest after the Mexican Revolution, 1940–1952." *Past and Present*, no. 206 (February 2010): 175–211.

Gillingham, Paul, and Benjamin T. Smith, eds. *Dictablanda: Politics, Work, and Culture in Mexico, 1938–1968*. Durham, NC: Duke University Press, 2014.

Gilly, Adolfo. *The Mexican Revolution*. London: Verso, 1983.

Gojman de Backal, Alicia. *Camisas, escudos y desfiles militares: Los Dorados y el antisemitismo en México (1934–1940)*. Mexico City: Fondo de Cultura Económica, 2000.

Gómez-Galvarriato Freer, Aurora. *Industry and Revolution: Social and Economic Change in the Orizaba Valley, Mexico*. Cambridge, MA: Harvard University Press, 2013.

Gómez-Galvarriato Freer, Aurora, and Emilio Kourí. "La reforma económica: Finanzas públicas, mercados y tierras." In *Nación, constitución y reforma, 1821–1908*, edited by Erika Pani, 63–119. Mexico City: Fondo de Cultura Economica / CIDE / INEHRM / CONACULTA, 2010.

Gómez-Galvarriato Freer, Aurora, and Aldo Musacchio. "Un Nuevo Índice de Precios para México, 1886–1929." *El Trimestre Económico* 67 (January–March 2000): 45–91.

Gonzales, Michael J. *The Mexican Revolution, 1910–1940.* Albuquerque: University of New Mexico Press, 2002.

González y González, Luis. "La Revolución Mexicana desde el punto de vista de los revolucionados." *Historias* 8–9 (1985): 5–13.

González y González, Luis, Emma Cosío Villegas, and Guadalupe Monroy. *La República Restaurada: Vida social.* Vol. 3 of *Historia moderna de México*, edited by Daniel Cosío Villegas. Mexico City: Hermes, 1957.

Gordon, Gary Isaac. "Peddlers, Pesos, and Power: The Political Economy of Street Vending in Mexico City." PhD diss., History Department, University of Chicago, 1997.

Gortari Rabiela, Hira de. "Política y Administración en la Ciudad de México: Relaciones entre el Ayuntamiento y el Gobierno del Distrito Federal y el Departamental: 1824–1843." In *La Ciudad de México en la primera mitad del siglo XIX*, edited by Regina Hernández Franyuti, 2:166–83. Mexico City: Instituto de Investigaciones Dr. José Luis Mora, 1994.

Gortari Rabiela, Hira de, and Regina Hernández Franyuti, eds. *Memoria y encuentros: La Ciudad de México y el Distrito Federal, 1824–1928.* 4 vols. Mexico City: Departamento del Distrito Federal / Instituto de Investigaciones Dr. José María Luis Mora, 1988.

Götz, Norbert. "'Moral Economy': Its Conceptual History and Analytical Prospects." *Journal of Global Ethics* 11, no. 2 (2015): 147–62.

Guadarrama, Rocío. *Los sindicatos y la política en México: La CROM, 1918–1928.* Mexico City: Ediciones Era, 1981.

Guerra, François-Xavier, and Annick Lempérière. Introducción to *Los espacios públicos en Iberoamérica: Ambigüedades y problemas, siglos XVIII–XIX*, edited by François-Xavier Guerra, Annick Lempérière, et al., 5–21. Mexico City: Fondo de Cultura Económica, 1998.

Habermas, Jürgen. *The Structural Transformation of the Public Sphere.* Cambridge: Polity Press, 1989. First published in 1962.

Hale, Charles A. *The Transformation of Liberalism in Late Nineteenth-Century Mexico.* Princeton, NJ: Princeton University Press, 1989.

Hamilton, Nora. *The Limits of State Autonomy: Post-revolutionary Mexico.* Princeton, NJ: Princeton University Press, 1982.

Hamnett, Brian R. *Juárez.* London: Longman, 1994.

———. "Liberalism Divided: Regional Politics and the National Project during the Mexican Restored Republic, 1867–1876." *Hispanic American Historical Review* 76, no. 4 (November 1996): 659–89.

Hansen, Roger D. *The Politics of Mexican Development.* Baltimore: Johns Hopkins University Press, 1971.

Hart, John M. *Anarchism and the Mexican Working Class, 1860–1931.* Austin: University of Texas Press, 1978.

———. *Empire and Revolution: The Americans in Mexico since the Civil War.* Berkeley: University of California Press, 2002.

Hefley, James C. *Aarón Sáenz, Mexico's Revolutionary Capitalist.* Waco, TX: Word Books, 1970.

Hernández, Sonia. "Women in Mexican Politics since 1953." *Oxford Research Encyclopedia of Latin American History.* February 26, 2018.

Hernández Chávez, Alicia. *La Mecánica Cardenista.* Vol. 16 of *Historia de la Revolución Mexicana.* Mexico City: El Colegio de México, 1979.

———. *Mexico: A Brief History.* Berkeley: University of California Press, 2006.

Hernández Franyuti, Regina, ed. *La Ciudad de México en la primera mitad del siglo XIX.* 2 vols. Mexico City: Instituto de Investigaciones Dr. José Luis Mora, 1994.

Hoffmann Calo, Juan. *Crónica Política del Ayuntamiento de la Ciudad de México, 1917-1928: Los partidos, las elecciones, los gobernantes.* Mexico City: Gobierno de la Ciudad de México, 2000.

Holden, Robert. *Mexico and the Survey of Public Lands: The Management of Modernization.* DeKalb: Northern Illinois University Press, 1987.

Illades, Carlos. "Composición de la fuerza de trabajo y de las unidades productivas en la Ciudad de México, 1788-1873." In *La Ciudad de México en la primera mitad del siglo XIX*, edited by Regina Hernández Franyuti, 2:250-78. Mexico City: Instituto de Investigaciones Dr. José Luis Mora, 1994.

———. "Organizaciones laborales y discurso asociativo en el siglo XIX." In *Ciudad de México: Instituciones, actores sociales y conflicto político, 1774-1931*, edited by Carlos Illades and Ariel Rodríguez Kuri, 245-74. Zamora, Michoacán: El Colegio de Michoacán / UAM, 1996.

Illades, Carlos, and Ariel Rodríguez Kuri, eds. *Ciudad de México: Instituciones, actores sociales y conflicto político, 1774-1931.* Zamora, Michoacán: El Colegio de Michoacán / UAM, 1996.

Isbister, John. "Urban Employment and Wages in a Developing Economy: The Case of Mexico." *Economic Development and Cultural Change* 20, no. 1 (October 1971): 24-46.

Iturriaga, José E. *La estructura social y cultural de México.* Mexico City: Instituto Nacional de Estudios Históricos de la Revolución Mexicana, 2003. First published in 1951.

Jiménez, Christina M. "Performing Their Right to the City: Political Uses of Public Space in a Mexican City, 1880-1910s." *Urban History* 33, no. 3 (2006): 435-56.

———. "Popular Organizing for Public Services: Residents Modernize Morelia, Mexico, 1880-1920." *Journal of Urban History* 30, no. 4 (May 2004): 495-518.

Jiménez Muñoz, Jorge H. *La traza del poder: Historia de la política y los negocios urbanos en el Distrito Federal, de sus orígenes a la desaparición del Ayuntamiento (1824-1928).* Mexico City: Dedalo, 1993.

Jones, Halbert. *The War Has Brought Peace to Mexico: World War II and the Consolidation of the Post-Revolutionary State.* Albuquerque: University of New Mexico Press, 2014.

Joseph, Gilbert M., and Daniel Nugent, eds. *Everyday Forms of State Formation: Revolution and the Negotiation of Rule in Modern Mexico*. Durham, NC: Duke University Press, 1994.

Katz, Friedrich. "Algunos rasgos esenciales de la política del imperialismo alemán en América Latina." In *Hitler sobre America Latina: El fascismo alemán en Latinoamérica, 1933-1943*, edited by Jürgen Hell et al., 9-96. Mexico City: Editorial Fondo de Cultura Popular, 1968.

———. "La guerra fría en América Latina." In *Espejos de la guerra fría: México, América Central y el Caribe*, edited by Daniela Spencer, 11-28. Mexico City: Porrúa, 2004.

———. "The Liberal Republic and the Porfiriato." In *Mexico since Independence*, edited by Leslie Bethell, 49-124. Cambridge: Cambridge University Press, 1991.

———. *The Life and Times of Pancho Villa*. Stanford, CA: Stanford University Press, 1998.

———. *The Secret War in Mexico: Europe, the United States, and the Mexican Revolution*. Chicago: University of Chicago Press, 1981.

Keremitsis, Dawn. *La industria textil mexicana en el siglo XIX*. Mexico City: Secretaría de Educación Pública, 1973.

Knapp, Frank A. *The Life of Sebastián Lerdo de Tejada, 1823-1889*. Austin: University of Texas Press, 1951.

Knight, Alan. "Cardenismo: Juggernaut or Jalopy?" *Journal of Latin American Studies* 26, no. 1 (February 1994): 73-107.

———. "Interpretaciones recientes de la Revolución mexicana." *Secuencia* 13 (1989): 23-43.

———. "El liberalismo mexicano, de la Reforma a hasta la Revolución (una interpretación)." *Historia Mexicana* 35, no. 1 (July-September 1985): 59-91.

———. *The Mexican Revolution*, 2 vols. Cambridge: Cambridge University Press, 1986.

———. "Mexico's Elite Settlement: Conjuncture and Consequences." In *Elites and Democratic Consolidation in Latin America and Southern Europe*, edited by John Higley and Richard Gunther, 113-45. Cambridge: Cambridge University Press, 1992.

———. "Revisionism and Revolution: Mexico Compared to England and France." *Past and Present*, no. 134 (February 1992): 159-99.

———. "The Rise and Fall of Cardenismo." In *Mexico since Independence*, edited by Leslie Bethell, 241-320. Cambridge: Cambridge University Press, 1991.

———. "The Weight of the State in Modern Mexico." In *Studies in the Formation of the Nation-State in Latin America*, edited by James Dunkerley, 212-53. London: ILAS, 2002.

Kocka, Jürgen, and Marvel van del Linden, eds. *Capitalism: The Reemergence of a Historical Concept*. London: Bloomsbury Academic, 2016.

Kofas, Jon V. *Foreign Debt and Underdevelopment: U.S.-Peru Economic Relations, 1930-1970*. Lanham, MD: University Press of America, 1996.

Komlosy, Andrea. *Work: The Last 1,000 Years*. London: Verso, 2018.

Konove, Andrew. *Black Market Capital: Urban Politics and the Shadow Economy in Mexico City*. Berkeley: University of California Press, 2018.

Kram Villarreal, Rachel. "Gladiolas for the Children of Sánchez: Ernesto P. Uruchurtu's Mexico City." PhD diss., History Department, University of Arizona, 2008.

Kuntz Ficker, Sandra. *Empresa Extranjera y Mercado Interno: El Ferrocarril Central Mexicano (1880-1907)*. Mexico City: El Colegio de México, 1995.

———. "Los ferrocarriles y la formación del espacio económico en México." In *Ferrocarriles y obras públicas*, edited by Sandra Kuntz Ficker and Priscilla Connolly, 105-37. Mexico City: Instituto de Investigaciones Dr. José Luis Mora / El Colegio de Michoacán / El Colegio de México / IIH-UNAM, 1999.

———. "Las nuevas series del comercio exterior de México." *Revista de Historia Económica* 20, no. 2 (2002): 213-70.

Kuntz Ficker, Sandra, and Priscilla Connolly, eds. *Ferrocarriles y obras públicas*. Mexico City: Instituto de Investigaciones Dr. José Luis Mora / El Colegio de Michoacán / El Colegio de México/ IIH-UNAM, 1999.

La Porta, Rafael, and Andrei Shleifer. "Informality and Development." *Journal of Economic Perspectives* 28, no. 3 (Summer 2014): 109-26.

Leal, Juan Felipe, and José Villaseñor, *La clase obrera en las historia de México: En la Revolución, 1910-1917*. Mexico City: Siglo XXI, 1988.

Lear, John. "Mexico City: Space and Class in the Porfirian Capital, 1884-1910." *Journal of Urban History* 22, no. 4 (May 1996): 454-92.

———. "Del mutualismo a la resistencia: Organizaciones laborales en la Ciudad de México de fines del Porfiriato a la Revolución." In *Ciudad de México: Instituciones, actores sociales y conflicto político, 1774-1931*, edited by Carlos Illades and Ariel Rodríguez Kuri, 275-309. Zamora, Michoacán: El Colegio de Michoacán / UAM, 1996.

———. *Workers, Neighbors, and Citizens: The Revolution in Mexico City*. Lincoln: University of Nebraska Press, 2001.

Levy, Santiago. *Good Intentions, Bad Outcomes: Social Policy, Informality, and Economic Growth in Mexico*. Washington, DC: Brookings Institution Press, 2008.

Lewis, Arthur. *The Theory of Economic Growth*. London: Allen and Unwin, 1959.

Lieuwen, Edwin. *Mexican Militarism: The Political Rise and Fall of the Revolutionary Army, 1910-1940*. Albuquerque: University of New Mexico Press, 1968.

Loaeza, Soledad. *Clases medias y política en México: La querella escolar, 1959-1963*. Mexico City: Colegio de México, 1988.

———. "Modernización autoritaria a la sombra de la superpotencia, 1944-1968." In *La Nueva Historia General de México*, 653-98. Mexico City: Colegio de México, 2010.

———. *El Partido Acción Nacional, la larga marcha, 1939-1994: Oposición leal y partido de protesta*. Mexico City: Fondo de Cultura Económica, 1999.

López Cámara, Francisco. *La estructura económica y social de México en la época de la reforma*. Mexico City: Siglo XXI, 1976.

López Monjardin, Adriana. "El espacio en la producción: Ciudad de México, 1850." In *Ciudad de México: Ensayo de construcción de una historia*, edited by Alejandra Moreno Toscano, 56–66. Mexico City: Instituto Nacional de Antropología e Historia, 1978.

López Rosado, Diego G. *El abasto de productos alimenticios en la Ciudad de Mexico*. Mexico City: Fondo de Cultura Económica, 1988.

———. *Los mercados de la Ciudad de México*. Mexico City: Secretaría de Comercio, 1982.

———. *Los servicios públicos de la Ciudad de México*. Mexico City: Porrúa, 1976.

MacIntyre, Alasdair. *Three Rival Versions of Moral Enquiry: Encyclopaedia, Genealogy, and Tradition*. Notre Dame, IN: Notre Dame University, 1990.

MacLachlan, Colin M., and William H. Beezley. *Mexico's Crucial Century, 1810–1910: An Introduction*. Lincoln: University of Nebraska Press, 2010.

Macpherson, C. B. *Burke*. Oxford: Oxford University Press, 1980.

Marichal, Carlos. "The Construction of Credibility: Financial Market Reform and Renegotiation of Mexico's External Debt in the 1880s." In *The Mexican Economy, 1879–1930: Essays on the Economic History of Institutions, Revolution, and Growth*, edited by Jeffrey Bortz and Stephen Haber, 93–119. Stanford: Stanford University Press, 2002.

Marichal, Carlos, Manuel Miño Grijalva, and Paolo Riguzzi. *El primer siglo de la hacienda pública del Estado de México, 1824–1923*. Mexico City: El Colegio Mexiquense / Gobierno del Estado de México, 1994.

Márquez Colín, Graciela. "Entre dos mundos: Las finanzas de la Cuidad de México." Paper presented at the XIV Reunión Internacional de Historiadores de México, Katz Center–University of Chicago, Chicago, IL, September 18–21, 2014.

Martí, Judith E. "Nineteenth-Century Views of Women's Participation in Mexico's Markets." In *Women Traders in Cross-Cultural Perspective*, edited by Linda Seligmann. Stanford, CA: Stanford University Press, 2001.

———. "Subsistence and the State: Municipal Government Policies and Urban Markets in Developing Nations: The Case of Mexico City and Guadalajara, 1877–1910." PhD diss., Anthropology Department, University of California, Los Angeles, 1990.

Matute Aguirre, Álvaro. "Orígenes del revisionismo historiográfico de la Revolución mexicana." *Signos Históricos* 2, no. 3 (June 2000): 29–48.

McCool, Gerald A. *Catholic Theology in the Nineteenth Century: The Search for a Unitary Method*. New York: Seabury Press, 1977.

McCormick, Gladys Irene. *The Logic of Compromise: Authoritarianism, Betrayal, and Revolution in Rural Mexico, 1935–1965*. Chapel Hill: University of North Carolina Press, 2016.

Medina Peña, Luis. *Civilismo y modernización del autoritarismo*. Vol. 20 of *Historia de la Revolución Mexicana*. Mexico City: El Colegio de México, 1979.

Mendiola García, Sandra C. *Street Democracy: Vendors, Violence, and Public Space in Late Twentieth-Century Mexico*. Lincoln: University of Nebraska Press, 2017.

Meyer, Jean A. *The Cristero Rebellion: The Mexican People between Church and State, 1926–1929*. Cambridge: Cambridge University Press, 1976.

———. *El Sinarquismo: ¿Un fascismo mexicano? 1937–1947*. Mexico City: Joaquín Mortiz, 1979.
Meyer, Lorenzo. "El conflicto petrolero entre México y los Estados Unidos (1934–1942)." *Foro Internacional* 7, no. 1–2 (July–December 1966): 99–159.
———. *Mexico y Estados Unidos en el conflicto petrolero, 1917–1942*. Mexico City: Colegio de México, 1972.
Meyer, Michael C. "The Militarization of Mexico, 1913–1914." *The Americas* 27, no. 3 (January 1971): 293–306.
Michaels, Albert L. "Las Elecciones de 1940." *Historia Mexicana* 81 (July–September 1971): 80–134.
———. *The Mexican Election of 1940*. Buffalo: State University of New York at Buffalo, 1971.
Middlebrook, Kevin J. *The Paradox of Revolution: Labor, the State, and Authoritarianism in Mexico*. Baltimore: Johns Hopkins University Press, 1995.
Miranda Pacheco, Sergio. "Conflicto político, finanzas federales y municipales en la Ciudad de México, 1846–1855." In *De Colonia a Nación: Impuestos y política en México, 1750–1860*, edited by Carlos Marichal and Daniela Marino, 215–45. Mexico City: El Colegio de México, 2001.
———. *La creación del Departamento del Distrito Federal: Urbanización, política y cambio institucional, 1920–1934*. Mexico City: Universidad Nacional Autónoma de México, 2008.
———. *Historia de la desaparición del Municipio en el Distrito Federal*. Mexico City: Unidad Obrera y Socialista, 1998.
Molina de Villar, América. "El Tifo en la Ciudad de México en tiempos de la Revolución Mexicana, 1913–1916." *Historia Mexicana* 64, no. 3 (January–March 2015): 1163–247.
Moncada González, Gisela. "La gestión municipal: ¿Cómo adminitrar las plazas y mercados de la Ciudad de México? 1824–1840." *Secuencia* 95 (May–August 2016): 39–62.
———. *La libertad comercial: El sistema de abasto de alimentos de la Ciudad de México, 1810–1835*. Mexico City: Instituto Mora, 2013.
Morales, María Dolores. "Espacio, propiedad y órganos de poder en la ciudad de México en el siglo XIX." In *Ciudad de México: Instituciones, actores sociales y conflicto político, 1774–1931*, edited by Carlos Illades and Ariel Rodríguez Kuri, 155–90. Zamora, Michoacán: El Colegio de Michoacán / UAM, 1996.
———. "Estructura urbana y distribución de la propiedad de la Ciudad de México en 1813." *Historia Mexicana* 25, no. 3 (January–March 1976): 363–402.
———. "La expansion de la ciudad de México (1858–1910)." In *Atlas de la Ciudad de México*, edited by Gustavo Garza, 64–68. Mexico City: Departamento del Distrito Federal / Colegio de México, 1987.
———. "La expansion de la ciudad de México en el siglo XIX: El caso de los fraccionamientos." In *Ciudad de México: Ensayo de construcción de una historia*, edited by Alejandra Moreno Toscano, 189–200. Mexico City: Instituto Nacional de Antropología e Historia, 1978.

Moreno, Julio. *Yankee Don't Go Home! Mexican Nationalism, American Business Culture, and the Shaping of Modern Mexico, 1920–1950*. Chapel Hill: University of North Carolina Press, 2003.

Moreno Toscano, Alejandra, ed. *Ciudad de México: Ensayo de construcción de una historia*. Mexico City: Instituto Nacional de Antropología e Historia, 1978.

Mosk, Stanford A. *Industrial Revolution in Mexico*. Berkeley: University of California Press, 1950.

Navarro, Aaron W. *Political Intelligence and the Creation of Modern Mexico, 1938–1954*. University Park: Pennsylvania State University Press, 2010.

Neruda, Pablo. "México florido y espinudo." In *Confieso que he vivido: Memorias*. Barcelona: Seix Barral, 1974.

Niblo, Stephen R. *Mexico in the 1940s: Modernity, Politics, and Corruption*. Wilmington, DE: Scholarly Resources, 1999.

———. *War, Diplomacy, and Development: The United States and Mexico, 1939–1954*. Wilmington, DE: Scholarly Resources, 1995.

Nussbaum, Martha. "Compassion: The Basic Social Emotion." *Social Philosophy and Policy* 13, no. 1 (1996): 27–58.

Ochoa, Enrique C. *Feeding Mexico: The Political Uses of Food since 1910*. Wilmington, DE: Scholarly Resources, 2002.

———. "Reappraising State Intervention and Social Policy in Mexico: The Case of Milk in the Distrito Federal during the Twentieth Century." *Mexican Studies / Estudios Mexicanos* 15, no. 1 (Winter 1999): 73–99.

Oikión Solano, Verónica. "La oposición Henriqusita en Michoacán, 1950–54." *Tzintzun* 29 (January–June 1999): 91–110.

Oldman, Oliver, Henry T. Aaron, Richard M. Bird, and Stephen L. Kass. *Financing Urban Development in Mexico City: A Case Study of Property Tax, Land Use, Housing, and Urban Planning*. Cambridge, MA: Harvard University Press, 1967.

Oles, James. "Noguchi in Mexico: International Themes for a Working-Class Market." *American Art* 15, no. 2 (Summer 2001): 10–33.

Olsen, Patrice Elizabeth. *Artifacts of Revolution: Architecture, Society, and Politics in Mexico City, 1920–1940*. Lanham, MD: Rowman and Littlefield, 2008.

Olvera Ramos, Jorge. *Los mercados de la Plaza Mayor de México*. Mexico City: Cal y Arena, 2007.

Osorio Marbán, Miguel. *El sector popular del PRI*. Mexico City: Coordinación Nacional de Estudios Históricos, Políticos y Sociales—PRI, 1994.

Padilla, Tanalís. *Rural Resistance in the Land of Zapata: The Jaramillista Movement and the Myth of the Pax PRIísta, 1940–1962*. Durham, NC: Duke University Press, 2008.

Padilla, Tanalís, and Louise Walker. "In the Archives: History and Politics." *Journal of Iberian and Latin American Research* 19, no. 1 (2013): 1–10.

Palti, Elías José. "Guerra y Habermas: Ilusiones y realidad de la esfera pública Latinoamericana." In *Conceptualizar lo que se ve: François-Xavier Guerra, historiador: Homenaje*, edited by Erika Pani and Alicia Salmerón, 461–83. Mexico City: Instituto Mora, 2004.

———. "La transformación del liberalismo mexicano en el siglo XIX: Del modelo jurídico de la opinión pública al modelo estratégico de la sociedad civil." In *Actores, espacios y debates en la historia de la esfera pública en la Ciudad de México*, edited by Cristina Sacristán and Pablo Piccato, 67–95. Mexico City: Instituto de Investigaciones Dr. José Luis Mora / Universidad Nacional Autónoma de México, 2005.

Pani, Erika. *Para mexicanizar el segundo imperio: El imaginario político de los imperialistas*. Mexico City: El Colegio de México / Instituto Mora, 2001.

Paxman, Andrew, ed. *Los Gobernadores: Caciques del pasado y del presente*. Mexico City: Grijalbo / Penguin Random House, 2018.

Pensado, Jaime. *Rebel Mexico: Student Unrest and Authoritarian Political Culture during the Long Sixties*. Stanford, CA: Stanford University Press, 2013.

Perló Cohen, Manuel. *El paradigma porfiriano: Historia del desagüe del Valle de México*. Mexico City: Porrúa, 1999.

Perry, Laurens Ballard. *Juárez and Díaz: Machine Politics in Mexico*. DeKalb: Northern Illinois University Press, 1978.

Peschard, Jacqueline. "Las elecciones en el Distrito Federal (1946–1970). *Revista Mexicana de Sociología* 50, no. 3 (July–September 1988): 229–46.

Piccato, Pablo. *City of Suspects: Crime in Mexico City, 1900–1931*. Durham, NC: Duke University Press, 2001.

———. "Honor y opinión pública: La moral de los periodistas durante el porfiriato temprano." In *Actores, espacios y debates en la historia de la esfera pública en la Ciudad de México*, edited by Cristina Sacristán and Pablo Piccato, 145–78. Mexico City: Instituto de Investigaciones Dr. José Luis Mora / Universidad Nacional Autónoma de México, 2005.

———. "Introducción: ¿Modelo para armar? Hacia un acercamiento crítico a la teoría de la esfera pública." In *Actores, espacios y debates en la historia de la esfera pública en la Ciudad de México*, edited by Cristina Sacristán and Pablo Piccato, 9–39. Mexico City: Instituto de Investigaciones Dr. José Luis Mora / Universidad Nacional Autónoma de México, 2005.

———. "Murders of *Nota Roja*: Truth and Justice in Mexican Crime News." *Past and Present* 223, no. 1 (2014): 195–231.

———. "Public Sphere in Latin America: A Map of the Historiography." *Social History* 35, no. 2 (2010): 165–92.

———. *The Tyranny of Opinion: Honor in the Construction of the Mexican Public Sphere*. Durham, NC: Duke University Press, 2010.

———. "Urbanistas, Ambulantes, and Mendigos: The Dispute for Urban Space in Mexico City, 1890–1930." In *Reconstructing Criminality in Latin America*, edited by Carlos Aguirre and Robert Buffington, 113–48. Wilmington, DE: Scholarly Resources, 2000.

Pick James B., and Edgar W. Butler. *Mexico Megacity*. Boulder, CO: Westview Press, 1997.

Pilcher, Jeffrey M. "Fajitas and the Failure of Refrigerated Meatpacking in Mexico: Consumer Culture and Porfirian Capitalism." *The Americas* 60, no. 3 (January 2004): 411–29.

———. *The Sausage Rebellion: Public Health, Private Enterprise, and Meat in Mexico City, 1890–1917*. Albuquerque: University of New Mexico Press, 2006.

Pletcher, David M. "The Fall of Silver in Mexico, 1870–1910, and Its Effect on American Investments." *Journal of Economic History* 18, no. 1 (March 1958): 33–55.

———. *Rails, Mines, and Progress: Seven American Promoters in Mexico, 1867–1911*. Ithaca, NY: Cornell University Press, 1958.

Porter, Susie S. "And That It Is Custom Makes It Law: Class Conflict and Gender Ideology in the Public Sphere, Mexico City 1880–1910." *Social Science History* 24, no. 1 (Spring 2000): 111–48.

———. *From Angel to Office Worker: Middle-Class Identity and Female Consciousness in Mexico, 1890–1950*. Lincoln: University of Nebraska Press, 2018.

———. *Working Women in Mexico City: Public Discourses and Material Conditions, 1879–1931*. Tucson: University of Arizona Press, 2003.

Portes, Alejandro, Manuel Castells, and Lauren A. Benton, eds. *The Informal Economy: Studies in Advanced and Less Developed Countries*. Baltimore: Johns Hopkins University Press, 1989.

Portes, Alejandro, and Richard Schauffler. "Competing Perspectives on the Latin American Informal Sector." *Population and Development Review* 19, no. 1 (March 1993): 33–60.

Puga, Cristina. "La controversia sobre el proteccionismo en México." In *Algunos debates sobre política económica en México: Siglos XIX y XX*, edited by María Eugenia Romero Sotelo, 195–239. Mexico City: Facultad de Economía, UNAM, 2008.

Pyle, Jane. "The Public Markets of Mexico City." PhD diss., Geography Department, University of Oregon, 1968.

Quiroz, Enriqueta. *Entre el lujo y la subsistencia: Mercado, abastecimiento, y precio de la carne en la Ciudad de México, 1750–1812*. Mexico City: El Colegio de México / Centro de Estudios Históricos Instituto Dr. José María Luis Mora, 2005.

Ramírez Plancarte, Francisco. *La Ciudad de México durante la revolución constitucionalista*. Mexico City: Botas, 1941.

Rath, Thomas. *Myths of Demilitarization in Postrevolutionary Mexico, 1920–1960*. Chapel Hill: University of North Carolina Press, 2013.

Reyna, José Luis, and Raúl Trejo Delarbre. *De Adolfo Ruiz Cortines a Adolfo López Mateos (1952–1964)*. Vol. 12 of *La clase obrera en la historia de México*, edited by Pablo González Casanova. Mexico City: Siglo XXI Editores, 1981.

Reynolds, Clark W. *The Mexican Economy: Twentieth-Century Structure and Growth*. New Haven, CT: Yale University Press, 1970.

Riguzzi, Paolo. "Los caminos del atraso: Tecnología, instituciones en inversión en los ferrocarriles mexicanos, 1850–1900." In *Ferrocarriles y vida económica en México, 1850–1950: Del surgimiento tardío al decaimiento precoz*, edited by Sandra Kuntz Ficker and Paolo Riguzzi, 31–97. Mexico City: El Colegio Mexiquense / Ferrocarriles Nacionales de México / Universidad Autónoma Metropolitana-Azcapotzalco, 1996.

———. "México, Estados Unidos y Gran Bretaña, 1867–1910: Una difícil relación triangular." *Historia Mexicana* 41 (1992): 365–436.

———. *¿La reciprocidad imposible? La política del comercio entre México y Estados Unidos, 1877–1938*. Mexico City: Colegio de México / Instituto de Investigaciones Dr. José Luis Mora, 2003.

Rivera Castro, José. *La clase obrera en la historia de México: En la presidencia del Plutarco Elías Calles, 1924–1928*. Mexico City: Siglo XXI / Instituto de Investigaciones Sociales de la UNAM, 1983.

Rodea, Marcelo N. *Historia del movimiento obrero ferrocarrilero en México, 1890–1943*. Mexico City: Ex-Libris M. Rodea, 1944.

Rodríguez Kuri, Ariel. "El año cero: El Ayuntamiento de México y las facciones revolucionarias (agosto 1914–agosto 1915)." In *Ciudad de México: Instituciones, actores sociales y conflicto político, 1774–1931*, edited by Carlos Illades and Ariel Rodríguez Kuri, 191–220. Zamora, Michoacán: El Colegio de Michoacán / UAM, 1996.

———. "Ciudad oficial, 1930–1979." In *Historia political de la Ciudad de México*, edited by Ariel Rodríguez Kuri, 417–81. Mexico City: El Colegio de México, 2012.

———. "Desabasto de agua y violencia política: El motín del 30 de noviembre de 1922 en la ciudad de México; Economía moral y cultura política." In *Formas de descontento y movimientos sociales: Siglos XIX y XX*, edited by José Ronzón and Carmen Valdez, 167–201. Mexico City: Universidad Autónoma Metropolitana, Azcapotzalco, 2005.

———. "Desabasto, hambre y respuesta política, 1915." In *Instituciones y Ciudad: Ocho estudios históricos sobre la Ciudad de México*, edited by Carlos Illades and Ariel Rodríguez Kuri, 133–61. Mexico City: Unidad Obrera y Socialista, 2000.

———. *La experiencia olvidada, el Ayuntamiento de México: Política y gobierno, 1876–1912*. Mexico City: El Colegio de México / Universidad Autónoma Metropolitana, Azcapotzalco, 1996.

———. "Gobierno local y empresas de servicios: La experiencia de la Ciudad de México en el Porfiriato." In *Ferrocarriles y obras públicas*, edited by Sandra Kuntz Ficker and Priscilla Connolly, 165–90. Mexico City: Instituto de Investigaciones Dr. José Luis Mora / El Colegio de Michoacán / El Colegio de México / IIH-UNAM, 1999.

———. *Historia del desasosiego: La revolución en la ciudad de México, 1911–1922*. Mexico City: El Colegio de México, 2010.

———. "Política e institucionalidad: El Ayuntamiento de México y la evolución del conflicto jurisdiccional, 1808–1850." In *La Ciudad de México en la primera mitad del siglo XIX*, edited by Regina Hernández Franyuti, 2:51–94. Mexico City: Instituto de Investigaciones Dr. José Luis Mora, 1994.

Rodríguez, Miles Vincent. "The Beginnings of a Movement: Leagues of Agrarian Communities, Unions of Industrial Workers, and Their Struggles in Mexico, 1920–1929." PhD diss., History Department, Harvard University, 2010.

Roxborough, Ian. "Mexico." In *Latin America between the Second World War and the Cold War, 1944–1948*, edited by Leslie Bethell and Ian Roxborough, 190–216. Cambridge: Cambridge University Press, 1992.

Rubin, Jeffrey W. *Decentering the Regime: Ethnicity, Radicalism, and Democracy in Juchitán, Mexico.* Durham, NC: Duke University Press, 1997.

Sabet, Daniel M. *Police Reform in Mexico: Informal Politics and the Challenge of Institutional Change.* Stanford, CA: Stanford University Press, 2012.

Sacristán, Cristina, and Pablo Piccato, eds. *Actores, espacios y debates en la historia de la esfera pública en la Ciudad de México.* Mexico City: Instituto de Investigaciones Dr. José Luis Mora / Universidad Nacional Autónoma de México, 2005.

Salazar, Rosendo. *Historia de las luchas proletarias de México, 1923 a 1936.* 2 vols. Mexico City: Avante, 1938–1956.

Salazar, Rosendo, and José G. Escobedo. *Las pugnas de la Gleba, 1907–1922.* 2 vols. Mexico City: Avante, 1923.

Salmerón Sanginés, Pedro. *Aarón Sáenz Garza: Militar, diplomático, político, empresario.* Mexico City: Porrúa, 2001.

Sánchez Mejorada, María Cristina. *Rezago de la modernidad: Memorias de una ciudad presente.* Mexico City: Universidad Autónoma Metropolitana, 2005.

Sanders, Nichole. *Gender and Welfare in Mexico: The Consolidation of a Postrevolutionary State.* University Park: Pennsylvania State University Press, 2011.

Schell, William, Jr. *Integral Outsiders: The America Colony in Mexico City, 1876–1911.* Wilmington, DE: Scholarly Resources, 2001.

Schers, David *The Popular Sector of the Partido Revolucionario Institucional in Mexico.* Tel Aviv: David Horowitz Institute for the Research of Developing Countries, Tel Aviv University, 1972.

Schwentesius, Rita, and Manuel Ángel Gómez. "Supermarkets in Mexico: Impacts on Horticulture Systems." *Development Policy Review* 20, no. 4 (2002): 487–502.

Scott, James C. *Domination and the Arts of Resistance: The Hidden Transcript of Subordinate Groups.* New Haven, CT: Yale University Press, 1990.

———. *The Moral Economy of the Peasant: Rebellion and Subsistence in Southeast Asia.* New Haven, CT: Yale University Press, 1976.

Selee, Andrew. *Decentralization, Democratization, and Informal Power in Mexico.* University Park: Pennsylvania State University Press, 2011.

Shadlen, Kenneth C. *Democratization without Representation: The Politics of Small Industry in Mexico.* University Park: Pennsylvania State University Press, 2004.

Silva Londoño, Diana A. "Comercio ambulante en el Centro Histórico de la ciudad de México (1990–2002)." *Revista Mexicana de Sociología* 72, no. 2 (April–June 2010): 195–224.

Silva Riquer, Jorge. "El abasto al mercado urbano de la Ciudad de México, 1830–1860." In *La Ciudad de México en la primera mitad del siglo XIX*, edited by Regina Hernández Franyuti, 1:64–115. Mexico City: Instituto de Investigaciones Dr. José Luis Mora, 1994.

Sinkin, Richard N. *The Mexican Reform, 1855–1876: A Study in Liberal Nation-Building.* Austin: University of Texas Press, 1979.

Skirius, John. *José Vasconcelos y la cruzada de 1929.* Mexico City: Siglo XXI, 1982.

Sluis, Ageeth. *Deco Body, Deco City: Female Spectacle and Modernity in Mexico City, 1900–1939.* Lincoln: University of Nebraska Press, 2016.

Smith, Benjamin T. *Pistoleros and Popular Movements: The Politics of State Formation in Postrevolutionary Oaxaca*. Lincoln: University of Nebraska Press, 2009.
Smith, Peter. *Talons of the Eagle: Dynamics of U.S.-Latin American Relations*. New York: Oxford University Press, 2000.
Smith, Robert Freeman. *The United States and Revolutionary Nationalism in Mexico, 1916–1932*. Chicago: University of Chicago Press, 1972.
Snodgrass, Michael. *Deference and Defiance in Monterrey: Workers, Paternalism, and Revolution in Mexico, 1890–1950*. Cambridge: Cambridge University Press, 2003.
Spenser, Daniela. *Unidad a toda costa: La tercera Internacional en México durante la presidencia de Lázaro Cárdenas*. Mexico City: CIESAS, 2007.
Stern, Steve J. "Feudalism, Capitalism, and the World-System in the Perspective of Latin America and the Caribbean." *American Historical Review* 93, no. 4 (October 1988): 829–72.
Stevens, Donald F. "Riot, Rebellion, and Instability in Nineteenth-Century Mexico." In *Five Centuries of Mexican History / Cinco Siglos de Historia Mexicana*, 2 vols., edited by Virginia Guedea and Jaime E. Rodríguez O., 1:344–54. Mexico City: Instituto de Investigaciones Dr. José Luis Mora / University of California, Irvine, 1992.
Suarez-Potts, William J. *The Making of Law: The Supreme Court and Labor Legislation in Mexico, 1875–1931*. Stanford, CA: Stanford University Press, 2012.
Téllez Contreras, León Felipe. "Los mercados de San Juan: Bienes colectivos en transformación." *Alteridades* 26, no. 51 (January–June 2016): 15–27.
Téllez Guerrero, Francisco, and Elvira Brito Martínez, "La hacienda municipal de Puebla en el siglo XIX." *Historia Mexicana* 39 (April–June 1990): 951–78.
Tenorio Trillo, Mauricio. *Artilugio de la nación moderna: México en las exposiciones universales, 1880–1930*. Mexico City: Fondo de Cultura Económica, 1998.
———. "1910 Mexico City: Space and Nation in the City of the Centenario." *Journal of Latin American Studies* 28, no. 1 (February 1996): 75–104.
Thompson, E. P. "The Moral Economy of the English Crowd in the Eighteenth Century." *Past and Present*, no. 50 (February 1971): 76–136.
———. "The Moral Economy Reviewed." In *Customs in Common*, 259–351. Pontypool, Wales: Merlin Press, 1991.
Thompson, Lanny. "Artisans, Marginals, and Proletarians: The Households of the Popular Classes in Mexico City, 1876–1950." In *Five Centuries of Mexican History / Cinco Siglos de Historia Mexicana*, 2 vols., edited by Virginia Guedea and Jaime E. Rodríguez O., 2:307–24. Mexico City: Instituto de Investigaciones Dr. José Luis Mora / University of California Irvine, 1992.
Thomson, Guy P. C. "Popular Aspects of Liberalism in Mexico, 1848–1888." *Bulletin of Latin American Research* 10, no. 3 (1991): 265–92.
Tilly, Chris. "Wal-Mart in Mexico: The Limits of Growth." In *Wal-Mart: The Face of Twenty-First Century Capitalism*, edited by Nelson Lichtenstein, 189–209. New York: New Press, 2006.
Tischendorf, Alfred. *Great Britain and Mexico in the Era of Porfirio Díaz*. Durham, NC: Duke University Press, 1961.

Treviño Rangel, Javier. "Los 'hijos del cielo' en el infierno: Un reporte sobre el racismo hacia las comunidades chinas en México, 1880–1930." *Foro Internacional* 45, no. 3 (July–September 2005): 409–44.

Turrent Díaz, Eduardo. *México en Bretton Woods*. Mexico City: Banco de México, 2009.

Tutino, John. *Making a New World: Founding Capitalism in the Bajío and Spanish North America*. Durham, NC: Duke University Press, 2011.

Unikel, Luis. *La dinámica del crecimiento de la Ciudad de México*. Mexico City: Fundación para Estudios de la Población, 1972.

Valadés, José C. *El Porfirismo, historia de un regimen*. 2 vols. Mexico City: Universidad Nacional Autónoma de México, 1977.

Van der Linden, Marcel. *Workers of the World: Essays toward a Global Labor History*. Leiden: Brill, 2008.

Vassallo, Roberta. "La construcción de los mercados públicos de estructura metálica en la Ciudad de México durante el Porfiriato." *Boletín de Monumentos Históricos / Tercera Época* 38 (September–December 2016): 78–99.

Vázquez Ramírez, Esther Martina. *Organización y resistencia popular en la Ciudad de México durante la crisis de 1929–1932*. Mexico City: Instituto Nacional de Estudios Históricos de la Revolución Mexicana, 1998.

Veeser, Cyrus. *A World Safe for Capitalism: Dollar Diplomacy and America's Rise to Global Power*. New York: Columbia University Press: 2002.

Vernon, Raymond. *The Dilemma of Mexico's Development: The Roles of the Private and Public Sectors*. Cambridge, MA: Harvard University Press, 1963.

Walker, David. "Porfirian Labor Politics: Working-Class Organizations in Mexico City and Porfirio Díaz, 1876–1902." *The Americas* 37, no. 3 (1981): 257–89.

Walker, Louise E. *Waking from the Dream: Mexico's Middle Classes after 1968*. Stanford, CA: Stanford University Press, 2013.

Warren, Richard A. "Desafío y trastorno en el gobierno municipal: El Ayuntamiento de México y la dinámica política nacional, 1821–1855." In *Ciudad de México: Instituciones, actores sociales y conflicto político, 1774–1931*, edited by Carlos Illades and Ariel Rodríguez Kuri, 167–83. Zamora, Michoacán: El Colegio de Michoacán / UAM, 1996.

———. *Vagrants and Citizens: Politics and the Masses in Mexico City from Colony to Republic*. Wilmington, DE: Scholarly Resources, 2001.

Weiner, Richard. "Battle for Survival: Porfirian Views of the International Marketplace." *Journal of Latin American Studies* 32, no. 3 (October 2000): 645–70.

Weis, Robert G. *Bakers and Basques: A Social History of Bread in Mexico*. Albuquerque: University of New Mexico Press, 2012.

———. "Immigrant Entrepreneurs, Bread, and Class Negotiation in Postrevolutionary Mexico City." *Mexican Studies / Estudios Mexicanos* 25, no. 1 (Winter 2009): 71–100.

———. "The Revolution on Trial: Assassination, Christianity, and the Rule of Law in 1920s Mexico." *Hispanic American Historical Review* 96, no. 2 (May 2016): 319–53.

Wells, Allen, and Gilbert Joseph. *Summer of Discontent, Seasons of Upheaval: Elite Politics and Rural Insurgency in Yucatán, 1876–1915*. Stanford, CA: Stanford University Press, 1996.

Wilkie, James W. *The Mexican Revolution: Federal Expenditure and Social Change since 1910*. Berkeley: University of California Press, 1970.

Wionczek, Miguel S. *Nacionalismo mexicano e inversion extranjera*. Mexico City: Siglo Veintiuno Editores, 1967.

Womack, John, Jr. "Luchas sindicales y liberalismos sociales, 1867–1993." In *Para una historia de América: Los nudos*. 2 vols., edited by Marcello Carmagnani, Alicia Hernández Chavez, and Ruggiero Romano, 1:417–60. Mexico City: Fondo de Cultura Económica, 1999.

———. "The Mexican Revolution." In *Mexico since Independence*, edited by Leslie Bethell, 125–200. Cambridge: Cambridge University Press, 1991.

———. *Zapata and the Mexican Revolution*. New York: Alfred A. Knopf, 1969.

Yoma Medina, María Rebeca, and Luis Alberto Martos López. *Dos mercados de en la historia de la Ciudad de México: El Volador y La Merced*. Mexico City: Instituto Nacional de Antropología e Historia, 1990.

Zabludovsky, Jaime. "La deuda externa pública." In *Un siglo de deuda pública en México*, edited by Leonor Ludlow and Carlos Marichal, 152–189. Mexico City: El Colegio de México / Instituto de Investigaciones Dr. José Luis Mora / El Colegio de Michoacán / IIH-UNAM, 1998.

Zebadúa, Emilio. "El Banco de la Revolución." *Historia Mexicana* 45, no. 1 (July–September 1995): 67–98.

———. *Banqueros y revolucionarios: La soberanía financiera de México*. Mexico City: Fondo de Cultura Económica, 1994.

Index

Abelardo Rodríguez Market, 9; inauguration and praise, 106–7, 111–12; jail, used as, 114–15; murals, 112n82–84; undersubscribed, due to competition among vendors, 95, 112–13
Acevedo, Esther, 194n83
Acordada Revolt, 167n18
Adelman, Jeremy, 5–6
agrarian reform, 71–72, 113, 194n95
Alemán, Miguel, 126–27, 199n24, 199–200n31; Banco Pequeño Comercio, 140–44; high cost of living, actions against 130–31; vendors' complaints, against mercados agrícolas, 134–36; vendors' demands to, 139–40, 201n66
Alianza de Camioneros, 190n15
Alianza de Comerciantes del Distrito Federal, 152
Alianza de Comerciantes en Pequeño del Mercado Hidalgo, 120
Alianza de Comerciantes en Pequeño del Mercado de Jamaica, 145, 204n114
Alianza de Comerciantes en Pequeño del Primer Cuadro, 103

Almazán, Juan Andreu, 95, 120–22
Alonzo Romero, Miguel, 82–84; and water riots, 85, 187n77
Álvaro Obregón Market, 104
ambulantes (vendedores), 49, 157; attempted banning of, 155, 165n34; customary rights, 61; differentiation from locatarios, 56, 58, 125; licenses, 54–55, 143, 180n85, 180n89; police repression of 67, 74; reglamento (bylaw), 101–4; relocations, 112, 114
Ampudia Market, 196–97n149
Anderson, Clayton & Co., 127
anticlericalism, 14, 27, 95
Aquinas, Thomas, 27, 171n65–67
Arana, Ángel, 114
arbitrios, 22. See also Ayuntamiento de la Ciudad de México
Arena, Benito, 45
Arredondo, Benito, 89–90
arrendamientos, 23. See also public markets
Arteaga, Eduardo F., 29, 172n77; and compassion, 172n76

Asociación Nacional de Almacenistas Comerciantes de Víveres y Similares, 118
Asociación Nacional de Cosecheros de Cereales y Productos Alimenticios (National Association of Cereal and Foodstuff Producers) (ANC), 131; against La Merced wholesalers, 133–36
Augustine, 27
Ávila Camacho, Manuel, 95, 121, 196n139; Banco Pequeño Comercio, creation of, 122
Ávila, Víctor Manuel, 146, 151–52
Ayuntamiento de la Ciudad de México, 6–8, 12, 25, 38–39, 69, 89, 105, 182n6; advisory board, reduced to, 60, 64; compassion, 27, 29, 53–54, 61; decline of, 42–43, 47, 54, 59–60, 62, 80; custom, undoing of, 56–57, 61; *Discursos*, 42, 53; as epicenter, of labor politics after 1917, 81; exclusionary benevolence, 13–14, 34–37; factional power struggles after 1917, 80–81, 85; final abolishing of, 96; fiscal revenues, including from markets, 22–24; foreign debt, taking of, 45; governorship, clash with over use of streets as markets, 48–50; jurisdiction of, 170n50, 170n53, 171n63, 178–79n61; market vendors, 31–33, 56–57, 82–84; during Mexican revolution, 78–79; moral economy, 26; Porfirian market project, role in, 45, 50–51, 52–53; privatizations, consideration of, 44; public markets, management of, 13, 17, 20–23, 26, 32–33, 57, 169–70n44; reinstatement in 1917, 80; unregulated street sales, campaign against, 50, 55–56; urban social relations, as arbiter of, 20, 30, 52, 57, 60; and viento vendors, 50–51, 55

Banco de México, 184n40; Bureau of Industrial Research, 127
Banco Nacional Hipotecario Urbano y de Obras Públicas, 106, 192n59
Banco Nacional Mexicano, 44–45
Banco del Pequeño Comercio del Distrito Federal (Bank of Small Commerce), 5, 122, 140–43, 154
Banco Refaccionario del Pequeño Comerciante de los Mercados del Distrito Federal, 105
Barbosa Cruz, Mario, 55, 163n15, 182n6
Bautista, Jesús, 122–23, 139–41, 143
Benítez, José, 110–1, 113
Bertaccini, Tiziana, 195–96n127
Beteta, Ramón, 141
Blancarte, Guillermo, 116
Blanco, Francisco R., 46, 48, 52
Bloque de Acción Revolucionaria Pro-Pequeño Comercio y Industria, 195–96n127
Blum, Ann, 171n63, 176n13
Bojórquez, Juan de Dios, 141–43, 203n102
Bretton Woods Conference, 125
Buffington, Robert, 27, 59
Bugambilia Market, 141
Bulman, Francisco, 100
Burke, Edmund, 172n74

Cabrera, Luis, 79
cajones: interiores, 17, 19; *exteriores*, 18
Chalco Canal, 20, 25
Calles, Plutarco Elías, 72, 107, 114; ayuntamiento politics, 80–82, 85, 89, 91; Consejo Consultivo, creation of, 97–98; final abolition, of ayuntamiento, 96–97; PNR, creation of, 95
Cámara de Comercio de la Ciudad de México (Chamber of Commerce of Mexico City), 104; street commerce, attack on, 100–101

Cámara Israelita de Industria y Comercio de México, 195–96n127
Cámara Nacional de Comercio (National Chamber of Commerce) (CANACO), 137–38, 202n80
Cámara Nacional de Industrias de Transformación (National Chamber of Transformation Industries) (CANACINTRA), 122, 126
capitalism, 2; custom, undoing of, 61; expansion of, 1, 3, 38–41, 93, 108, 126–28, 163n13
Cárdenas, Alberto, 114, 116–17, 194n101
Cárdenas, Lázaro, 106, 111, 113; Mexico City markets, management of, 114–16, 121, 129, 195–96n127; oil industry, nationalizing of, 119; price controls, imposing of, 9, 95, 117; and vendors, 116–21
Carranza, Venustiano, 71–72, 77–79, 81; ayuntamiento, reinstatement of, 80, 186n68
Casa del Obrero, 79, 185n56
Casas Alemán, Fernando, 130, 132, 138, 199–200n31
Castañares, Francisco P., 35
Catholic Church, 14, 22, 26, 71; social teachings, 27
Catholicism, 7, 13–14, 26; public importance of, 27–28
Cedillo, Saturnino, 121
CEIMSA (state food agency), 129, 136, 199n30, 202n76; in management of industrial relations, 164n27; surveillance of reactions to, 204n115
Centro Cosmopolita de Dependientes de Comercio, 90
Centro Escolar Revolución, 107
CEPAL (United Nations' Economic Commission for Latin America), 127
charity, 171n63, 176n13; and compassion, 27; good works, emphasis on, 27

Chihuahua (Mexico), 71
chinampas, 20
Cifuentes, Agapito, 117
Clayton, William L., 127, 197–98n4
Clayton Plan, 126, 197–98n4
Cohen, Manuel Perló, 176n13
Cold War, 126, 128
Colonia ex-Hipódromo de Peralvillo Market, 134
Colonia del Valle Market, 110–11; mercado agrícola in, 131, 133–34
Colonia Española, La (newspaper), 35
Comité Pro-Raza, 195–96n127
Comité Regulador del Mercado de las Subsistencias, 119
Communist International: Popular Front strategy, 114
Communists, purging unions of, 128
Compañía de Carnes Refrigeradas El Popo, 75; monopolistic practices, accusations of, 76
Compañía Empacadora La Internacional, 185n53
Compañía Empacadora Nacional Mexicana, 185n53
Compañía de Fomento y Urbanización, 107
compassion, 7, 13, 28, 35–37, 56, 69, 171n63, 172n76, 183n30; and ayuntamiento, 29–30, 52–54, 61; as Catholic duty, 27, 172n69; and moral economy, 26
Confederación de la Clase Media, 195–96n127
Confederación General de Trabajadores (General Confederation of Workers) (CGT), 81; vendor organizations in, 88, 189n105
Confederación Nacional Campesina (National Campesino Confederation) (CNC), 127–28, 131, 135–36

Confederación Nacional de Organizaciones Populares (CNOP), 5–6, 123–24, 127–28, 162n8, 165n30; vendors, as part of, 10, 144–45, 149, 154, 204n115
Confederación Nacional de la Pequeña Propiedad Agrícola, 131
Confederación Patronal de La Republica Mexicana, 133
Confederación Regional Obrera Mexicana (Mexican Regional Labor Confederation (CROM), 81, 85, 97, 120, 187n77, 189n105; Federación de Sindicatos Obreros del D.F., 91, 117; vendor organizations in, 88–90
Confederación de Trabajadores Mexicanos (Confederation of Mexican Workers) (CTM), 121–22, 126–27, 133, 145, 201n57; electoral competition with CNOP, 148–49; against high cost of living, 117; Popular Frontism, commitment to, 114
Confederation of Mexican Workers. *See* Confederación de Trabajadores Mexicanos (CTM)
Consejo Consultivo, 9, 94, 97–98, 107–8, 110, 118, 120–21, 138, 190n16; conflicts among vendors, 115; reglamento de ambulantes, 100–104; reglamento del pan, 99–100; as truncated experiment, 106
Consejo Superior de Gobierno del Distrito Federal (Superior Council of Government of the Federal District), 66, 76
Consejo Superior de Salubridad Pública (Superior Council of Public Health), 6, 60; and markets 66–69, 73, 76
Constitution (of 1857), 14, 22, 170n48; separation of Church and state, 26, 166n4
Constitution (of 1917), 8, 80
Constitutionalist Army, 71, 77–78
contratas, 44

Convencionista forces, 77
Convention of Aguacalientes, 71
Cooperativistas, 81, 187n77. *See also* Partido Cooperativista
Corral, Ramón, 64
Cota, Enrique, 86
Cristero rebellion, 72, 90, 95
Cross, John C., 144
custom: capitalism and undoing of, 61–62; as contested, 56–57, 61; "since time immemorial," 39, 61

Dávila, José María, 112
Davis, Diane, 97, 120, 162n6, 190n15, 196n135, 205n1
de la Huerta, Adolfo, 80
delahuertista rebellion, 84
del Moral, Enrique, 150
Demócrata, El (newspaper), 63, 86, 88
Departmento del Distrito Federal (Department of the Federal District), 21, 94, 96, 102, 106, 114, 144; Consejo Superior de Gobierno of, 66; Departamento de Protección al Pequeño Comerciante, 91; market construction, 9, 11, 138, 150, 154; mercados agrícolas, transfer of responsibility for, 135–36; population of, 129, 202n82–83; price controls, 131; vendor movement, 95, 132, 139–40, 143, 145–47, 157
derechos municipales, 22. *See also* Ayuntamiento de la Ciudad de México
developmentalism (*desarrollismo*), 124, 127, 131, 145, 154; as conflictual, 128; in Mexico City, 129, 139; underbelly of, 155
Díaz, Dámaso F., 88–89
Díaz, Porfirio 14, 39, 40, 70; exile of, 70; urban renewal, including markets, 48, 52–53, 64–65, 92, 176n13; vendors appeal to, 57, 69
Dirección Federal de Seguridad (Directorate of Federal Security) (DFS), 6;

as political communication channels, 147–48; surveillance, of markets and vendors, 145–47, 204n115
Dirección General de Investigaciones Políticas y Sociales (General Directorate of Political and Social Investigations) (DGIPS), 6; surveillance of markets, 129–30, 196–97n149, 204n115
Dos de Abril Market, 147, 182n, 205n129
Durán, Rafael Barajas, 27

ejidatarios, 113. See also agrarian reform
El Jardín Market, 17
El Parián Market, 167n18
El Volador Market, 12, 17–19, 169–70n44; collective action, 33, 87, 107; and custom, 61; disparaging of, 47, 61, 92; fire at 25, 31; upgrading, proposal for, 48; viento vendors at, 23–24
Enríquez Guzmán, Adolfo, 154
Enríquez, Ignacio C., 78–79, 186n68
Escamilla, Fernando, 89
Escamilla, José, 105
Escobar, José Gonzalo, 96
Escuela Nacional de Bellas Artes, 27
Espíndola de Cal y Mayor, María Luisa Reyes, 110
Estrada Cajigal, Vicente, 104
Excélsior (newspaper), 86, 131–34, 136, 152
exclusionary benevolence, 7, 13

Federación de Comerciantes e Industriales (Mexicanos) en Pequeño, 112, 118, 122
Federación de Comerciantes en Pequeño de los Mercados del Distrito Federal, 146, 154
Federación de Ligas del Sector Popular del Distrito Federal, 122
Federación Mexicana del Trabajo, 116
Federación Nacional de Comerciantes e Industriales (Mexicanos) en Pequeño, 105, 113, 132, 134–35, 138–39, 142, 201n66
Federación de Sindicatos de Comerciantes del Exterior de los Mercados del Distrito Federal (FSC), 83–84, 87–90, 189n105
Federación de Sindicatos Obreros del Distrito Federal, 91, 189n105, 190n15
Federación de Sindicatos de Trabajadores al Servicio del Estado (Federation of Unions of State Employees), 119
Federal Labor Law, 187n83, 190n17
Federalista, El (newspaper), 35
Federation of Workers Unions of the Federal District, 79. See also Federación de Sindicatos Obreros del Distrito Federal
Fernández, José Luis, 107
Fernández, Ramón, 43, 45; ayuntamiento, pressure on, 47, 49
food riots, 78, 122
Foodstuffs and Their Distribution along the Viga Canal (Greenwood, Marion), 112
Ford, Eileen, 202n83
Foro, El (newspaper), 35
Fraga Ferreira, Ángel, 118
French intervention, 12, 14
Frente Coordinador de Unificación Nacional pro-Adolfo Ruiz Cortines, 145
Frente Femenil de Protección de Comerciantes, 145
Frente de Protección Mutua de Comerciantes en Pequeño de La Lagunilla, 146

Galicia Rodríguez, Pedro, 85, 88
Galindo Ochoa, Francisco, 146–47
Gamboa Ramírez, Ricardo, 170n46, 171n63
García Brito, Juan, 19–20; market upgrading proposals, 24–25

García Cubas, Antonio, 176n16
García Torres, Vicente, 174n98
Gasca, Celestino, 81
Gayol, Roberto, 48
Geiger, John Lewis, 15, 17
gentrification, 11, 158
Gillingham, Paul, 199n20, 199n25
Gojman de Backal, Alicia, 191–92n43, 195–96n127
González, Abraham, 82
González y González, Luis, 92
González, Manuel, 39, 44
González, Pablo, 80
Gordon, Gary, 165n32
Great Depression, 9, 94–95; consequences of, 126
Greenwood, Grace, 112
Greenwood, Marion, 112
Guadalajara (Jalisco, Mexico), 27, 121, 163n15
Guadalupe Hidalgo Market, 89–90, 130, 187n82
Guadarrama, Ramón Alva, 112
Guerrero Market, 31, 45
Guzmán Olmos, Jesús, 139–40

Habermas, Jürgen, 163n12, 173–74n96
Henríquez Guzmán, Miguel, 194n101
Hernández, Altagracia, 118
Hernández, Lamberto, 102
Hidalgo Catalán, Emigdio, 101, 108
Hill, Benjamín, 79
Hinojosa, Cosme, 114, 115
History as Seen from Mexico in 1936 (Noguchi), 112
Huerta, Victoriano, 71, 76, 78, 185n56; market policies, 77
hunger marches, 122
Hurtado, Elías, 103, 105–6

Ibáñez, Crisóforo, 102
Ibáñez, M. Romero, 76
Ibarrarán y Ponce, José María, 27

imperialism, 39, 69–70
industrialization, 126–27
Industrialization of the Countryside, The (Greenwood, Marion), 112
inequality, 11, 41, 91–92, 164n28
infalsificables, 79
inflation, 78–79, 95, 117, 119, 122, 125, 129, 131, 156
Insurgentes Market, 111
Islas, Francisco, 148–49
Iturbide Market, 17, 19, 22, 68. *See also* San Juan Market

Jamaica Market, 152, 193n66, 205n133; vendors request, for public works, 107
Jesuits: expulsion of, 28
Jesús Market, 17, 21, 31; critique of, 37
Jewish merchants, 191–92n43, 195–96n127
Jiménez, Christina, 163n15, 181n96
Jiménez Torres, Jesús, 152
Juaréz, Benito, 12, 14, 29, 171n63, 172–73n78
Juaréz Market, 82, 87
Junta de Mejoras Materiales, 44
Juvenal, 48

Knight, Alan, 195–96n127, 199n25

Labor Department, 76
labor movement, 9, 79–80, 127, 130, 186n70; splintering of, 81, 88, 198–99n17
La caridad en los primeros tiempos de la Iglesia (Ibarrarán y Ponce), 27
La Dalia Market, 87, 143, 187n82
Lago Garda Market, 141
La Lagunilla Market, 82, 102–3, 130; complaints against market officials, 146–47; conflicts among vendors, 115, 139–40, 191–92n43; vendors of, 69, 85, 87, 107–8, 196–97n149

La Merced Market: butchers, expulsion of, 68–69; disparaging of, 54–55, 67, 76–77; fire at, 158–59; gentrification, 158; inauguration of (1957), 150–52, 154–55; inflation management, 119, 130, 135–36; origins of, 17, 20, 23, 25, 31–32; political control of, 146–49, 195–96n127; Porfirian upgrade of, 45, 47–48, 52–53; vendor conflicts at, 56–57, 73–74, 143; vendor demonstrations, 87; vendor petitions, 58–59, 73–74; wholesalers, 131–33, 135–36, 149, 196–97n149

Landa y Escandón, Guillermo, 68–69, 183n30

La Reforma Laws, 26, 48

Lascano, Donasiano, 113

Lázaro Cárdenas Market, 132

Lear, John, 74, 78

Legión Mexicana Nacionalista, 195–96n127

León de la Barra, Francisco, 74–75

León, Miguel A., 68

léperos, 15, 166n8

Lerdo Law (1856), 22

Lerdo de Tejada, Sebastián, 172–73n78

Levy, Jonathan, 5–6

Ley de Dotación del Fondo Municipal, 22, 29, 33

Ley Orgánica del Distrito Federal y Territorios Federales (1928), 96

Ley de Planificación y Zonificación del Distrito Federal (1933), 192n53; Comisión de Planificación, creation of, 106

Liberal factionalism, 14, 34; end of 39

Liberalism, 14, 166n5

Liberals, 14, 27–28, 171n63; and the press, 34

Liga de la Pequeña Propiedad, 99–100

Liga Revolucionaria de Comerciantes en Pequeño del Mercado Martínez de la Torre, 118

Lizardi, Francisco, 35

Loaeza, Soledad, 165n30, 165n33

locatarios (market stallholders), 7–8, 63, 69, 73–74, 85, 87, 95, 110, 122, 132, 134, 139–40, 152, 154, 159, 195–96n127, 196–97n149; ambulantes and viento vendors, differentiation from, 58; collective action, 58–59; custom, language of, 56; identity of, 59; modernity, embracing of, 39, 56–57, 61; public sphere, transformation of, 59, 84, 92–93. *See also* market vendors

Lombardo Toledano, Vicente, 92, 198n7

López Mateos, Adolfo, 154

López Rosado, Diego G., 168n33, 187n82

Loreto Market, 48, 52; failure of, 53

Maderista uprising, 64, 70–71

Madero, Francisco, 70–71, 76; vendors appeal to, 74–75

maquiladoras, 157

markets. *See* public markets

market halls, 18–19, 41, 45, 47, 55, 91–92, 94–95, 109–10, 138, 156; construction, slowing down of, 82, 157; inauguration of, 22, 52–53, 82, 111, 150–51. *See also* public markets

market vendors, 9, 13, 34, 68, 121, 128, 205n1; ambulantes, differentiation from, 58, 125, 154–55; and ayuntamiento 6–7, 26, 30–32, 50–52; class conflicts, 3–4, 105–6; competition and conflicts among, 4, 58, 73, 94–95, 104–5, 115–18, 137–39; Consejo Consultivo, 97–98, 100–106; custom, 56–57, 61–62; demonstrations, 84–87, 133, 145; fee and rent reductions, petitions for, 4–5, 25–26, 33, 59, 63, 84, 123; grievances, 31, 64, 75, 91, 97, 123, 132–33; inflation, effects on, 78, 95, 117–19, 122, 129; market upgrading and renewal, support for, 83–84, 107–8, 140, 144; mercados agrícolas,

market vendors (*continued*)
resentment toward, 131–32, 134–35; and "Mexican miracle," 125; Mexican Revolution, 64, 72–74, 77–78; as orphaned by authorities, 69; overflow beyond halls, 92, 100; as passive "pueblo," portrayal of, 63, 86–87; police harassment of, 38, 49, 54, 67, 90, 114, 118, 147–48, 155; political life, exclusion from, 119; price controls, conflicts over, 117–20, 131–34, 136; public sphere, exclusion from, 33–36; public sphere, transformation of, 59, 84, 92–93; rate increase, cancellation of, 88; repression of, 145–46; and scribes, 173n86; social justice, 188n90; and strikes, 104; against Sunday rest decree, 90; as suppliers of wage goods, 156; surveillance of, 122, 196–97n149, 204n115; unions, formation of, 82–83; vendor movement, as fragmented, 104–5, 113, 123, 146; vendor movement, political incorporation of, 122–23, 146–47, 152–54; wage workers, differentiation from, 89–91, 98; wage workers, identification with, 74–75; wholesalers, conflicts with, 105, 132–33; xenophobia, 101–3, 191–92n43, 195–96n127. See also *locatarios*; viento vendors

Martí, Judith, 163n15
Martínez de la Torre Market, 52–53, 68, 77, 130, 147; butchers, expulsion of 67; vendor conflicts at, 116, 118, 196–97n149
Martínez Domínguez, Alfonso, 203n103
Martínez Domínguez, Guillermo, 140–42, 203n103
Maximilian, Emperor, 12
Medina, Ramón, 81–82
Melchor Ocampo Market, 110
mendicancy, 171n63
Mendiola, Sandra, 165n34
Mendoza, José, 110
Meneses, Pablo, 102
mercados agrícolas, 133–36, 179n63, 200n38; public markets, in direct competition with, 131–32
mercados sobre ruedas (mobile markets), 158
Mexican Central Railway, 40
Mexican miracle, 11, 125, 157
Mexican Revolution, 4, 6, 70–72, 97, 158; emergency food supply system, in Mexico City, 78–79; Mexico City vendors, 8, 64, 74–76, 92–93, 105, 123
Mexico, 5–6, 12, 14, 27, 69, 72, 79, 85, 95, 121, 124, 136; austerity, embracing of, 157; capitalism, expansion of, 38–41, 126–28; debt crisis, 157; informal economy of, 158, 161n4; Mexican miracle, 1, 11, 125, 157, 164n28; "order and progress," motto of, 40; public investment, collapse of, 157; public markets, 1–2, 156; supermarkets in, 137, 157–58. See also agrarian reform; Mexican Revolution; strikes
Mexico City (Mexico), 36, 71, 74, 79, 81, 121–22, 126, 128, 156, 198n15; aesthetics, 24, 44, 47, 55, 65, 92, 100, 108, 111–12, 138, 144, 150–52, 181n96; bakeries in, 99–100; capitalist modernization of, 7, 38, 40–43, 45, 64–65, 106, 129, 144; Catholicism, importance of, 26–28; cholera threat, 73; cosmopolitanism of, 65; cost of living, politics of, 117, 119–20, 129–31, 136; developmentalism in, 124, 129; floods, 31, 41, 148; food riots and hunger markets, 78, 122; food supply into, 20–21, 25, 78, 119, 131; locatarios, overflow of, 92; market vendors, 3–4, 10, 13; during Mexican Revolution, 73–80; migration to, 157, 202n82; militarization of, 76–79, 186n68; penny press, 59; political (re)organization of, 8,

21, 60, 62, 66, 69, 80, 96–97; population of, 15, 42–43, 82, 91, 129, 176n16, 202n82; public health, 31, 41, 44, 47, 51–52, 55, 57, 65–67, 69, 73, 76, 84, 92, 100, 108, 138, 152, 163n15; public spaces, "proper" use of, 38–39, 45, 65, 95, 98; socioeconomic structure of, 15–17, 43, 98, 158, 176n11; street stalls, as source of conflict, 54, 100–102, 154–55; subway system, 205n1; supermarkets in, 136–37, 157–58; tax base and structure, 22–23, 42–43, 66, 82, 144, 193n69, 194–95n110 ; tourism, 103, 111, 158; traffic circulation, 24, 41, 49–50, 55–56, 58, 68, 84, 92, 100–101, 103, 108, 111, 144; typhoid in, 78; water supply to, 22, 44–45, 65–66, 106, 139, 144, 187n77. See also *ambulantes*; public markets; viento vendors
Mexico Tramways Company, 76
Michoacán (Mexico), 27
Mijangos, Genaro, 118
Michaels, Albert, 195–96n127
Mining (Greenwood, Grace), 112
Mixcalco Market, 107, 114
Mixcoac Market, 87
modernization, 126; ayuntamiento, decline of, 56, 61–62; as exclusive, 157; locatarios, support for, 8, 39, 56–59, 139, 154; of markets, 45–47, 51, 108, 111, 151–52, 158; urban project of, 7, 38, 40–43, 64–65, 144
modes of production, 2–3
Monitor Republicano, El (newspaper), 35, 47, 174n98; Juvenal, 48
Monte de Piedad, 44–45
Monterrey (Nuevo León, Mexico), 114, 121, 136–37
Montes de Oca, Rodrigo, 101, 103–4
Monteverde, Francisco, 66–67
moral economy, 6, 7, 36, 48–49, 78, 162n9; Catholic ethics and doctrine, 26

Morelia (Michoacán, Mexico), 163n15, 181n96
Morelos (Mexico), 71
Morones, Luis N., 120
Municipio Libre, El (periodical), 49, 170n53
Muñoz García, Antonio, 108, 111, 193n62

Nacional, El (newspaper), 54, 131, 152
Nacional Financiera, 96, 106, 192n58
NADYRSA (state food agency), 164n27
Nájera, Pedro D., 87–88
Napoleon III, 12
National Bank for Urban Mortgages and Public Works, 192n59. See also Banco Nacional Hipotecario Urbano y de Obras Públicas
National Federation of Small-Scale Vendors and Industrialists, 140. See also Federación Nacional de Comerciantes e Industriales Mexicanos en Pequeño
National Music Conservatory, 49
National Palace, 25, 42, 47, 146
National Preparatory School, 185n56
Navarro, Francisco, 148–49
neoliberal turn, 157–58
Neruda, Pablo, 1
Nieto, Adán, 133
Noguchi, Isamu, 112
Nonoalco Market, 87
Noriega, Iñigo, 138–39
North American Free Trade Agreement (NAFTA), 157
Novedades (newspaper), 136

Obregón Álvaro, 72, 106, 184n40; assassination of, 95–97; postrevolutionary politics, 80–82; vendors' appeals to 83–84, 90
Obregonistas, 72, 80
Ocaranza, Antonio, 19
Ochoa, Enrique, 129, 164n27, 191n23

Office for the Promotion and Organization of Credit Associations, 141. *See also* Banco del Pequeño Comercio del Distrito Federal
Oficina de Agrupaciones y Asuntos Sindicales, 115
O'Higgins, Pablo, 112
Oles, James, 164n26
Olsen, Patrice, 106
Ordenanzas Municipales (1840), 21–22
Ortiz Rubio, Pascual, 96, 192n56; reglamento de ambulantes, 103
Osorio Palacios, Juan José, 147

País, El (newspaper), 63, 86
Palace of Fine Arts, 106
Palti, Elías José, 45
Partido Acción Nacional (Party of National Action) (PAN), 121, 149
Partido Autonomista Mexicano, 196–97n149
Partido Cívico Progresista (PCP), 84–86
Partido Cooperativista, 81–82, 84, 92
Partido Laborista Mexicano (Mexican Laborist Party) (PLM), 81, 84–87, 89, 92, 97, 187n77
Partido Liberal Constitucionalista (PLC), 81–82, 84, 86, 187n77
Partido Nacional Revolucionario (National Revolutionary Party) (PNR), 96, 102, 107, 113, 119
Partido Revolucionario Institucional (Institutional Revolutionary Party) (PRI), 5, 10, 124–25, 127–28; congressional politics, 147–49; and middle classes, 165n33; vendor movement, incorporation of, 140, 143–47, 154, 165n34; vendors, surveillance of, 155, 204n115
Partido de la Revolución Mexicana (Party of the Mexican Revolution) (PRM), 119–21, 127; Comité Central Ejecutivo del D.F., 123

Patria, La (newspaper), 35, 67, 174n98
pauperism, 27
Pax Porfiriana, 40
Paz, Ireneo, 174n98
Paz, Pascual, 88
peddlers, 15, 17, 25, 38, 82; market vendors, clash with, 74, 104, 124; numbers, increase in, 124; untaxed, 49–50, 67. *See also ambulantes*
Peña Manterola, Gonzalo, 143–49, 152, 154–55, 203–4n110
penny press, 28, 59
Permanecer en La Merced (documentary), 158
petates, 168n32
Piccato, Pablo, 36, 65, 163n15, 164n22
Pilcher, Jeffrey, 185nn52–53
Pimentel y Fagoaga, Fernando, 62
Piña Soria, Rodolfo, 117
Pius IX, 14, 166n4
Plan de San Luis Potosí, 70, 75
PNR. *See* Partido Nacional Revolucionario
Polanco, Samuel, 88
Popular, El (newspaper), 133
Porfirian elite, 7, 38, 49, 55–56, 70; civic piety, identification with, 171n63; laboring classes, control of, 45, 65; urban renewal, 41, 53, 58, 176n13
Porfiriato: economic development, 38–41, 163n13; urban inequality, 41, 65, and vendors, 69, 92–93, 105, 163n15
Portal de Mercaderes, 15
Porter, Susie, 54, 163n15
Portes Gil, Emilio, 96, 190n17
Posadas, Odilón, 149
Prensa, La (newspaper), 132–34
Prieto Laurens, Jorge, 84, 92, 187n77
PRM. *See* Partido de la Revolución Mexicana
Production of Charcoal, The (Guadarrama), 112

propios, 22. See also Ayuntamiento de la Ciudad de México
proprietary mode of production, 2–4
proprietary traders, 6; capitalist merchants, disputes with 9, 94, 99, 136–37; competition among, 7–8, 101, 137–38; in Consejo Consultivo, 98; and CROM, 97; deserving compassion, 13, 26, 32; middle-class aspirations 11, 125, 154; in modern city, 52, 54, 150–51; political representation, lack of, 106, 117, 120–21; and PRI, 5, 10, 144–45; and PRM, 95, 122–23; wage workers, differentiation from 91, 93, 98; wage workers, identification with, 75–76, 82. See also *ambulantes*; *locatarios*; market vendors
proprietary vendors, 19–20, 36. See also proprietary traders
protectionism, 39–40, 126–27, 129
public markets, 5, 26, 37, 93, 154, 167n18, 168n33; administrator, role of, 20; arrendamientos, 23; Ayuntamiento de la Ciudad de México, jurisdiction over, 13, 20–22, 80, 169–70n44; class conflict, outlets of, 122; closing time of, 57; under Consejo Superior de Gobierno, 66–68; customary arrangements in, 61–62; gentrification, threats of, 11; as heterogeneous places, 17–18, 20; management of, 1–2, 30, 66, 68, 73, 138; meaning of, clash over, 48–49; mercados agrícolas, in direct competition with, 131–32; during Mexican Revolution, 73, 76–78; modernization and reorganization of, 45, 61, 66, 94, 107, 140, 144, 158; police presence in, 8, 38, 49, 54, 67, 74, 90, 112, 114, 118, 139, 151; privatization, fear of, 159; public health officials, presence in, 66, 68, 73; as public service, 4, 13, 108; regulations and bylaws, 18–19, 61, 68, 103; as revenue source, 13, 20, 23–25, 29–30, 66, 179n63; social and cultural services, provision of, 110–11, 150–51; social and physical boundaries of, 18–19, 38, 48–49, 56, 58, 82, 92, 189n107; Sunday rest, conflict over, 90; supermarkets, competition from, 136–37, 157–58; types of, 19–20; viento sales, as part of, 23–24, 47–48, 55, 82, 179n63, 193n69. See also market halls; *puestos eventuales*; *sombras*; *zonas de mercado*
public sphere, 9, 36–37, 81, 86, 163n12, 173–74n96, 188n90; and ayuntamiento, 7; transformation of, 8, 59, 64, 156; vendors, exclusion from, 13, 34
puestos eventuales (movable booths), 17–20, 23
Puig Casauranc, José Manuel, 98, 190n17

Raya, Marcos E., 84–86, 88
Red Battalion, 79
Rego, José María, 48
Restored Republic, 6
Revista de Obras Públicas (periodical), 100
Rincón Gallardo, Pedro, 43–44, 52–53
Rivera, Diego, 111, 194n83
Riveroll, Ramón, 92
Robles Rodríguez, Francisco, 149
Rocha, Federico, 85–86
Rodríguez, Abelardo, 96; urban renewal, 106, 111
Rodríguez Kuri, Ariel, 21, 42, 74, 78, 176n17, 184n49, 186n68
Rojo Gómez, Javier, 147
Romero Rubio, Manuel, 52–53
Ross, Ramón, 81, 90
Róvalo, Agustín, 47
Ruiz Cortines, Adolfo, 127, 144, 199n30, 199–200n31; market inaugurations, 151–52; vendor movement, 145–46
Ruvalcaba, Francisco, 143–44

Sáenz, Aarón, 106–8, 114, 192n61; public markets, 110–11
Salas Valencia, Leonardo, 154
Salazar, Rosendo, 107
Salcedo, Armando, 103
Salgado, Javier, 152
San Ángel, 91
Sánchez Madariaga, Alfonso, 149
Sánchez Mejorada, María Cristina, 147
San Cosme Market, 52, 73, 87, 130
San Juan Market, 17, 21–22, 32, 102, 130; gentrification of, 166n35; Porfirian upgrade of, 48, 52, 55; vendors from, 76–77, 83, 87, 141
San Lucas Market, 52, 66, 84, 87, 112
Santa Ana Market, 66, 147
Santa Anna, Antonio López de, 167n18
Santa Catarina Market, 17, 22, 82
Santa Julia Market, 130
Saracho, Arturo de, 89
Scott, James C., 162n9
Sears Roebuck, 202
Serrano, Francisco, 81
Servín de Peralta, María, 120
Sierra, Justo, 188n90
Sinarquista movement, 121, 199n24
Sindicato de Comerciantes del Exterior del Mercado de San Juan, 83
Sindicato de Comerciantes en Pequeño del Interior y Exterior del Mercado de la Merced y Calles Adyacentes, 123
Sindicato Independiente de Comerciantes en Pequeño del Mercado de la Merced, 148–49
Sindicato Mexicano de Electricistas, 79, 117
Sindicato de Redactores de Prensa, 190n15
Siqueiros, David Alfaro, 194n83
Sluis, Ageeth, 112
social justice, 128, 152, 188n90
sombras (tripod parasols), 18–19, 23, 169–70n44
Spanish Empire, 21, 173–74n96
squatter settlements: bulldozing of, 157
state capitalism, 5, 126–27; dismantling of, 157–58
State Food Agency, 119, 129, 131, 134, 199n30. *See also* CEIMSA; NADYRSA
street vendors, 59, 66, 157–58, 165n32, 165n34; criminalization of, 38, 65; marginalization of, 56, 61; market vendors, competition and conflicts with, 9, 11; repression of, 114–16, 145–46, 154–55; tradition, invoking of, 61. *See also ambulantes*; viento vendors
strikes, 72, 76, 79, 91, 114, 122, 130; workers' right to, 80; vendors, 104
Suarez, Eduardo, 125
supermarkets, 4, 137, 157–58
Super Mercados S.A. (SUMESA), 137

Tacuba Market, 87, 130
Tacubaya Market, 87, 130, 196–97n149
Tapia de Gómez, Sra. 115
Teatro del Pueblo, 111
Tenorio Trillo, Mauricio, 40, 65, 176n13
Tepito Market, 130, 147
Thomism, 27
Thompson, E. P., 26, 162n9
Thompson, Lanny, 177n26
tianguis (outdoor markets), 54, 92, 158
Tiempo, El (newspaper), 48
trabajadores por cuenta propria, 2

UC. *See* Unión de Comerciantes del Exterior de los Mercados
Unión de Comerciantes del Distrito Federal., 113
Unión de Comerciantes Detallistas de La Mercad, 149

Unión de Comerciantes del Exterior de los Mercados (UC), 87–88, 91, 188n102, 189n105
Unión de Comerciantes del Mercado de la Lagunilla (Union of Small-Scale Vendors of La Lagunilla Market), 107, 139
Unión de Comerciantes del Mercado Martínez de la Torre, 135
Unión de Comerciantes Semifijos en el Mercado Insurgentes, 110
Unión Femenina de Comerciantes y Madres de Familia del Mercado de la Lagunilla, 115
Unión de Locatarios del Mercado Hidalgo y Comerciantes en Pequeño, 89–90
Unión de Locatarios de Puestos Aislados de la Ciudad de México, 112
Unión Mexicana de Comerciantes en Pequeño del Martínez de la Torre, 116–17
Unión Nacional de Transportes Ejidales, 135
Unión de Pequeños Comerciantes del Mercado Río Blanco, 135
Unión de Proprietarios de Panaderías, 100
Unión de Resistencia de Comerciantes Semifijos y Ambulantes, 103
United Nations (UN): Economic Commission for Latin America, 127
United States, 14, 39–41, 48, 70, 72, 121, 125, 130
Universal, El (newspaper), 54, 103, 130–31, 152
Universal Exhibition (Paris, 1889), 172n70
urban renewal, 1, 11, 37–38, 41, 44, 54, 58, 107, 125, 146
Uruchurtu, Ernesto P., 162n8, 203–4n110, 205n1; market construction 149–52; ousting of, 157; vendor movement 144–47, 154–55

Vagancy Tribunal, 171n63
Vallejo Market, 130
Vasconcelos, José, 96
Velarde, Gonzalo, 103–4
Velarde, Ramón, 85, 88
Velasco, Luis R., 118
Velázquez, Fidel, 117
vendedores ambulantes. See *ambulantes*
vendors: compassion, 26, 69; criminalization of, 38, 65; cultural crusade, to reshape behavior of, 38, 45, 51; and custom, 61–62. See also *ambulantes*; *locatarios*; market vendors; viento vendors
Vera, Abraham, 133
Veracruz (Mexico), 71, 169n38
Vera, Julio, 133
Vernon, Raymond, 198n11
viento (account), 23, 29–30, 47, 50. See also public markets
viento vendors, 23, 25, 56, 58; compassion for, 26, 29, 50–51; "horrified gaze" toward, 55; marginalization of, 54–55; sales, protection of, 50; v. unregulated peddlers, 30, 49–50
Vigil, José María, 174n98
Villa, Francisco, 71, 77
Villalobos, Antonio, 114–15
Villamil Market, 22
Villarreal, Rachel Kram, 162n8
Villegas, Pedro, 101
Villistas, 184n38. See also Villa, Francisco
voluntary associations, 173n92

Walker, Louise, 162n8, 165n33
Walmart, 11, 157–58
Warren, Richard A., 171n63
Weis, Robert, 99, 190n11

Womack, John Jr., 2–3, 161n3, 164n19, 183n30, 185n54, 186n70
Workers' Struggle against Monopolies (O'Higgins), 112
World's Columbian Exposition (Chicago, 1893), 172n70
World War I, 72

World War II, 10, 121–22, 124, 125–26, 196–97n149

Zapata, Emiliano, 71, 77
Zapatistas, 71, 184n38, 198n17
zonas de mercado (market areas), 138–39, 143, 147, 202n85; mapping of, 115